PHILANTHROPY

PHILANTHROPY

VOLUNTARY ACTION FOR THE PUBLIC GOOD

Robert L. Payton

AMERICAN COUNCIL **M** MACMILLAN PUBLISHING
ON EDUCATION **M** COMPANY
NEW YORK
Collier Macmillan Publishers
LONDON

The American Council on Education/Macmillan Series on Higher Education

Macmillan Publishing Company
A Division of Macmillan, Inc.
866 Third Avenue, New York, N.Y. 10022

Collier Macmillan Canada, Inc.

Library of Congress Catalog Card Number: 88-881

Printed in the United States of America

Printing number
1 2 3 4 5 6 7 8 9 10

Library of Congress Cataloging in Publication Data
Payton, Robert L.
    Philanthropy.

    (The American Council on Education/Macmillan series
on higher education)
    Includes index.
    1. Endowments—United States. 2. Charities—United
States. 3. Philanthropists—United States. I. Title.
II. Series: American Council on Education/Macmillan
series in higher education.
HV97.A3P39 1988   361.7'0973   88-881
ISBN 0-02-896490-X

The death of my brother Don two years ago at the hands of a drunk driver reminded me yet again of the vulnerability of all of us. He was 18 months older than I and had worked very hard all of his life so that he could devote his retirement to his family. Those plans evaporated at midnight on July 18, 1986.

I do not live as if I were expecting to die any time soon. Actuarially, the odds are pretty good for me. But prudence cautions me that this may be my only book, the only opportunity I will have to dedicate something of great importance to me to the two families of my life: the one in which I grew up, and the one that Polly and I have shared. All of those people, and all of our friends, would understand my dedicating this book very specifically to our three sons:

Joseph Keith Payton
October 15, 1949–November 2, 1982

Matthew William Payton
May 24, 1955–May 29, 1973

David Edward Payton
September 4, 1961–

and to our grandson:

Joseph William Payton Grant
May 24, 1983–

Contents

Foreword

Is Robert Payton the guru of contemporary American philanthropy? In its original meaning in Hinduism, *guru* denotes a spiritual teacher. In everyday speech in this country, however, its meaning is probably correctly rendered by the *American Heritage Dictionary* as "a charismatic leader or guide." Bob Payton clearly qualifies, but equally clearly any such label would embarrass him greatly. For he is an unassuming man, more given to listening than to preaching, in fact. One thing that strikes one about this book is the tendency to address the reader conversationally—"You should try to bear in mind, too, as I have, that it isn't possible to design a definitive outline of a dynamic tradition. (I welcome your improvements of it.)" The whole approach is one of engaging the reader, not seeking to indoctrinate.

The last several years have seen the development, at what appears to be an accelerating pace, of interest in understanding philanthropy and its role in American society. There are a number of reasons for this. The Reagan administration, both by preaching the virtues of philanthropy and by cutting the budgets of specific philanthropies, has called attention to the phenomenon. Before that, periodic investigations such as the Filer Commission had served to raise consciousness on the subject—and just as well, since consciousness in this instance started at a very low ebb indeed; having taken philanthropy for granted for so long, Americans were startled to hear it analyzed, praised and criticized, puzzled over—much as Molière's Bourgeois Gentilhomme was amazed and gratified to discover that all his life he had been speaking prose.

Academic interest has followed along, and Payton has
been prodding it, probing it, looking for ways to guide it and
stimulate it. He is currently a Scholar in Residence at the
University of Virginia, in Charlottesville. During his concluding years in New York he directed one of the famous
Columbia University Seminars, looking at the subject of philanthropy. These seminars enlist academics and interested
lay persons—in this case often practitioners in philanthropy—for three-to-four-hour sessions, eight or nine times a year,
at which individuals members may be called upon for papers
or presentations, and out of which can come all sorts of by-
products, from teaching materials for university courses to
publications of general interest. Payton thinks this could
provide a useful model by which to organize the study of the
philanthropic sector elsewhere. It has several virtues in this
context: openness and nonexclusivity; flexibility; and the capacity to bring theorists, empirical researchers and day-to-
day practitioners together in a setting that is ideal for mutual
enlightenment.

Would the creation of several, or several dozen, Columbia-
style seminars on philanthropy lead to the creation of a field
of study, to be called "philanthropics," analogous to economics or aesthetics? Payton specially likes the latter analogy, "because aesthetics fits comfortably within art history
and philosophy as well as fine arts; philanthropics has even
more opportunities."

Prediction is hazardous, midst the shifting sands of academic disciplines. Clearly thus far, scholars get their serious
rewards from performance in their traditionally established
disciplines; if a historian writes about philanthropy, she or
he will win praise or encounter criticism more significantly
from fellow historians than from students of philanthropics.
It will be to the fellow historians that deans and others responsible for approving promotions and setting compensation levels will listen.

One has the impression that Payton cares far more about
whether the fog of ignorance that envelops the subject can
be lifted than he does about who does the lifting, and through
what organizational or disciplinary mechanisms:

There are probably other fields where the general level of shared knowledge and values is lower than in this sector, but I can't think of any offhand. There are few fields of such vast magnitude that have stimulated so little curiosity among scholars.

Especially lacking are serious scholarly efforts to get at the underlying philosophical questions and to probe the assumptions that people who work in philanthropy make about what they are doing and why. Payton's essays make some useful beginnings. The one entitled, "Tainted Money: The Ethics and Rhetoric of Divestment," is particularly incisive, not to say courageous, given the emotions stirred by the issue of U.S. corporate involvement in South Africa—and stirred nowhere more energetically than on the campuses where, presumably, most serious academic study of philanthropy must originate.

In "The Ethics of Corporate Grantmaking" he pursues the practical outcome of failure to examine the assumptions and value judgments that govern much decision making in philanthropy, as elsewhere in the world:

> Making decisions ethically involves the process as well as the result. Almost every decision is made in the context of uncertainty about the facts and the consequences. There is a tendency to resolve the ambiguity by pretending that the matter is clearer than it is. We seek to be consistent by forcing cases into predetermined and comfortable categories; we find such comfort in certainty that we blind ourselves to the ambiguity that won't go away.
>
> In my experience, the most common expression of that tendency is to hide behind guidelines, to make them so precise and inflexible that they make the decisions for us.

Among the many good reasons for desiring more serious attention to philanthropy is that without such attention we are left with little more than celebratory rhetoric that cannot withstand the slightest evidence that all is not well with the philanthropic sector. In an early section called "Gleanings" (Payton clearly likes introductions, since this section might be seen as a sequel to this foreword, the author's preface that follows, and the general introduction that follows *that*) we have an arresting series of glimpses into the diverse reality of the philanthropic impulse and its expressions in practice. Included are brief news items, such as the one about "the United Cancer Council (UCC), an Indiana-based charity, [which] raised more than $5.1 million from contributions, but spent only $20,000 on cancer research, according to the watchdog National Charities Information Bureau. Ninety-seven percent of the money went for fundraising or management expenses, the Bureau said." But downers like that are interspersed with the items having the opposite thrust: the success, year after year for over a century, of the Fresh Air Fund's work to give slum kids the chance to experience life in the country, or the ingenuity of Benjamin Eisenstadt, developer of the artificial sweetner, Sweet 'N' Low, and part-time president of the Maimonides Medical Center, in finding ways to persuade people to donate much-needed blood. Still other entries offer individual insights, offbeat ironies, examples of charitable and philanthropic behavior from the sublime to well past the ridiculous, with numerous way stations in between. Payton is certainly not out to convince us that philanthropy is an unmixed blessing.

But he is convinced, and the conviction is infectious, "that philanthropy is simply essential to the survival of this country as a free and open and democratic society." This is not because it represents necessarily the most efficient or even the most equitable way of allocating resources, but because of its "voluntary dimension":

> By organizing our society so that important work depends on voluntary action, we activate the moral imagination. We employ the model of voluntary action as a means of teaching virtue: of caring for others, in its simplest and most familiar expression.

The essay entitled, "Virtue and its Consequences," begins, "This is an exercise in exploratory discourse." So, indeed, is this entire volume, including the chapter contributed by Virginia Hodgkinson that surveys the present state of research on the third sector. Bob Payton's instinct is to raise questions rather than to provide answers. He is especially wary of simple answers. No doubt new fields of study have on occasion been opened up by dogmatists who provoke reactions and so a dialectic. But it seems more appropriate to go about the business as Bob Payton does, by raising questions, reminding us of how much we do not yet know, and providing an example of restless curiosity that is nevertheless rooted in commitment. His commitment is both to public service, as his own remarkable and varied career has shown, and to the pursuit of complex and elusive truth, in an area hitherto more noted for its reliance on cliché and unexamined assumption.

These essays, then, deserve our attention both for their manner as well as their matter—and most of all for the admirable spirit in which their author conducts his explorations. May his tribe increase!

Richard W. Lyman, Ph.D.
President, The Rockefeller Foundation
President Emeritus, Stanford University

Preface

The purpose of this book is to stimulate reflection and discussion on the philanthropic tradition. The material thus mixes—as reality does—the uncomfortable combinations of high aspiration and low technique that emerge from the spirit of benevolence.

The perspective of the book is from within the American tradition of voluntary service, voluntary association, and voluntary giving. There is no apology for that, although there is little scholarly work on which to build an understanding of how the American tradition and practice compare with those of other societies and cultures.

My own experience in philanthropy began in 1957, when I wrote a speech (for someone else) on the future of the urban university for a convocation launching a capital campaign. Philanthropy is not a two-sided desk, but a many-sided table, and I have sat in most of the chairs: hospital board; family service agency board; and international technical assistance organization board. I have made fund-raising calls on corporations, foundations, and individuals. I have argued the case for public support of private higher education. I have lent my support to a symphony orchestra and to an organization that supports the art of jazz; to an organization concerned with dropout prevention and another committed to advancing personal excellence among young people. I have always welcomed the opportunity to work with those helping international educational exchange or the advancement of foreign language study. For ten years, I was privileged to be president of a corporate foundation.

Along with 90 million other Americans, in other words, I

have found time and other resources—some of my resources of time and money along with those provided by other people—to participate in the work of voluntary associations for the public good, just as Tocqueville said Americans do.

Over the course of time I began to realize that the philanthropic tradition is just that—a tradition, with some coherence, sense of direction, and abiding values. It is far more coherent than its diversity would suggest. There is a core to be found within the tradition, just as there is a constant process of testing its boundaries and the limits of its practices.

The first part of this book, "Major Challenges to Philanthropy," reprinted here with minor corrections, sketches an overview of that tradition. Preliminary to it is a brief chapter entitled "Gleanings," an effort to indicate the wonderful richness and perplexing problems that characterize philanthropy in America.

The second part is a collection of essays within the philanthropic tradition, intended to explore in varying degrees of depth some aspects of philanthropic theory and practice that are touched upon in other ways in Part I.

Part II includes an important chapter by Dr. Virginia A. Hodgkinson, Vice President for Research of Independent Sector, on the current status of research on philanthropy. Her essay is adapted from her report to the Independent Sector Research Committee, and I know of no one better qualified to present such a status report.

The "Afterword" discusses briefly three themes that are important to me: the notion of an intellectual domain that might be called *philanthropics;* the place of philanthropy in general education; and a model for continuing serious inquiry into "America's most distinctive virtue." ("I often quote myself," Shaw once said; "it adds spice to my conversation.")

I will caution the reader to treat this book as one would treat a work by Will Durant or other popularizers: as an encouragement to look further into the subject.

As I. A. Richards once wrote in *The Philosophy of Rhetoric:*

> I recall the painful shock I suffered when I first came across, in a book by Dr. Bosanquet, what he called the Golden Rule of Scholarship. "Never to quote or comment on anything

in a book which you have not read from cover to cover." As with other Golden Rules a strange peace would fall upon the world if that were observed. I cannot say that I practice the Rule or recommend it. There is a middle way wiser for Children of This World. However, as I neither am nor hope to be a scholar, I have no occasion to practice it. (Oxford University Press, 1936, p. 32)

In the "Afterword," I warn the reader that I am already engaged in writing a second book on this subject (entitled *Philanthropics*), and two other books may have grown out of this one. It is also the case that as an ENTP (extraverted intuitive thinking perceiving) personality type, my ambition tends to exceed my ability. I prefer to be overcommitted, as do many of my peers in this work. To be committed to philanthropy as volunteer and professional is to work harder—if not more efficiently—than most people.

That continuing expenditure of energy is even more rewarding when one feels part of a great and noble tradition. This book is a tentative introduction to it.

Acknowledgments

This book grows out of and expands along a discussion paper entitled *Major Challenges to Philanthropy*, commissioned by Independent Sector for its annual meeting in 1984. Without the personal intervention of Brian O'Connell, President of Independent Sector, there would have been neither opportunity nor encouragement to write what is presented here as Part I.

James A. Fisher, then President of the Council for Advancement and Support of Education, and Robert L. Gale, President of the Association of Governing Boards of Universities and Colleges, persuaded ACE/Macmillan to publish this expanded version. The late James Lipscomb, then President of the George Gund Foundation, provided funds for a research assistant, Susan Leicher.

Virginia A. Hodgkinson, Vice President for Research of Independent Sector, has also been a constant source of suggestions and support and is the author of the chapter on the status of research in this volume.

James Murray, Director of Publications for the American Council on Education, brought his rich background in publishing to bear at crucial points—as the labor pains became unbearable, so to speak.

The first versions of the manuscript were shared with—imposed upon—three colleagues and good friends at Exxon Education Foundation: Caryn G. Korshin, editor and critic of infinite patience; William J. McKeough, word processing adviser, wit, and old friend from Hofstra University; and Arnold R. Shore, now Executive Director of the Foundation and an endless source of insights into the meaning behind the murky convolutions of my prose. John Simon made detailed and helpful comments on the original paper and on one of the essays in Part II. Robert Parsley prepared the index.

These formal acknowledgements are as minimal as I can make them. To do more than that would require a description of the network of scholars, professionals, and volunteers in which I play a small but eager part. Even to list the organizations would require a page; the names of individuals would expand that to a chapter of its own. I feel particularly indebted to the people who have so generously helped me with advice, counsel, and occasional criticism.

And so I will choose to fumble for excuses for not naming names beyond those few directly concerned with bringing this book into being.

Because there are traces of my tenure with Exxon Education Foundation throughout the book, I must add a disclaimer and stress again that the opinions offered are mine and not necessarily those of my former employer. Even so, the high value I continue to put on corporate philanthropy owes a great deal to Exxon's proud tradition in the field.

Gleanings

The fields belonging to the royal estates of the
king were harvested by hired laborers, serv-
ants, and slaves (see 1 Sam. 8–14; 1 Chron.
27:26). What was left in the field after reaping
could be gathered ("gleaned") by widows, orphans, the poor, or alien residents (see Ruth
2). Hebrew religious law provided for the
practice of gleaning by prohibiting the owner
of a field from clearing it completely (Lev.
19:9–10; Deut. 24:19–21).

Madeleine S. and J. Lane Miller,
Harper's Encyclopedia of Bible Life,
Harper & Row, 1978, p. 179.

What follows is a miscellany, gathered from a wide variety
of newspapers, magazines, and other publications. The ex-
cerpts are not organized by category or theme because their
very randomness helps to bring out the diversity and complexity of the field. Most of them, however, relate to topics
in the pages that follow. It may be preferable to sample this
selection rather than read it through, and return to it from
time to time as a way of testing the themes and arguments
of the book itself.

*Undoubtedly, many theories will be advanced to ac-
count for the events of recent months. Some followers*

of conservative social philosopher Allan Bloom may blame it on social decay. A few economists may believe it has something to do with the opening of the London commodities market—the Big Bang—making it possible to speculate 24 hours a day. And some scientists may attribute these eerie happenings to leaks in the ozone layer, permitting dangerous rays to enter the atmosphere unfiltered.

The latter theory comes close, but the truth seems to lie beyond—in a previously undiscovered and invisible protective ring around the plant called the Bozone Layer.

When the bozone is frayed, random rays cause disturbances on earth. What's especially alarming is that there is no known way to protect oneself against the deterioration of the bozone. Sunglasses and wide hats, as prescribed by Interior Secretary Donald Hodel, have, for example, so far proved ineffective.

Consider: An unusual bozone leakage seems to have occurred over Fort Mill, S.C., where Jim and Tammy Bakker. . . .

—Sidney Blumenthal, "Lost in the Bozone,"
Washington Post, August 21, 1987.

By the 1880s opinion leaders, particularly in the North, had changed their tune. No longer should America be different from the world; its mission was to beat it. These advocates of research-oriented scientific medicine won a sympathetic hearing among civic worthies and philanthropists, eager to fund the future.

No ear proved more receptive than that of John D. Rockefeller. Wishing to invest millions to put American medicine on the map, Rockefeller wholeheartedly accepted the view of his advisers, the Flexner brothers, that science held the key. . . .

—Roy Porter, "Making an American Medicine," review of
Elizabeth Fee, *Disease and Discovery* in *Times Literary Supplement* (London), August 7, 1987.

Sumner B. Irish, retired engineer of Charlottesville, tutors fifth-grade students in arithmetic. He also serves as a volunteer with Meals on Wheels. "I have to admit I don't understand elementary education now," Irish said. "The experiences I had as a youngster in school are so different from what they have now." Growing up in the South Bronx with children who were mostly Jewish immigrant children, were "from families that placed a high value on education."

Irish believes volunteers are essential in the 21st century as the population ages and fewer people will be working to pay taxes to support government services. . . . "The human service agencies will use volunteers more. It's the only way we will be economically viable."
—*Daily Progress* (Charlottesville, Virginia), April 26, 1987.

Sociologists may tell us that we are becoming more isolated and atomized as individuals, but this is still a country of irrepressible joiners. Thousands of clubs, societies, associations, coalitions and confederacies exist to answer our organizational impulses, whether they flow along personal, professional or political lines, as I found out recently. . . .

I was directed to an extraordinary book called The Encyclopedia of Associations, which lists more than 20,000 organizations nationwide. . . .

Intellectually assertive types can approach Mensa International, *open to those who score within the top 2 percent of the general population in a standardized intelligence test. . . .*

Any university professor can join the Association of Concern for Ultimate Reality and Meaning, *whose meetings might be blamed for setting the conversational tone of too many faculty cocktail parties. . . .*

The Society for the Eradication of Television *opens its arms to anyone willing to carry a card that reads "I*

*do not have a working TV set in my home and encourage
others to do the same"....*
    —William McGowan, "A Sense of Belonging," *New York
Times Sunday Magazine,* August 23, 1987.

*In 1985, the United Cancer Council (UCC), an In-
diana-based charity, raised more than $5.1 million from
contributions, but spent only $20,000 on cancer re-
search, according to the watchdog National Charities
Information Bureau. Ninety-seven percent of the money
went for fund raising or management expenses, the bureau said.*
    —*Washington Post,* April 18, 1987.

*[Percy] Ross's obvious talent for self-promotion has
earned him a fair number of critics, particularly in Minneapolis, where he is known for his bankruptcies as
much as his philanthropy. He has been accused of tax
evasion, of giving only when the cameras are rolling, of
being an incurable show-off.*
    *"Percy is not a malicious person, but he is a flam-
boyant publicity-seeker," said Robert T. Smith, a col-
umnist for the Star-Tribune and one of the most persistent critics. "Take that stunt where he threw the silver
dollars out of the car. Not since Marie Antoinette said
'Let them eat cake' has anyone been so insensitive."*
    *Ross is unperturbed by the carping. If he ever again
feels unloved, he can take refuge in the warehouse full
of thank-you notes that he has accumulated over the
years. Filed away neatly and never thrown away, they
have become a paper monument to his philanthropy.*
    —Michael Dobbs, "Giving While the Giving's Good,"
Washington Post, August 22, 1987.

[Daniel] Smith, 25, has finally ended a solo two-year walk across the United States, accompanied by the skirl of his doodlesack . . . Smith played the bagpipe.

On the back of Smith's backpack are the words "Piping Across the USA for Cancer." But raising money for the American Cancer Society, he says, is only the "catalyst" for a trip that takes a little more explaining.

So far, he estimates that through donations, playing benefits and the occasional gig on a street corner he's raised about $25,000 for the American Cancer Society. . . . Smith figures he's walked about 6,000 miles since leaving Quoggy Head Park in Maine.

—Daily Progress (AP), April 9, 1987.

A corporation can't perform a charitable act any more than it can fall in love. But sometimes when corporations invest in charity—the way they invest, say, in advertising or in a new fleet of trucks—the dividends can be immense.

Consider the Dayton-Hudson Corp. of Minneapolis . . . [who] got wind of a possible takeover attempt by the awkwardly named Dart Group Corp. of suburban Washington. . . .

The keys to Dayton's success were that it employs 34,000 people (although two-thirds of them work part time) and that it gives away at least five percent of its profits each years to arts organizations and other worthy causes. . . .

Last year Dayton's earned $310 million in profits on $9.3 billion in sales. It gave away $20.8 million to charity—roughly half that in Minnesota. [Dayton chairman Kenneth Macke] and the other top managers of Dayton's had the pleasure of being philanthropic without giving away any of their own money. They aren't alone. The heads of most major corporations are lauded and feted for their generosity with their shareholders' cash. . . . No

one in management owns more than $1 million worth of stock, so when the directors vote to give away $20 million, it costs them less than $20,000—not to mention the tax benefit.
—James K. Glassman, "Free Gifts," *The New Republic,*
July 27, 1987.

At first hearing, it's a worthy enough request. Support your local police and at the same time help some underprivileged children.

But the fund-raising tactics of professionals brought in by the local Fraternal Order of Police lean too heavily on raising the funds and too lightly on sharing those funds with charity.

The group hopes to sell 2,400 tickets at $6 each for a May 10 performance of "the Golden Goose." Telephone solicitors are asking people to buy tickets for underprivileged children and for themselves.

The FOP's contract with the firm will give FOP 80 percent of the profits—expected to be about 33 cents on the dollar. That 33 percent is what actually will go to charity.

Two years ago, 6,000 tickets at $4 were sold for the B&B production of "Rumplestiltskin"—but fewer than 2,500 people attended the program. . . . If those figures hold true for the inevitable no-shows this year, nearly 6,000 tickets will be wasted.

How much better for each donor simply to write a $6 check to the FOP. There would be no bothersome telephone solicitations, no middle men, no waste. Donors would have the satisfaction of knowing that 100 percent, not 33 percent, of their contributions went to charity.
—Editorial, "Fund-Raisers Lack Efficiency,"
Daily Progress, April 15, 1987.

Mayor Koch had been demanding it for months. William J. Grinker, the Mayor's Human Resources Admin-

istrator, responded by drafting a specific plan. Finally, on June 30, the Board of Estimate approved it: an imaginative jobs program to get up to 3,000 people off welfare without government subsidies.

The program required that, beginning July 1, every contractor doing business with the Human Resources Administration would have to hire one welfare recipient for every $250,000 in contract fees received from the city.

How many have been hired since?

One, Mr. Grinker said somewhat sheepishly last week—a 20-year-old Brooklyn mother who has been on welfare for two years and went to work two weeks ago as a clerk-typist for a child-care agency.

The employment program makes sense, if properly monitored, and by bureaucratic benchmarks it all but rocketed into being. Yet the city's modest progress so far, in the relatively short time since it attempted to redefine its bargain with social service contractors, illustrates again what it takes to make even a dent in the welfare system. . . .
—Sam Roberts, "Welfare Costs: Spending Money to Save Money," *New York Times*, August 27, 1987.

One thing I have discovered is that attitudes and values that I acquired in China long before I came to the United States have had a great bearing on the way I do business. These values have much in common with the virtues of Confucianism, the system of Chinese thought that stresses proper behavior and moderation.
—Dr. An Wang, in *Northwest*, April 1987, p. 64.

One of the things that I've made very clear to all my clients [sports agent Leigh Steinberg says] is that I feel professional athletes should serve as role models. And I won't take on a player unless he is willing to give back substantially to the community, whether in terms of scholarship programs to his school, charity, what-ever. . . .

I've talked to some athletes who don't want to be in-volved. One told me that he was his own favorite charity, and I told him, "Fine, go get yourself another agent."
—*Los Angeles Times Magazine,* April 12, 1987.

Get all the information you need to develop and maintain a successful telephone fund-raising program. This book will work for you regardless of your cause or the size of your program.

Find out the key elements of a model telephone fund-raising program:

- *how to plan and administer a telephone fund-raising program, large or small*
- *how to find the best callers*
- *what a perfect caller would do in almost every situation*
- *how to develop a targeted list of potential contributors*
- *20 keys to upgrade pledges to larger amounts*
- *how to conduct a flawless training session*
- *how to set up the ideal pledge collection system*

Learn the rules for setting up a perfect telephone fund-raising program, and then follow the rationale behind these rules to insure your success.

There is virtually no limit to the amount of money telephone fund raising will bring to your organization. Order your book today! $29.95.
—From a Public Management Institute brochure.

Q. As one who belongs to a number of museums and other cultural institutions, and who has done volunteer work, I am much concerned about their survival in our city. However, I am equally concerned over the manners of some of the fund-raisers.

Of late, we have received several calls and have had to allocate our priorities; in the case of the large, well-known and hitherto well-endowed entities, we have felt that the annual membership subscription is sufficient, and prefer to make special donations to equally worthy but often overlooked grass-roots organizations.

I have had some difficulty conveying this to some of the more persistent callers. One said that she was sure "the federal government would take care of them" (not so if a religious organization or the local community is their sponsor). How can one respond with a gracious "no" to requests that one presently cannot grant?

A. Miss Manners is also appalled by rude and aggressive fund-raising techniques, but concerned that teaching people to deflect them will result in fewer charitable contributions. Please, let us separate the rudeness of the caller from the worthiness of the organization.

In any case you need not discuss your philanthropy with anyone. Telling why you are not giving money to a particular organization, or what you plan to support instead, constitutes a discussion and therefore invites argument.

The way to avoid one, when a refusal is questioned, is to say directly, "I'm sorry—I give what I can, but I never talk about my charitable contributions."

—Miss Manners, "Saying 'No' to Requests for Donations," United Features Syndicate, *Washington Post*, August 26, 1987.

Homelessness is often a function of joblessness. That's why, after considerable prodding, New York City's Department of Employment last year began trying to place homeless men in permanent jobs. Now the agency deserves credit for a small success.

The effort started with a three-month pilot program that found work for 104 residents of the Harlem Men's Shelter. After a full year, it has placed 364 men in full-time unsubsidized jobs averaging $4.23 an hour. With steady work, 262 men have moved out of the shelters.
—New York Times, "Topics of the Times," April 8, 1987.

AMERICA, AMERICA
[From the Marin County (Calif.) Pacific Sun]
DOGGIE BRUNCH
Reverend Philip Roundtree of St. Francis of Assisi Episcopal Church will bless your pet after it brunches on kibble quiche and sugarless dog cookies (cameras suggested). Your $5 donation goes to the Marin Humane Society; 11 a.m. For Paws, Larkspur Landing.
—The New Yorker, June 29, 1987.

The prophet. *Time and again in its 150-year history, Union [Theological Seminary] has been the scene of a prophetic witness against the shortcomings of the church and society. In the 1800s, its students and faculty were among the most vocal supporters of the abolition movement. In the 1980s, its championing of independent biblical scholarship led its faculty and board to declare themselves independent of the Presbyterian Church. From the early 1900s to the present, it has steadily supplied leadership for the movement toward unity among Christians around the world. Except for a regrettable lapse into over-fervent patriotism in the period of World War I, its students and faculty have kept a critical stance toward the excesses of nationalism in American life. In the teaching of Reinhold Niebuhr and Harry Ward, in the 1930s, it reached out to the economic and political crisis of the time to call for justice for poor people in the United States and in the world. In the 1950s, it gathered together an unprecedented number of young church leaders from the "emerging nations" of the post-war world; and in the 1960s its campus became a national center of church protest against the Vietnam war. Then, in the 1970s, its faculty and students and board came to a new appreciation of the new theological, ethical, and political priority which Christians should place on the needs of people neglected in American and world society—black people, women, and the multitude of the poor. Neither theology nor political perspective remains still in the Union tradition. Ours is a prophetic tradition, in which past and present are always raising questions of each other.*

—From a speech by Donald W. Shriver Jr., President of Union Theological Seminary.

For many of Ulster's Catholics, help from across the Atlantic threatens to become too much of a good thing. What troubles them is a growing campaign by Irish Americans to force action by U.S.-owned firms against anti-Catholic job discrimination. Naturally, they agree on the goal: A fair shake for the Catholic minority in the British-ruled province. But they are divided over how to reach it. The U.S. already confronts the question of whether economic sanctions can force political change in South Africa. Both there and in Ulster the risk is similar: A costly backlash from well-intended pressure. . . .

—Pamela Sherrid, "Why Irish eyes frown at U.S. help," *U.S. News and World Report,* August 24, 1987.

The Maryland House of Delegates approved today and sent to the governor's desk a measure that would permit the return of slot machines to eight counties on the Eastern Shore, as long as they are used by nonprofit groups for charitable purposes.

—*Washington Post,* April 7, 1987.

A more sophisticated version of this theory [Arthur Schlesinger on "simple mood-swings between public and private career preferences as the source for the see-saw pattern of American politics"] has been offered by Samuel Huntington, who thinks that the exaggerated moral expectations of the "American Creed" constitute a permanent reservoir of rebellion which must from time to time assert itself against the practices of interest-group politics. Some permanent reforms are achieved, and then, in exhaustion, politics as usual are resumed.
—Judith Shklar reviewing Arthur M. Schelsinger Jr., *The Cycles of American History,* in (London) *Times Literary Supplement,* March 13, 1987, p. 267.

The profiles of "the world's 500 biggest industrial CEOs" in Fortune *Magazine (August 3, 1987) include no reference to CEO involvement in nonprofit activity or to corporate philanthropy.*

You travel around the country, and no matter where you go, people say, Don't waste your time, nothing changes, you can't fight the powers that be—no one can. You hear it a lot from young people. I hear it from my own kids: Daddy, you're so quaint to believe in hope. Kids today live with awful nightmares: AIDS will wipe us out; the polar ice cap will melt; the nuclear bomb will go off at any minute. Even the best tend to believe we are helpless to affect matters. It's no wonder teenage suicide is at a record level. Young people are detached from history, the planet, and, most important, the future. I maintain to you that this detachment from the future, the lack of hope, and the high suicide rate among youth are connected.
—Abbie Hoffmann, "The Future is Yours (Still)," in *Harper's Magazine,* July 1987.

Benjamin Eisenstadt says he hates begging money for his favorite local charity, Maimonides Medical Center in the Borough Park section of Brooklyn.

But he doesn't mind asking for blood, a lot of it. And he has devised an incentive scheme to persuade people to give—seats at a baseball game or a lottery chance at an overseas trip for two.

The lottery is but the newest stratagem in the 80-year-old Mr. Eisenstadt's three-day-a-week job as president of Maimonides. He spends the other weekdays at the Cumberland Packing Corporation, the family-owned company he built into a multimillion-dollar business with his development of Sweet 'N Low, an artificial sweetener. . . .

The chronic shortage of blood donors is his latest concern because the center spends $1.5 million on blood yearly. It uses 25,000 pints but only 10 percent comes from donors in the community.

By offering pairs of tickets for a Mets game, donations were increased by 1,000 this year, he said. But the baseball season ends, and then what? Hence the lottery. . . .
—Kathleen Teltsch, "Hospital Patient Becomes Its Patron," *New York Times*, August 23, 1987.

Sometimes after 1095, a single schoolmaster established himself at Oxford.

The new splendour [of 16th century Oxford] derived from an increase in benefactions, which in turn produced more, as nostalgic alumni and rich widows donated money that could no longer be absorbed by the dissolved monasteries and chantries of post-Reformation England.

What Oxford men wanted was government patronage and protection: the price was co-operation and a willingness to conform.

[In the 18th century] the prime extenuating factor [for falling enrollment] is that in this period—and most

unusually—Oxford was in bondage to the British State without being very much assisted by it.
—Linda Colley reviewing three of the volumes of the new
History of the University of Oxford in (London) *Times Literary Supplement*, March 13, 1987, p. 261.

The bus pulled in, and children laden with duffel bags bounded into the waiting area. After a few seconds of scanning the crowd, cries of "Mommy, hi!" and "Hey, Ma, over here!" pierced the steamy air.

The scene was repeated every day last week as the Fresh Air Fund wrapped up its 111th summer of vacations for inner-city children. This year, 11,000 children experienced country pleasures by visiting host families in upstate New York and Pennsylvania in the Friendly Towns program or attending the sleep-away camps. . . .
—"Children End Their Season of Fresh Air," *New York Times*, August 23, 1987.

The Pharisee in this story made three very basic mistakes: he thought his heart was pure; he thought ethics was a simple matter; and he thought God was a mere bookkeeper. Unfortunately, I'm always making these same mistakes. . . .

In my more naive moods, I, too, think ethics is a simple matter. I'm a good family man; I try to live altruistically; I have surrendered my life to "the higher calling." In the Pharisee's words, "I am not like other men, extortioners, unjust, adulterers"—or even like the panhandlers. My life is structured, balanced, controlled, constructive.

I am part of humanity, part of the intricate web of global affairs. I have a home and have not taken in the homeless. I have money and I have not bought food for the hungry. I have arms and I have not embraced the outcasts.
—John Killinger, Lenten Meditation, *The Christian Century*, April 1, 1987, pp. 301–302.

Opponents of animal experimentation are taking a militant turn. "We're not just little old ladies in tennis shoes," says Donald Barnes of the National Anti-Vivisection Society. And across the country, researchers say that a growing level of intimidation, along with impending federal rules that would further restrict the use of animals in experimentation, is having a sudden—and chilling—effect on critical work. Many scientists acknowledge that past pressure from animal advocates has led to better care and treatment of laboratory animals. "But now it has gone beyond that," says Dr. Hibbard Williams, dean of the School of Medicine at the University of California at Davis. No longer is the issue humane treatment of animals: It's now the very right of researchers to use animals at all.
—Stephen Budiansky, "Winning Through Intimidation?"
in *U.S. News and World Report*, August 31, 1987.

Readers contemplating a tour of English cathedrals this coming summer should be pleased to learn that a parliamentary report has recommended that the cathedrals receive government grants to ensure their preservation. This is splendidly heartening news for hard-pressed deans and chapters, since the government is now receiving many appeals for astronomical sums. There is a snag, however. To gain the grants, the cathedrals must attempt to secure more money from their great multitude of visitors. . . . Rumor had it that there would be a "compulsory entrance fee before qualifying for state aid," but now it appears that a "recommended" fee would be enough.
—Kenneth Slack, *The Christian Century*, April 1, 1987.

The Fiesta Bowl, in which Pennsylvania State University defeated the University of Miami in January for the unofficial national championship in college football, was a huge financial success.

*The game set records for net payments to the two in-
stitutions, had the highest television rating in the history
of college sports, and pumped $75 million into the econ-
omy of the state of Arizona. . . .
Penn State and Miami each received $2.4 million.*
—Chronicle of Higher Education, December 3, 1986.

*If I had money—say I got lucky and hit the Pick 6,"
said Mr. Ellis, "two types of people I'd look out for. The
elderly and the kids."*
—Michael Winerip in "Our Towns," New York Times,
April 3, 1987.

*In this increasingly technological society, college ed-
ucation will have to play the role previously played by
the factories: providing access to the entry-level jobs that
helped to lift recent generations of America's poor out
of their poverty.
That being the case, we had better stop thinking of
college access for the nation's minorities as a form of
charity we can no longer afford and start thinking of it
as an investment we can't afford not to make.*
—William Raspberry, Washington Post, April 1, 1987.

*Dr. [William F.] Baker, formerly the president of
Group W Television, is taking a pay cut of more than
half, to about $150,000 a year. He said this week that
the WNET job is his way of "giving at the office."
Whether this is another version of commercial television or whether it will truly be a commitment to serving
the public need—that will be the test.
On fund-raising, perhaps the most important aspect
of his job and the one most unfamiliar to him, Mr. Baker*

said, "Hopefully, that's just part of the job. I would find raising money generally abhorrent if it weren't for a cause that I believe in."
— Peter J. Boyer, "New Chief, Hard Job at WNET,"
New York Times, April 2, 1987.

[The Washington Journalism Review will move to the University of Maryland College of Journalism this summer.]

Columbia Journalism Review editor Spencer Klaw said recently to one newspaper reporter that his magazine had turned down a similar proposal because "even if the money were laundered through an endowment, we didn't think we could take money from people we write about."
— *Washington Post,* April 2, 1987.

Willie Nelson is on the road again, plowing ahead with plans for Farm Aid III.

"Naturally, there is not enough money raised to pay off a $225 billion farm debt," the singer-songwriter-guitarist-actor said. "We can't pay off people's notes. But we could send them a little money and we can call attention to the problem. And that's mainly what we're trying to do."
— *Daily Progress* (AP), March 26, 1987.

"Eighty percent of the $82.5 million raised by the hunger anthem, 'We Are the World' and the Hands Across America human chain will be funneled to programs for the needy by May," organizers said Wednesday. USA for Africa released an independent audit which showed that "91 cents out of every dollar donated since the charity's effort inception two years ago was being

spent on programs to help the hungry and homeless in the United States and Africa and not on administration and overhead."

Most important, [USA for Africa President Ken] Kragen stressed, was that the charity efforts raised the national awareness of hunger and homelessness.

—AP, *Daily Progress*, March 26, 1987.

Four former members of a large Northeast Washington Pentecostal church have filed a class-action suit against the ministers there, charging that the church leaders used fraud, coercion and threats to induce the congregation to make large gifts.

The lawsuit . . . . charges that ministers at Evangel Temple on Rhode Island Avenue have pressured church members to sell their homes and encouraged them to fraudulently obtain bank loans to make donations. At the same time, the suit contends, Evangel Temple's ministers have used church funds to enrich themselves.

—*Washington Post*, March 26, 1987.

Sometimes a politician has to get out of the heat and head for the kitchen. Which is what 15 teams of celebrity chefs did Tuesday night during the fifth annual March of Dimes Gourmet Gala at the Sheraton Washington, which raised $200,000 for the cause. "Fables and Fairy Tales" was the theme of the evening, which saw the "culinary magicians" performing for prizes in specially built fantasy mini-kitchens, created by members of the American Society of Interior Designers' local chapter.

—"Chef's Surprise: Serving It Up for the March of Dimes," *Washington Post*, March 26, 1987.

No vision haunts America's conscience more than the sight of the street people, those lonely souls, huddled

*atop a warm grate or slumped in a doorway, their shop-
ping carts piled with despair.*

*It is a national problem that we Americans, in our
compassion, must overcome. Yet because of its random
nature, it is a problem that government has found difficult to handle.*

What can we do?

*Working with a spectrum of mental health groups, I
have developed legislation that is specific to the long-
term problems of the mentally ill among the homeless.
It envisions a five-year effort based on five principles.*

*First, there must be "outreach." We must search the
parks and bus stations. . . .*

Next, we must provide a roof, some real shelter. . . .

Third, we must offer treatment. . . .

*Further, there is "case management." With proper
medicines and attention, most of the estimated 1.6 million Americans who are schizophrenic can function in
society. . . .*

*Finally, there is training. . . . to help medical, social,
and government workers identify persons suffering mental problems. . . .*

—Sen. Pete V. Domenici, Rep., New Mexico, *Washington
Post*, March 26, 1987.

*The activities of university administrators in sanc-
tioning the rental of a university laboratory, along with
the students and researchers therein, may constitute a
serious danger to the university. Many laboratories, formerly institutions producing knowledge of use to all in
society—consumers, workers, farmers, businesspeople—
have become captives of a single corporation. The result
is that the freely usable knowledge base is shrunk, and
this could lead to a lack of information for those unable
to purchase it. The frenzied courting of industry by university administrators and faculty willing to sell nearly
anything seems particularly inappropriate, since these
same administrators are charged with the responsibility*

of acting for the good of the great university community, and the university has a self-proclaimed obligation to serve the greater good of society.

The point is not only that the knowledge being sold was paid for by the public but, even more important, that the university, a peculiar and fragile social institution that can trace its history back to early feudalism, is being subsumed by industry, one of the very institutions with which it should, to some degree, be in conflict. When university and industry become partners, the entire society is endangered, for the demise of the university as an independent institution will lead to the crippling of the tradition of an independent university. . . .

Perhaps the cruelest irony will be experienced by U.S. industry itself. As the university is bought and parceled out, basic science in the university will increasingly suffer. The speculative, noncommercial scholar will be at a disadvantage, and the intellectual commons so important for producing a trained labor force and the birthplace of new ideas will be eroded and polluted. Industry will then discover that by being congenitally unable to control itself and having no restraints placed on it by the public sector it has polluted its own reservoir.

—Martin Kenney, Ohio State University (Department of Agricultural Economics and Rural Sociology), from *Biotechnology: The University-Industrial Complex,* Yale University Press, in *Chronicle of Higher Education*, January 7, 1987, p. 43.

As a nation, we must expand both the private and public sectors to meet the needs of a high-tech international economy. As a nation, we must be both liberal and conservative simultaneously—but be able to distinguish clearly and effectively which of these qualities to apply to basic human needs and which to apply to our

limited but expanding human and environmental re-
sources.

> —Wilbur J. Cohen, former Secretary HEW, in
> "Rostrum," *US News and World Report,*
> March 18, 1987.

So far as I know, William Golding, the British author,
never visited—probably never even thought about—the
violence-wracked inner cities of America.

And yet, when I think about what is happening in
so many places—emphatically including Detroit, where
black teenagers are shooting each other at the appalling
rate of nearly one a day—I find myself reflecting on a
theme that runs through practically all the 76-year-old
Golding's fiction.

The theme is this: the moral order we call civilization
is a delicate skin-deep thing that, left untended, peels
away to expose us for the amoral savages we really
are. . . .

> —William Strawberry, "Children of the Streets,"
> *Washington Post,* May 4, 1987.

In May 1829, a small advertisement in a Paris review
announced a remarkable discovery that would quadruple
national revenues, eliminate national debts, free black
slaves and enrich writers, artists and teachers. "Chi-
meras, visions, you will say! No, it is a new and highly
methodical science." Charles Fourier, who elaborated
this his new science, was then 57 years old. Offspring
of a provincial family, ruined by the French Revolution
and his own fecklessness, he had spent most of his life
in what he called the jailhouse of commerce as a clerk,
broker or traveling salesman. Emancipated by a small
annuity that his mother left and his sisters paid reluc-

tantly, supported by contributions from a few friends and admirers, he was able to present his discoveries in writings that struck their few readers—as they did the American consul in Paris—as "either a genuine curiosity or the emanation of a disturbed brain."
> —Eugen Weber, "Here's to Sexual Philanthropy," review
> of Jonathan Beecher, *Charles Fourier: The Visionary and
> His World,* in *The New York Times Book Review* (n.d.).

When police arrived at James Turley's apartment in Southeast Washington on Friday night, his 22-year-old son Tommy was standing in the yard holding a handgun. People were running for cover. Tommy had allegedly shot two neighbors and had emptied the gun firing at others.

As far as police matters go, it was a routine occurrence for the first of the month, or "Mother's Day," as welfare check day is called. Within 48 hours, nearly $5.7 million in public assistance funds had been funneled into the poorest neighborhoods of the city, causing as much chaos as comfort. . . .
> —Courtland Milloy, " 'Mother's Day' Madness,"
> *Washington Post,* May 3, 1987.

A. H. Robins Co. and its leaders have been sturdy pillars of numerous civic and charitable enterprises in Richmond—so much so that in 1983, Town and Country magazine listed Chairman E. Claiborne Robins Sr. among the five "Most Generous Americans."

But the good works of the 121-year-old company and the family were of no consequence to Kansas courts when judges recently scorned Robins' argument that philanthropy demonstrated an absence of knowing and willful wrongdoing in connection with the Dalkon Shield.

"A person who is ordinarily a philanthropist and hu-

manitarian does not receive thereby a license to commit intentional wrongs on his days off," the Kansas Supreme Court said in a 7–0 decision upholding a record $9.2 million award to a victim of the Dalkon Shield.
—*Washington Post*, July 1, 1987.

In the context of the Ivan Boesky scandal and the decision by Jewish Theological Seminary to remove his name from a building, there is this passage in Jefferson's letter of September 23, 1800 to Benjamin Rush: "Death alone can seal the title of any man to this honor [of having something named for him], by putting it out of his power to forfeit it."
—*Thomas Jefferson*, Library of America, p. 1081.

PART I

Major
Challenges to
Philanthropy

A Reader's
Guide

This guide is not an executive summary; it merely highlights some of the points and questions that arise in Part I of this book. Its purpose is to help the reader keep in mind some of the common themes Part I lays out and discusses.

And this section is a discussion. It asks questions, offers some opinions, but gives few answers.

My starting point was the establishment of Independent Sector* itself: why there should be such an organization, and who should belong to it. The months of discussion and debate that led up to the creation of Independent Sector were summarized in a very useful essay prepared by the Organizing Committee. It is now almost five years later. It is timely to reflect on some of the original understandings and assumptions.

Format

My own first and most fundamental question is one of definition: When we talk about the independent sector, about philanthropy, volunteering, pluralism, and related terms, to what do we refer? Is there any agreement among us about what is included and what is excluded? This is not simply a matter of a taxonomy of organizations. It also raises questions of values.

*Founded a decade ago, Independent Sector is the umbrella organization of the field: its 600 members include nonprofit organizations (50%); foundations (25%), and corporations (25%).

27

The Introduction to Part I explains that it is a search for common themes and values and ideas, with an effort to bring to the surface some of the problems such a search reveals.

The chapter entitled "The Varieties of Philanthropic Experience" is an effort to identify the major elements of the field. Early in that chapter, there is an outline I devised headed "The Philanthropic Tradition." The chapter is a commentary on that outline, with one major exception: the professional dimension of our work, and the relations between professionals and volunteers and among the people served by them, are the subjects of a separate chapter, "Philanthropy as a Vocation."

There is also a separate chapter on some of the problems that come to mind in thinking at length about the independent sector. That is entitled "Philanthropy and Its Discontents."

Approach

At the center of the whole discussion is the tension that exists in almost every aspect of the field. The first law of philanthropy, like the first law of medicine, is *Do no harm.* That poses a question, then, that must precede any action.

It isn't an easy question. Nor are others. A friend just called who is a trustee of a not-for-profit organization that is in the midst of a severe financial crisis. She wants to help it survive.

Should it survive? Is it the responsibility of this funding source to see to it that it has a chance to survive?

Every decision like that has an opportunity cost. One decision will preclude another, and the second choice may be "more important"—what do I mean by that?—than the first.

A provocative challenge was made by one reader to the talk about "compassion" in the essay. "Charity is the enemy of philanthropy," he said. The purpose of philanthropy, by his argument, is "strategic capital investment in economic betterment." Diverting scarce resources to emergencies simply prevents the development of solutions that will prevent similar emergencies in the future.

Item 5 of the "philanthropic tradition" outline identifies

some of the dialectical aspects of our work. The commentary argues, among other things, that acts of mercy and acts of justice are often in conflict. Another example that turns up time and again, on the theme of poverty and welfare, is the conflict between what is received (or denied) by voluntary action, and what can be claimed as a right.

At several different points the political dimension of philanthropy comes up. How independent is the independent sector, for example. How independent can organizations be, asked one reader of this paper, that depend on the government for practically all of their income?

The ancient books of the Jews are filled with "and on the other hand" kinds of comments. St. Thomas Aquinas organized his vast theological system around arguments for and against.

This essay is an unsystematic effort to do the same thing. Chris Argyris of Yale, a specialist in organizational behavior and development, wrote somewhere about "optimal fuzziness." That's what this emphasis on tension, contradiction, paradox—the dialectical quality—is intended to achieve.

There are no final, fixed, certain answers. There are some unavoidable questions.

Why Bother?

Why should we go to all this trouble? Why should we carve out several hours of valuable meeting time at the annual meeting that could better be given to the hard problems facing us?

My assumption is that most of the people in the country who ought to know about and understand these issues will be involved in the work of Independent Sector, and that you will be among them. You and I are among the few thousand professionals who share the principal burden of defending the philanthropic tradition.

That was John Gardner's pregnant insight: Some of the people within the sector must come together and act in behalf of the system as a whole.

There are probably other fields where the general level

of shared knowledge and values is lower than in this sector, but I can't call any to mind offhand. There are few fields of such vast magnitude that have stimulated so little curiosity among scholars . . .

But I digress again, chasing off after things that come up in the chapter on "Discontents."

Professionals have a moral obligation to understand what they do and why they do it, as well as how they might do it better and—at some point—even how they might better their own condition in the process.

That's why I wrote this essay, and that's why I hope you'll read it.

Introduction

When the day of judgement comes we shall be
examined about what we have done, not what
we have read; whether we have lived consci-
entiously, not whether we have learned fine
phrases.

Thomas à Kempis
The Imitation of Christ

One purpose of this essay is to provide some common themes
for discussion, both in terms of concrete issues and problems
and in terms of abiding questions that are sometimes vex-
atious and at other times illuminating.

Because one person was commissioned to write it, the essay will reflect one person's wanderings, ruminations, and
opinions. What is said is personal, not institutional or collective: It does not present the views of Independent Sector,
Exxon Education Foundation, the Independent Sector Research Committee, the Columbia University Seminar on Philanthropy, Catholic Relief Services, or of the Garden City
Community Church Theology and Track Club; nor does it
claim to represent the views of Brian O'Connell, Richard Lyman, John Gardner, Virginia Hodgkinson, or of those quoted
herein—all of which and whom have some current influence
on what I think about these matters.

"These matters" are labeled "Major Challenges to Philanthropy" in the announcements for the annual members'
meeting of Independent Sector for which this essay was

written. That usage solves one problem of terminology. In this text the word *philanthropy* will be used in two ways: first, as a comprehensive term that includes voluntary giving, voluntary service, and voluntary association, primarily for the benefit of others; and second as the prudent sister of charity, philanthropy and charity being intertwined threads throughout most of the 3,500 years of the philanthropic tradition in Western civilization.

The most difficult assumptions to examine are your own, especially when they are beneath the surface of consciousness. A second purpose of this essay is to bring some assumptions about philanthropy to the surface for examination and discussion.

There are many areas of disagreement among us, and many unresolved problems. Yet beyond our domestic quarrels are enemies and critics whose points of view are not compatible with ours. Critics and enemies can almost always claim some validity for what they say; it is incumbent on us, if we are to contend with them, to be able to answer the legitimate charges. This essay may be as good a place as any to try to bring out some of the arguments against what we claim to do (there always being some gap between our words and our deeds, in any event).

This will be an exercise in which we examine our own assumptions and those of others who come to different conclusions. It will involve two different kinds of source material: gleanings from reports published by people within the sector and from newspapers, magazines, and journals; it will also draw on the literature and language of the tradition. I find it enlightening, somehow, to alternate between thinking about almsgiving in Jeremy Taylor's *The Rules and Exercises of Holy Living* from 1650 and a guidebook to modern fund raising; to compare the language of a corporation's report on its 1983 contributions with that of Charles Loch's summary of the principles of charity in 1895.

Philanthropy is not a firmly fixed and settled compendium of values and practices. The most common observation about the independent sector and the philanthropic tradition is that generalizations about them are almost always wrong. The quickest way to sense that is to do as I did shortly after I agreed to write this paper: I looked through the alphabetical list of the member organizations of Independent Sector. (Try "O"–Older Women's League, Olin Corporation, Open Space Institute, Opera America, Organization of Chinese Women, etc.)

The main purpose of the essay, then, is to consider whether there is a common set of themes that we might discuss—beyond being tax exempt and not-for-profit.

But Aristotle warns us not to impose greater order on a subject than the subject permits; the philanthropic tradition is just such a subject. Its origins are as complex as the words *compassion* and *community*, and if I impose order on them it is to help me reduce great complexity to some manageable simplicity—the test for both of us is to remember that that's what I've done.

Another way to delimit the field is to turn to the statements of Independent Sector itself. The Organizing Committee Report reflects a point of view:

> On the most basic level the central task of this new organization will be to strengthen the nation's traditions of giving, volunteering, and not-for-profit initiative.

In thinking it through, the Committee came to the now-familiar list of five tasks:

- Public education,
- Communication,
- Relationships with government,
- Research, and
- Effective sector management.

The board and membership of the new Independent Sector then added a sixth task:

- Measurable growth in giving and volunteering.

The Organizing Committee Report also concluded that Independent Sector should foster certain values:

- Commitment beyond self,
- Worth and dignity of the individual,
- Individual responsibility,

- Tolerance,
- Freedom,
- Justice, and
- Responsibilities of citizenship.

Finally, the Report listed eight problems:

1. Relative decline in giving,
2. Encroachments on the freedom of citizens to organize,
3. Negative impact of changes in tax policy,
4. Greater dependence on government funding by independent institutions,
5. Governmental influence on the agenda of the independent sector,
6. The limitations of some of the organizations in the sector,
7. Limited public understanding of the sector, and
8. Inadequate recognition of the importance of having alternatives and multiple sources of giving.

It isn't really possible to keep such an array of themes, topics, and issues in mind; you may find it useful, as I have, to return to them from time to time. It is also helpful to rank and order them or re-order them according to your own understanding of what makes the most sense. I tend to approach this subject from the perspective of ideas: *Ideas Have Consequences*, as Richard Weaver put it. Behind or beneath tax policy or giving levels and organizational dependency are more fundamental questions. Philanthropy is one of three sectors; it does not stand alone. (It may even be, as someone suggested the other day, not really a "sector" at all, but merely the frazzled edges of the other two.)

"Public education" would come first on my list, probably because of my professional background. But before education is possible in the sense of teaching someone something, it is necessary to know and understand, even to master the underlying principles and methods of the subject. Prior to "public education," then, there is "professional education"— even though I don't believe most of us can claim the right to call ourselves professionals. (Perhaps, as you'll discover later, you may not want to.)

We should set about educating ourselves about the reasons why there is a philanthropic tradition, and whether it should be encouraged or is instead merely the artifact of an earlier and less enlightened level of social development. The practice of private giving for public purposes appears to be in good shape in this country: Our own research indicates that the level continues to rise steadily—and $90 billion is a lot of money. The practice of voluntary service also appears to be vigorous: The estimates indicate as many as 90 million volunteers. The condition of an estimated 870,000 voluntary associations seems to resist all efforts to suppress them or even to dampen their creation and expansion.

Who can find evidence for concern in such statistics?

Let me report a few of the kinds of statements we've all heard that could give us cause for concern:

- The relative decline in giving may reflect a weakening of the habit of giving and a weakening of the binding force of religion.
- We may be victims of our own initiatives: The emphasis on tax incentives may leave us without stronger reasons for our generosity.
- The public commitment to the philanthropic tradition grows weaker each generation.
- The experience of other developed and democratic societies proves that a third sector isn't really necessary.
- Fund raising is turning away from face-to-face contact and relying increasingly on direct mail and even television.
- Paid staff are becoming more expert in the growing complexity of large-scale philanthropy. The unhappy fact of life is that there is no longer a useful place for the volunteer.
- Fund raising is becoming prohibitively expensive, especially given the scale of needs to be met.
- Responsible stewardship argues for vastly increased government funding (even if through voluntary agencies) and a sharp reduction in the number of voluntary organizations. Let only the well-managed survive.

- The sector cannot be relied on to police itself; if we do expect it to police itself, we must insist on fuller accountability.
- Corporations are turning inward; they are less and less interested in the causes they support and more interested in turning their grants into sources of profit.

That is another kind of list. It absorbs and restates some of the "problems" identified by the Organizing Committee five years ago. The purpose it is supposed to serve at this point is to suggest something less than unanimity about the sector, in spite of its apparent health and vitality.

Someone asked me a few weeks ago, after listening to me go on through lunch about the importance of philanthropy as a theme of general education, what it is that makes me give this subject so much importance. One answer might be cast in terms of my self-interest—the way we usually assess other people's motives. My job depends on it. If the sector thrives, I will. I will benefit economically. I will also benefit in terms of self-esteem and self-importance if philanthropy becomes a positive and constant image in the public mind. The subject is presumably of some intellectual interest to me, also, and in this way I am able to enjoy the pleasures of research and be paid for it. I am able to participate in meetings such as the annual meeting of Independent Sector, and that brings me into personal contact with others who share my interests and my prejudices. I have a good job, that is, and my personal interests fit closely and comfortably with my professional interests.

The self-interest of each of us is catalogued something like that: It is both revealing and distorting of what makes us tick. There is an assumption of something beyond self-interest; it shapes our lives and guides our careers. It also encourages us to believe that there is something beyond self-interest in most people, and that we can appeal to it in them as it provides motivation for us.

The Varieties of Philanthropic Experience

No one denies that a system needs enough indifference to hold it together and enough involvement to make it move. The question is:
how much is enough?

Dennis F. Thompson
The Democratic Citizen

The title is borrowed from *The Varieties of Religious Experience* by William James. James drew from a vast array of
writings of responsible people and tried to infer from what
they said about their own religious experiences and understandings a classification of the principal forms that emerged.

This essay is an attempt to make a map of the territory.
What do we include within the definition of the word *philanthropy?* What must we leave out? Why?

In addition to boundaries, what are the practices and values that we may justly call *philanthropic?*

What follows is an outline of the philanthropic tradition:

37

an outline in the literal sense, first, followed by commentary and interpretation.

I think it is important to seek a rough consensus about such an outline, knowing that it is too simple and arbitrary and also that it is constantly changing. Our work will suffer unless we achieve some greater shared understanding—suffer from avoidable internal conflict and suffer from external attacks and intrusions.

Philanthropy is one aspect of religion; there are also philanthropic dimensions to economics and politics. One can approach philanthropy from the perspective of any of the humanities and social sciences: history, literature, anthropology, and so on. One can also look at its functions: how money is raised, how it is given, and how it is used. There are also the people involved: the volunteers and professionals. Some approach philanthropy from the vantage point of the structure of the society and its institutions, and see in it only the expression of class struggle, domination, alienation, and false consciousness. Others look on philanthropy as a subset of exchange—social as well as economic—ruling out the sublime emotions in favor of what they term more rigorous analysis.

This long chapter (not half long enough!) attempts to relate to the following outline of the philanthropic traditions. You will notice that some categories overlap and are not as distinct as the outline suggests. You should try to bear in mind, too, as I have, that it isn't possible to design a definitive outline of a dynamic tradition. (I welcome your improvements of it.)

The Philanthropic Tradition

1. A living tradition
   a. Core values and themes
   b. Constantly changing
2. Philanthropy will always be with us, because
   a. Things go wrong, and some people need help
   b. Things could always be better for all of us

3. The need for public goods
    a. Limitations on the marketplace
    b. Limitations on government
4. Philanthropy is the manifestation of two values
    a. Compassion (charity)
    b. Community (philanthropy)
5. The philanthropic dialectic
    a. Self and other
    b. Love and fear
    c. Mercy and justice
    d. Voluntary and obligatory
    e. Relief and development
6. The works of mercy
    a. Corporal
    b. Spiritual
7. Methods of philanthropy
    a. Mutual aid
    b. Empowerment and self-help
    c. Without strings
    d. A mixed economy (welfare issues)
8. The dynamic of philanthropy
    a. From impulse to habit
    b. From simple to complex
    c. From individual to collective
    d. From voluntary to obligatory
    e. From private to public
    f. From relief to development
9. There are two basic types of philanthropic activity
    a. Organizing, recruiting, fund-raising
    b. Contributing services, expertise, money
10. There are six major areas of philanthropic activity
    a. Religion
    b. Health
    c. Education
    d. Welfare
    e. Culture
    f. Civic and community affairs

11. There are two categories of personal participation
    a. Volunteer
       (1) Expert
       (2) Non-expert
    b. Paid
       (1) Professional/managerial/technical
       (2) Secretarial/clerical/maintenance

A Living Tradition

Philanthropy is a tradition, "a sequence of variations on received and transmitted themes," as Edward Shils put it in *Tradition*. It is not a body of laws, nor is it a fixed set of institutions. As a tradition it has common roots, themes, practices, and values. As a tradition it is also dynamic and changing, and the themes, practices, and values change so that even tracing the roots becomes a continuing problem. It is "the social history of the moral imagination" (to borrow a wonderful phrase from Clifford Geertz's *Local Knowledge*, p. 8), or at least one prominent thread in it.

Philanthropy in some organized form appears in all the major cultural and religious traditions, and it might be argued that *philanthropy is an essential defining characteristic of civilized society.*

Things Go Wrong

The disturbances of our domestic tranquillity in the late 1960s and early 1970s serve as a reminder that things can go seriously wrong even in a society as blessed and favored as this one. Given the right circumstances, in every society there will be opportunities to improve the quality of life in the community and there will be reasons for acts of mercy and compassion. In sum, as John Gall declared, "All systems operate in a failure mode most of the time." That is a caution to all the idealists, optimists, Utopians, and other true believers that "the best-laid schemes o' mice and men gang aft a-gley." Religion sometimes puts a good face on it, and declares that the poor offer opportunities for charity that will win us credit in heaven.

The reason this simple idea is important is because there are two fallacies of the modern age that would eliminate philanthropy entirely. Both are blindly Utopian. The first is a misinterpretation of the "invisible hand" that applies economic self-interest as the criterion of *all* behavior. The second is an interpretation that argues that the state best understands the needs of the society and of individuals and has the primary responsibility for their welfare; the state, therefore, must have the power and authority to plan and provide for them as necessary. Whatever labels we put on them, neither has a place for philanthropy.

Self-interest as the principal acceptable motive for economic behavior seems to me far superior to the notion that the state can plan economic activity with such wisdom as to produce a humane and free society. But the self-interested society tends to pay for its wealth by a loss of humanity; the planned society certainly pays for distributive justice by the loss of freedom, political as well as economic.

Philanthropy—to paraphrase James Douglas's splendid book, *Why Charity?*—is the instrument that societies have used to compensate for the indifference of the marketplace and the incompetence of the state. *Voluntary acts of compassion and acts of community are always needed, in all societies, and always will be.*

Public Goods

The quality of life even in modern America and in other economically advanced societies makes the scale of resources required beyond the reach of private, voluntary giving. Churches, corporations, universities, artists, and intellectuals willingly and properly accept government funds: It is in their self-interest to do so; most will argue that it is also in the public interest for them to do so. The scale of need is so great that voluntary contributions inevitably fall short.

Less often voiced is a second theme: Many of the needs of community are what economists call *public goods* which

. . . bestow benefits that are often so widely diffused that
it is impossible to allocate their costs to the individual ben-
eficiaries in a commensurate proportion. Moreover, in the
case of pure public goods their enjoyment by some will not
curtail their enjoyment by others. The market will not produce such goods for a variety of reasons, but chiefly because
if everyone can enjoy what it produced for someone else,
no one will want to reveal his demand for a public good.
(Henry W. Spiegel, *The Growth of Economic Thought*)

If someone else will pay for something that I will then be
able to use, why should I pay for it? Mr. Jones built a private
road and a private bridge; when others began to use it, Mr.
Jones concluded that the next road and bridge would be built
by someone else. When no one stepped forward—when no
one volunteered—"the public" had to pay for it, or it wasn't
built at all.

The reason I prolong this is because not enough attention
is given to the range and variety of public goods, and which
among them should be provided by taxation and which might
be left to the marketplace and to private philanthropy. This
becomes a powerfully important question in my mind because it involves a determination of the best way to preserve
the freedom of thought. For example:

How Should Philosophers Be Paid?

If, as has been the case in recent years, philosophers are
primarily dependent on income derived from teaching, and
if it is true that there has been a decline in the number of
students who take courses in philosophy; and if it is the case
that those who provide financial support to colleges and universities through gifts and grants either neglect philosophy
or attach strings to their gifts to philosophers; and if the popular culture is bored with philosophy and philosophy can
claim little share of the vast sums generated by television
advertising, say, or the more profitable books clubs . . . Or if
philosophers have to spend so much time teaching in order
to earn a living that they have no time for reflection, dis-

cussion, debate, and research on questions that may not prove to be fruitful (the same problems plague mathematicians, by the way), then perhaps there is a place for philanthropic support. The marketplace usually ignores philosophy because it isn't "useful"; the state usually becomes very heavy-handed in making sure philosophers *are* useful, but in one Right Way.

Some philosophers now find employment as "ethicists" on the staffs of hospitals or an occasional business corporation. Some abandon philosophy for other, more practical and profitable occupations.

Almost everything about the work of philosophers must be subsidized. How? By whom? Philosophers, whether in the narrow professional sense of the term or more broadly considered, are the ones who advise us about the Good, the Beautiful, the True; about compassion, justice, and community. Do we have enough philosophers? Is their work as good as it ought to be? Are they working on the right problems?

The foundation with which I was associated considers these to be relevant and important questions, even though the corporation that supports the foundation is almost entirely engaged in the production of energy resources. Why should such a company make contributions to support the work of philosophers?

I raise the question here as a means of focusing on how things are paid for in American society, obscure things like philosophy as well as obvious things like health. The questions are usually segmented into questions of how money is raised, and by whom, and by whom it is given, and for what purposes. Philanthropic activity that thinks about health while ignoring philosophy, that thinks about science but not about religion, will lead us into the temptation of believing that only our bodies are important.

Two Values

"Words are tools that break in the hand."
We can press words too hard, misapply them, let them

lose their shape and utility. Trying to write about philanthropy makes painfully clear how many of our problems stem
from an inadequate, often rusted and even broken vocabu-
lary. It would be timely to find a word that could replace
philanthropy, much as philanthropy replaced charity. Awkward coinages like "voluntaryism" are unlikely to catch on;
others, like *pluralism*, leave too much out.

Until a better word is found, philanthropy will have to
do. It is a protean word, like *society* or *religion*. There are
two central ideas embraced by it in its present usage: *compassion* and *community*. Compassion is another of the many
terms we have employed to get around the hopeless ambiguity of the word *love*. It implies an understanding, sympathetic concern for another who is in some way in distress
or need, and who cannot cope with the situation alone, without help.

Community relates to the things that bring us and hold
us together. The emphasis is on mutuality and sharing, common values that override or discipline our self-interest and
competitiveness; a healthy community not only permits but
encourages vigorous individual development within a few
powerful constraints.

Compassion, then, has a strong emotional quality; it is
not thoughtless, but it is not calculating, either. *Community*
has a more rational tone, more reflective; it can be emotional—with a vengeance—but it implies organization, plan,
prudence, calculation.

Given that warning, one might accept an interpretation
that attributes the dimension of compassion in the philanthropic tradition to origins among the Jews and Christians
of the ancient Near East, and the origins of the dimension
of community to the Greeks and Romans of the classical period.

As a tradition in the Western world that emerged out of
the cultures of the ancient Near East and the Mediterranean
region, the philanthropic tradition is very old. It is difficult
for us to think in terms of decades, much less centuries and
millenia. It would be as easy to overestimate as to under-
estimate the importance of this fact: The philanthropic tra-

dition is older than democracy, older than Christianity, older than formal education, perhaps as much as 2,000 years older than the oldest university.

The Philanthropic Dialectic

There is tension, even conflict, within philanthropy. We often say that philanthropy expresses a concern for others, but the two notions of self and other are inseparable. As the Mishnah asks:

> If I am not for myself who is for me?
> and being for mine own self what am I?
>   and if not now, when?

Philanthropy, in my view, occurs at the juncture of economics and religion; it may appear at the juncture of politics and religion as well. "A fence about riches is alms," according to the Mishnah: The philanthropic is a restraint on self-interest, selfishness, acquisitiveness, greed. The philanthropic is also a bridle on power; it introduces compassion into community, but—and this has become increasingly important in the modern era—it is also a goad to the public conscience.

Kenneth Boulding has been an important contributor for me in trying to think about philanthropy. The original title of his principal book on the subject is *The Economy of Love and Fear.* There is a dialectical tension between the two.

Boulding's notions of "love" and "fear" are revealing of our values. The late 1960s and early 1970s were filled with dramatic evidence of philanthropic acts motivated by fear. There is, in fact, a long history of arguments for helping the poor (more recently including the foreign poor) based on fear: If you don't feed them now, the angry mobs will rise up and destroy you.

Why do we make gifts to others? Boulding speaks of gifts without return, gifts that may bring satisfaction but no compensating material benefit. He calls them "one-way transfers of exchangeables." With the poetry that Boulding has always brought to economics (and everything else he writes about), he describes the two basic motivations as love and fear.

But there are other kinds of fear that motivate philanthropic behavior: fear of divine retribution, fear of loss of self-esteem, fear of not "living on" in your works after your death.

Love is an accepted philanthropic motivation; fear probably isn't; greed never is. An act of compassion might prompt gratitude; an act of fear is likely to inspire contempt. Some philanthropic acts seem to rise out of both emotions.

What is the place of guilt in our philanthropic behavior? It is certainly a powerful motivator for many people, as is the desire to have our works survive us. To what extent are we expressing guilt not about our own behavior, but for that of earlier generations?

Are other psychological forces at work—sublimation, for example?

Memories of one's own past needs might prompt sympathy for the needs of another later on. How others responded to you yesterday may inspire or deflate your inclination to respond to others tomorrow.

Similar arguments appear in philanthropic service to the Third World. If we help underdeveloped countries to educate themselves, they will be able to develop economically; if they develop economically, they will provide markets for our goods and we will buy more of theirs.

Some will then assume, though not out loud: "and then they will owe us something for helping them." Foreign aid is a way of buying allies, according to such a rationale; it often becomes an exchange of food for military bases.

Does the present generation in western Europe "owe" the present generation in the United States for the Marshall Plan? Does one generation inherit the moral credit or guilt for the acts of an earlier generation? Do they inherit gratitude and resentment?

Can gratitude and friendship be bought? If so, why aren't we more popular? Is it because we've used our philanthropic resources for political purposes? People look at what we do and conclude that we are like the Water-man, in John Bunyan's *The Pilgrim's Progress*, looking one way and rowing another. Has the mixture of political, economic, and philanthropic motives simply won us a reputation for hypocrisy? Do we act from a sense of compassion and a concern for world community, or from fear and greed?

One-way transfers are not all philanthropic, but all philanthropic transfers are one-way.

Throughout the other chapters of Part I there is direct or indirect reference to the trade off between "mercy" and "righteousness," between compassion and justice. I won't expand on it here, except to offer a reminder that mercy and justice prompt very different responses: The anger of righteous indignation often overwhelms the tender concern of sympathy; mercy without justice may merely perpetuate the need for alms. Implicit in this dialectical tension are the struggles of the Roman Catholic Church in Latin America, to cite but one current example.

There seems to be an inexorable movement from the voluntary to the obligatory. It can be traced in the ancient books of the Jews, from a divine mandate to help the poor and defenseless to a precisely specified set of instructions about how much to give. (I would argue—although there is not room for it here—that the roots of the philanthropic tradition are religious; a distinguished anthropologist tells me that religion is not necessary to explain philanthropic behavior. I think there is an important issue involved, and not just a semantic dispute.)

Can an act mandated by God be thought of as "voluntary"? Is a charitable gift that responds to social pressure to be thought of as "voluntary"? Can a voluntary sector dominated by paid professionals be thought of as "voluntary"? These questions weaken a bit what might otherwise be thought to be a comfortable generalization about philanthropy: *All philanthropic giving is private and voluntary.*

Those questions seem to lead to some troubling conclusions: that *state philanthropy* is a contradiction in terms, for example. Such questions also seem to imply the conclusion that *corporate philanthropy* is a contradiction in terms as well. (Some people like to contend that corporate philanthropy is a tax on shareholders and employees, a tax imposed without giving them a right to decline to participate.) The critics of the idea of "public altruism" make their case on the grounds of the missing voluntary dimension in mobilizing the resources in the first place. If the funds are not voluntarily given, but collected, their transfer to someone else is not voluntary, therefore not philanthropic.* The state and the corporation are thus seen to be agents in giving away "other people's money," yours and mine, as taxpayers and share-holders, as employees of government and of corporations. The purpose of the gift is not determining, in other words; it is the voluntary initiative that makes the gift possible that makes it philanthropic.

Is an act philanthropic if it means that you merely have discretionary use of funds not your own? What credit or blame, if any, carries over from a collective act to the in-dividual's participation—especially central participation—in it?

If the government uses my taxes to pay for grants of food for starving Ethiopians, have I somehow participated in a charitable act? This is the other side of the argument of the good bishop who is withholding a share of his tax payments from the IRS to detach himself from arms expenditures by the government. The argument against the bishop is that he can't designate his taxes the way he might earmark a gift; the government may apply all the taxes the bishop does pay to armaments and apply none of it to welfare. That is the argument against my claiming a share in the aid to starving Ethiopians and denying a share of the military help to warring Salvadorans.

Is the voluntary dimension of collective giving by gov-ernments, corporations, and churches symbolic? Something that I read in an essay by a British theologian prompted this very awkward and troublesome question: "Does a Christian meet his Christian obligations to his fellow man by paying taxes in a welfare state?" (To phrase the question differently:

---

*A friend of mine recalled Robert Sherrill's line that "military justice is to justice as military music is to music." Does this, he asks, provide a parallel to corporate philanthropy? Is corporate philanthropy to *real* phi-lanthropy as corporate advertising is to literature?

Does a corporate employee share in the giving of his or her corporation in such a way that he or she can not only claim "I gave at the office," but even claim that "the office gave for me?")

Is it important? Americans allocate several hundred billions of tax dollars to welfare programs that include substantial sums for widows, orphans, and strangers as in ancient times, and for old age pensions, unemployment insurance, and other benefits of the modern era. If one expends 40%, say, of his or her gross income in taxes, and some substantial share of that is used for the poor, needy, and disabled (including some of those in other countries), why should one *voluntarily* give even more?

Answer: The requirements of compassion and community go far beyond what we are willing to tax ourselves for.

Must charity be coerced? In its simplest form, it says that the needs that we have sought to meet by voluntary giving in the past exceed what voluntary giving will ever produce. However we organize ourselves to raise money from private contributions, the demands of just economic distribution go far beyond what our voluntary efforts will generate.

The secular—that is, long-term—trend appears to be to shift the responsibility for the material needs of the poor from voluntary charity to public welfare. Compassion becomes bureaucratized.

The more recent trends would also indicate that efforts to improve the quality of life—the dimension of community—are also shifting from the private to the public sector, from voluntary to obligatory support of the arts, the humanities, the sciences, even to economically driven activities like engineering and technology.

The Works of Mercy

I speak with no authority about the work of St. Thomas Aquinas—but I greatly admire his work and find it useful in thinking about philanthropy. The volume on charity in the *Summa Theologiae* includes a "question" on almsgiving, and introduces a perspective that spells out what is meant by being personally and directly engaged in philanthropic work. The Roman Catholic tradition divides almsgiving into corporal and spiritual works of mercy, and makes convenient lists of them that Aquinas reduces to a few words. (It is worth comparing this list with those from the Organizing Committee Report mentioned in the "Introduction.")

The corporal works of mercy "are summed up," Thomas writes, "in the verse, *Visito, poto, cibo, redimo, tego, colligo, condo* [visit, give drink, feed, rescue, clothe, gather, bury]."

"Then," St. Thomas continues, "there are the seven kinds of spiritual almsgiving that are usually listed: instructing the ignorant, giving advice to those in doubt, consoling the sorrowful, reproving sinners, forgiving offenses, putting up with people who are burdensome and hard to get on with, and finally, praying for all." (*Consule, solare, castiga, remitte, fer, ora*, with the word *consule* covering both advice and instruction.)

The spiritual works of mercy cannot be wholesaled. We may be able to increase the amount and improve the distribution of corporal alms, but not the spiritual ones. Not, at least, if our purpose is to awaken and develop the moral imagination.

- Trevor Farrell is an 11-year-old from suburban Philadelphia who provides help to the homeless and derelict "street people" as part of a "family ministry." (*New York Times*)
- Since 1970 Lola Martin has run a program to provide volunteer tutors (whom she has trained) to help adults who cannot read or write. Lola Martin is herself legally blind. She has worked without public money, contributing from her own savings and raising money by selling cakes and crocheted dolls. Faced with loss of her storefront reading center, she said, "I was doing so good. I'm not ready to give up. I can't. There are too many people out there who need me." (*Newsday*)
- A volunteer at the Bowery Residents Committee center is himself a former derelict and alcoholic. "I've never felt so needed . . . since working here I've never felt so useful. I help people here as much as I can, but I help myself tenfold." (*New York Times*)

There is in such statements a reflection of experience that cannot be derived authentically as well as vicariously, merely from reading about it or observing it. Voluntary *service* is clearly critical to the philanthropic understanding.

Those who are personally involved speak to us with the authority of their witness; it may be the closest we can get to sharing the suffering we seek to alleviate.

We can attend to misfortune but we may also have to judge it: Not all sufferers are innocent.

In the mid-17th century, Jeremy Taylor attempted to elaborate on the lists of the corporal and spiritual works of mercy:

> According to thy ability give to all men that need: and, in equal needs, give first to good men, and then to bad men; and if the needs be unequal do so too; provided that the need of the poorest be not violent or extreme: but if an evil man be in extreme necessity, he is to be relieved rather than a good man who can tarry longer, and may subsist without it. . . . The best objects of charity are poor housekeepers, that labour hard, and are burdened with many children; or Gentlemen fallen into sad poverty, especially if by innocent misfortune . . . persecuted persons, widows, and fatherless children, putting them to honest trades or schools of learning . . . And search into the needs of numerous and meaner families: for there are many persons that have nothing left but misery and modesty. (P. 236)

Noel Timms, in his *Social Work Values*, discusses acceptance, self-determination, and respect for persons as positive values in social work, and identifies manipulation and paternalism as examples of "disvalues." The positive values are inseparable from personal contact; the disvalues thrive on the impersonal. It is only on the basis of personal involvement and understanding that we can make judgments of "desert," judgments of who should come first, judgments of when our help will be helpful and when it might undermine a tentative effort of someone to stand on his or her own feet.

Charles Loch and his fellow-Victorians are roughly treated in the literature, and "friendly visiting" became the target of scorn of authors like Charles Dickens. Yet in those days

volunteers—presumably "delicate and sensitive ladies"—
went into neighborhoods that even paid professionals are re-
luctant to enter these days. As many writers have pointed
out (such as Kathleen McCarthy in her book, *Noblesse Oblige*),
professionals replacing volunteers removed the necessity of
direct contact between the rich and the poor, between the
haves and have nots, the comfortable and the distressed.

To what extent do the personal needs of donors for self-
esteem affect the integrity of the relationship with recipients?
The resentment of "bureaucrats" makes it clear that relationships free of the germs of emotion are empty in part because of their antiseptic quality. Where can we turn for an
appropriate perspective?

I am an admirer of Adam Smith's *The Theory of Moral
Sentiments*. One of the intriguing ideas in it is that of the
"impartial spectator"—the notion that we should conduct
ourselves as if there were an impartial spectator, fully informed, observing us. Our self-respect should be based not
on how other men actually judge us, but how they would
judge us were they to be in the position of the impartial spectator.

To what extent are these intimate personal connections
appropriate to the dispassionate work of philanthropy? They
seem unavoidable in charitable relationships that grow out
of hardship and call for sympathetic understanding. How
well do they apply to the philanthropic relationship—in the
arts, say, or in education? The impartial spectator idea works
there, too, but we have less of an understanding of the pro-
tocol. Our expectations of ourselves and of those with whom
we deal are less well established.

For that reason, some applicants behave as supplicants,
and some grantmakers affect the airs of patrons.

Methods of Philanthropy

There is a "norm of reciprocity" that governs our lives.
A personal gift, once accepted, is likely to lead to an effort
to return the favor. Some cultures have built elaborate structures of relationships around such gifts. More familiar to us

is the tradition of mutual aid, the voluntary associations in which people contribute as a form of group insurance against the needs of members—assuming some equity of distribution, but not insisting on it.

If I help you with a loan when you're in distress, you not only have an obligation to repay me, you take on an obligation to make a loan to me should our circumstances be reversed. Carried further: If you don't ever need the loan from me, perhaps another will; my assistance to you is expected to serve as a model for your assistance to others later on. *Pass it on* is one of the philanthropic commonplaces of our culture.

Who knows where it will end? A scientist, I'm told, has written an article asking, when does an experiment end? A literary critic has asked, when does a poem end? When does "a teaching" end? When does a good deed end?

Self-help is another commonplace: "God helps those who help themselves" is trite for good reason. It is the central value of a culture that puts a premium on individualism. If these things ring true:

> First, there is the ultimate moral principle of the supreme and intrinsic value of the individual human being. . . .
> Distinct from the first idea is a second: the notion of individual self-development. . . .
> The third element of individualism might be called the idea of self-direction, or autonomy. . . .
> The fourth unit idea is the notion of privacy, of a private existence within a public world. (Steven Lukes, "Types of Individualism.")

If these things incur your assent and agreement, then self-help is obviously a central factor in your understanding of philanthropy. It is, as Maimonides put it in the 12th century, and as Rockefeller echoed early in the 20th, the highest form of charity to help someone become self-supporting and self-sustaining. It is the core idea of the effort to achieve equality of opportunity; the assumption is that one is owed no more— has no right or just claim to more—than a chance to help himself or herself.

There is an important implication in the emphasis on self-help: The least worthy condition in life is that of dependence on others.* Adulthood is the time of freedom to stand alone, liberated from dependency. "Liberation" in "liberation movements" is liberation from political or economic oppression in order to achieve a level of self-sufficiency.

Is it any wonder that *charity* as almsgiving became a word of shame? Is there any wonder that accepting aid becomes demeaning? If individualism and self-reliance are supreme values, dependency implies disgrace. Large numbers of people who are eligible for public assistance refuse it because their pride—their belief in individualism and self-help—prevents it. "I'd rather starve" is a statement sincerely felt by those to whom being able to stand on one's feet is more important than anything else. (Another variant appears in ethics courses in the questions about the man who steals a medicine to save his child's life, rather than let her die because he can't pay for it. Is the pharmacist culpable for not giving the medicine away in those circumstances? How could such circumstances exist in the first place?)

The asymmetries of the human condition, the mismatches of needs and resources, wants and abilities, desires and power, are corrected in three ways: by self-interest; by rights guaranteed by the state; and by philanthropy.

Welfare Issues

At the turn of the century there was an intense intellectual struggle to shift the burden of responsibility for such conditions as poverty from the individual to the society. The struggle has broadened to become a principal theme of contemporary society; it continues to be one of the main agenda items of political parties. As many commentators have observed, the argument has shifted attention from individual responsibilities to individual rights: Where past generations made claims that were too great for many individuals to

---

*There are said to be mendicant religious orders in the East whose dependence on alms helps their benefactors gain entrance to heaven.

meet, many in the current generation make claims of rights
that exceed the ability of the state to provide.

In 1895, C. S. Loch of the Charity Organization Society
in England said this:

> The truest charity often lies in the righteous fulfillment of
> duty, whether personal or public; and next to it must often
> be placed that charity which is vigilant to see duty done. . . .
> Charity that helps others to do their duty is the most gen-
> uine and salutary.

The best way to help people who have neglected their responsibilities to themselves and to their families is to put
them back on the right track, to call them back to their duty.
There is an assumption that among any number of people
who are idle, some are idle by choice. They are perhaps supported by others—not by relatives or friends, but by
strangers. Some are idle by birth defect, accident, or lack of
opportunity; others are idle by self-indulgence. One approach
is to deal with the problem presented by the idlers (some of
whom don't want our help) by trying to reform them; another
is by trying to reform society. In American history, one can
read about the debate under the heading of the "Social Gospel" movement in the religious literature, and in the histories
of the reforms of progressivism in the political literature.

One can read about this debate more currently, too, in
the pages of *To Promote Prosperity*, for example, a study of
domestic policy by the Hoover Institution, and in *Beyond the
Waste Land*, a wide-ranging critique and "democratic alternative to economic decline . . . 'by the three most interesting
economists of the left in the United States—or anywhere—
today' " (according to John Kenneth Galbraith). The Hoover
Institution excerpt that follows deals only with the issue of
poverty and welfare; the page drawn from *Beyond the Waste
Land* is the authors' outline of their proposed agenda of reform.

TOWARD WELFARE REFORM

Welfare reform is urgently needed. But to achieve reform
there first must be widespread agreement on the general

principles that shape and govern the welfare system. The following four principles seem eminently reasonable:

1. *Most people can and should take responsibility for supporting themselves and their families.* In the absence of physical or mental impairment, individuals should perceive that society expects them to support themselves and their families, and this perception should be reinforced by the operation of the welfare system.

2. *Short-term help should be available to many; long-term help should be reserved for a few.* A humane welfare system is one that readily provides temporary and emergency help to those in need. A responsible welfare system is one that provides permanent help to only the very few who cannot support themselves.

3. *The welfare system should not encourage the breakup of the family.* Family members should not find it in their economic self-interest to dissolve the family unit. One of the reasons why families exist in every culture is that there are economic advantages to specialization and division of labor within the family. The welfare system should not undermine these advantages.

4. *The goals of the welfare system should be achieved at minimum cost.* As with every other social goal, it is in our self-interest to find the most effective ways of operating welfare based on these principles.

(Reprinted from *To Promote Prosperity: U.S. Domestic Policy in the Mid-1980's* edited by John H. Moore, with permission of Hoover Institution Press. Copyright 1984 by the Board of Trustees of the Leland Stanford Jr. University.)

AN ECONOMIC BILL OF RIGHTS

I. Right to Economic Security and Equity
   1. Right to a Decent Job
   2. Solidarity Wages, Comparable Pay, and Equal Employment Opportunity
   3. Public Childcare and Community Service Centers
   4. A Shorter Standard Work Week and Flexible Work Hours
   5. Flexible Price Controls
II. Right to a Democratic Workplace
   6. Public Commitment to Democratic Trade Unions
   7. Workers' Right to Know and to Decide
   8. Democratic Production Incentives
   9. Promoting Community Enterprises

(Samuel Bowles et al., p. 270)

I chose these two examples, despite their incomparability, because they are current and because they reflect sharply contrasting perspectives. I chose them, too, because each of these positions seems to me to be further from the middle than close to it. More extreme positions often have the advantage of showing how the consequences of ideas work themselves out as they are carried further toward their implied conclusions.

The struggle implicit in "self-help," as discussed earlier, touches the most sensitive nerve of the philanthropic tradition. The continuing public policy debates are carried on, however, largely without reference to the philanthropic tradition, or in ways that simply draw on it for ammunition (by both sides). The issues are so important that they are considered broadly political—the Hoover Institution underwrote one study and the Progressive Alliance inspired and supported the other—yet there remains great difference of opinion about how directly ideas developed with philanthropic resources should influence political decisions.

The Dynamic of Philanthropy

The section on the "dialectic" of philanthropy stressed the tension between paired ideas and values. There is also a dynamic visible in the tradition, one that struck me first in reading about the early religious expression of these ideas.

The response to particular suffering amid widespread suffering probably meant that emotional sensitivity to the needs of others was a gradual but profoundly significant development. Two kinds of response may have appeared over the centuries: first, a spontaneous reaching out beyond the family, clan, or tribe to defenseless strangers; then a move to make that response more reliable, less quixotic.

My working hypothesis is that there is an inherent tendency in philanthropy to move from the spontaneous to the planned, from the impulsive acts of individuals to the organized acts of groups. That dynamic imposes order and reason on a powerful but notoriously unreliable emotion.

There is certainly anthropological evidence that I don't know about that would help to support or disprove such a hypothesis. The history of religions might reveal, in its study of tithing, how the voluntary gift was transformed into the coercive power of a tax. Philosophers could help me out of my confusion about the question of free will and its place in the voluntary act. Historians will correct my reading of the emergence of the Poor Laws in England, a still confusing history for the layperson of public and private, coercive and voluntary measures to cope with economic and social change. Political economists and others working on problems of the poor countries of the world are trying to find ways to link relief and development, to build on acts of mercy to create the means to avoid recurrent tragedy.

The modern expression of this dynamic is expressed in language more familiar in western Europe than in the United States: from "sentiment" or "privilege" to "right." The accepted interpretation of modern history among Europeans who hold such views sees the emergence first of basic political rights followed by equally valid basic economic rights.

My hypothesis is intuitive and tentative; what it seeks to provide is a framework for discussion of certain central issues for philanthropy: what should be voluntary and private, and what should be the role of the state. You should also bear in mind what I have passed over, and thought too little about as yet: how things sometimes flow in the other direction.

Gathering and Dispensing Organization, Leadership, Participation

There is another inseparable pair we should always keep in mind but seldom do: fund raising and grantmaking. Those are the most familiar aspects of two much more complex forms of philanthropic activity: Organizing determines the purpose; recruitment brings together the people who make things work; fund raising is essential to both.

There has been much less attention paid to the organizational aspects of grantmaking: Edwin Whitehead is only the most recent millionaire to claim that giving money away is more difficult than acquiring it in the first place. But planning and organizing are essential aspects of bringing resources to bear on problems. Without them there will be harm done rather than good, and certainly there will be waste rather than efficiency.

Organization requires leadership. The problems of leadership are important because the genius of American philanthropy—and of modern society generally—is organization.

In order to organize, one has to persuade others to come together in some common pursuit. That is the function of leadership. In order to enable the people who come together in the organization to pursue their goals, money has to be raised. All that is true of private, for-profit activity, too, of course; the differences lie in what happens to the surplus of income over expenditures.

We can't divide simply by purpose, although purpose is

an important element: Education, health, the arts, and most of the other things that fall in the independent sector have private, for-profit counterparts. A discussion of particular tension now is that of competition between for-profit and not-for-profit organizations offering similar services. The expenditures go for similar things: salaries, telephones, heat, word processors.

That controversy is mild compared to the struggle between services provided by government in competition with services provided by not-for-profit institutions. The best publicized controversy is in higher education, but there are serious disagreements in the health field as well.

How should such differences be resolved? Who speaks for the public interest in these matters? Politicians? Professionals? Trustees?

Democratic values have tended to reward modesty and to punish boldness; we may have created an environment in which anonymity—rather than modesty—is a virtue. An environment based on consensus is one that muffles the subtleties that would be revealed by disagreement. It presents to the outside world a deceptively bland consistency that the Russians, for example, seem to consider the highest form of social discourse.

Max Weber said that authority is based on one of three factors: tradition, charisma, and legality. I've come to the conclusion that *in a society that minimizes the past, tradition is no longer a guide; in a society that makes anonymity a virtue, leadership fades away; in a society that is governed not by laws but by legalism and litigiousness, life is bureaucratized.*

Independent sector organizations have more problems of democratization than do business corporations and government agencies. The dependence on voluntary participation means that paid leaders often risk stepping on the egos of volunteer leaders, leaving the volunteers in the dank shadows while claiming the place in the warm and nourishing sunshine for themselves. Volunteers, who are often people of great distinction and accomplishment in other spheres of activity, sometimes seek personal visibility by intruding on the proper terrain of the professional.

Some Preliminary Conclusions

Interrupting the commentary on the outline, some interim conclusions come to mind:

1. Philanthropy is an important theme of "the social history of the moral imagination." It is easy to lose sight of the moral dimension in the profusion of our activity—unlike a kaleidoscope, there is no way of shaking it down into some pleasing and rational pattern that might be called "moral."

2. There may be more efficient ways to allocate resources than the philanthropic. There may also be allocation procedures that achieve a more equal, even a more just and equitable distribution of wealth and services. If we focus on distribution, there are simply better alternatives than the philanthropic.

To choose philanthropy is to choose an option that has virtues that the marketplace and government lack—in some circumstances. The crucial difference is the voluntary dimension, and not simply doing something that may benefit others, because that can happen as an externality of our self-interest in the marketplace or as the result of redistribution of wealth by taxation.

3. The irreducible core of the sector is its voluntary dimension. By organizing our society so that important work depends on voluntary action, we activate the moral imagination. We employ the model of voluntary action as a means of teaching virtue: of caring for others, in its simplest and most familiar expression. Voluntary participation, however, must be more than reflex action, more than a once-a-year initialing of a payroll deduction form. Voluntary action must engage us personally and directly if it is to shape our values, beliefs, and principles.

Defining "Public Interest"

The independent sector offers a miscellany of activities that range from the most profound to the extremes of inane triviality. Senator Proxmire would find countless candidates for his "Golden Fleece Award" in our sector. To justify the sector in terms of purpose is to risk controversy at times, even ridicule.

Under the definition of not-for-profit, philanthropy provides an array of goods that allegedly will not be provided in sufficient measure by the marketplace or with sufficient discrimination by government. Such goods tend to be those that have no strong economic or political force behind them: reruns of old "Honeymooners" episodes at the Museum of Broadcasting; the preservation of a log cabin on Long Island (built in the 1920s, but Annie Oakley, Vernon and Irene Castle, and Will Rogers may have slept there); a study by a public policy foundation that argues that population growth is a "great triumph of humankind" even now; the *Encyclopedia of Southern Culture*, with biographies of race driver Richard Petty, novelist William Faulkner, and so on.

There is one now-famous question about the services that the marketplace, government, and voluntary service might each provide, a question that probably has become the best known question about philanthropy: How do we structure the relationship between donor and recipient when the gift is blood?

The contribution of blood is the most dramatic gift, yet one that has become routine in our society. A full-page advertisement in the *New York Times* is dominated by a photograph of eight people, each with a sleeve rolled up and holding a small piece of white cloth against the crook of the arm:

THESE TOP EXECUTIVES PROVE THEY DON'T HAVE ICE WATER
IN THEIR VEINS

You're looking at people with responsibilities like Chairman of the Board, President, and CEO.

But each one of them has a greater responsibility. The responsibility to life.

That's why they've volunteered to be the leaders of this year's blood donor campaign.

A baby is in open heart surgery. A little boy has leukemia. A grandmother is hit by a car.

Hour after hour, there are people here, neighbors, who are fighting for their lives.

They need you to join the fight. By giving blood. It's true, they won't know who you are. But you will.

LIFE IS WORTH FIGHTING FOR.
GIVE BLOOD.
The Greater New York Blood Program

All of the crucial elements are there: organization, volunteers, and money. Contributions of service, talent, and money are described in order to persuade donors to give their very blood, even for strangers. Moral purpose, voluntary action, and demonstrable need are present. If voluntary contributions fail to provide the supplies of blood that are needed, would a plan to buy blood work better? Should we organize a publicly funded national blood bank, centralizing in a single place information about the whereabouts of people with particular types of blood, and *require* them to give it when it is needed?

The Gift Relationship by Richard Titmuss started this debate years ago; *Tragic Choices* by Guido Calabresi and Philip Bobbitt is an interesting place to pursue the question further. Is the denial of the gift of blood when the consequences of the denial may be tragic a choice that society should permit professionals to make, or should we democratize the decision process?

Fund Raising

There is an abundant literature on how to raise money. It is a practical literature, written largely by practitioners. It rarely asks questions that might stir doubts or second thoughts in the minds of those it is intended to persuade. Much of it is written in a tone similar to that William James talked about in describing "the religion of healthy-mindedness." (Not all positive thinkers are good salespersons, but all good salespersons are positive thinkers.)

There are those, on one extreme, who consider fund raising enjoyable; they are in the minority. Most people don't like to ask other people for money; the trouble is that an attitude like that threatens a system based on voluntary contributions—of money, time, expertise, even of blood. One evidence of this may be in the trend that one professional fund-raising consultant called to my attention: the increasing reliance on direct-mail fund raising that eliminates the need for volunteers. The dramatic success of some efforts to raise money using televised appeals—World Vision is one of the best-known examples—suggests a further erosion of direct, personal, volunteer-to-volunteer fund raising.

Most academics detest fund raising; they often treat the campus fund-raising staff will ill-concealed disdain. The attitudes that work in fund raising don't work in scholarship; fund raising brings commercial values and commercial practices onto the campus; commercial values are thought to infect everything they touch with a corrupting profit motive; commercial techniques undermine the esteem in which scholarly work is held by the general public.

Yet only a few academics know much about fund raising, and most academics have not thought very much about the philanthropic relationship. They seem to be surprisingly willing to rely on opinion and anecdote in passing judgment in these matters—to an extent they would consider unpardonable in their own fields of specialization.

I don't know whether distaste for fund raising is the cause, but *the most serious barrier to public education we face in this field results from the widespread ignorance of the philanthropic tradition among college professors.*

In spite of such lack of support intellectually and educationally, those engaged in fund raising professionally are striving to raise standards, to become more "professional," to provide better training and "mentoring" for young people entering the field. Part of their efforts reflect their understanding that fund raising is often betrayed by the outrageous practices of some who find their way into it; the future of the serious professionals depends on raising the average level and finding ways to screen out the hustlers and con artists. (Disreputable fund raising often colludes with dishonest giving; some schemes are possible only because they are collusive.)

There is a vast gulf between donors and fund raisers; there

is not sufficient mutual respect based on shared knowledge and purposes. Fund raisers and donors too seldom realize that they are participants in *one* enterprise, not two.

The Philanthropic Agenda

EDUCATION

There is a recent and well-publicized example of the problem in the reports of conflict as well as competition between the public and private sectors of higher education. (Please bear in mind that neither term accurately describes either sector: Public institutions receive private funds and private institutions receive public funds.)

In the face of projected sharp declines in enrollments, private colleges and universities think they will be priced out of business by artificially low tuition charges in public institutions. Public institutions believe that they are already expected to do more in service to the public than the public provides funds for. Both sides argue their case in terms of the American tradition and the public interest.

Least often examined is the public policy question of how higher education should be organized in this country. The Hoover Institution and the Progressive Alliance will come to different conclusions and will seek to elicit our agreement. The independent sector becomes a useful source for generating prospective answers to such public questions, and it usually does so long before political parties decide to make particular recommendations or legislators are willing to risk re-election by proposing legislation.

Compassion is a powerful force in addressing issues of welfare; community is the determining influence in addressing issues of education. Compassion is determining in issues of the health of individuals; community values guide us in dealing with public health problems. Cultural and public policy question are almost exclusively matters building on the value of community.

When we tackle the question of who should go to college, for example, to study which subjects for how long, and who should pay for it, we are dealing not so much with mercy as with freedom and justice, with equity and excellence, with personal advantage and private as well as public gain.

Philanthropy can be helpful in supporting public discourse about the economics of our system of higher education. Philanthropy cannot be expected to solve the problems themselves. The base budgets of colleges and universities are met by income derived from enrollments, primarily, whether the institutions are public or private. Philanthropy works at the margin; it deals with special problems, it can help to introduce important improvements in quality, it can underwrite some experimentation and innovation. Philanthropy cannot replace tuition income and public allocations.

In that context, consider the role of philanthropy in shaping higher education today. This array of news was reported, for example, in the August 1984 issue of *The Chronicle of Higher Education:*

- A federal panel appointed by the U.S. Department of Education has concluded that Fisk University will require "bold steps" if it is to survive. Specific recommendations are forthcoming.
- The Law School of the University of California, Berkeley has set up a graduate program on "jurisprudence and public policy."
- Florida Memorial, another black college like Fisk, "rebounds from hard times," according to a *Chronicle* headline.
- "Recent legislative changes in the Tax Code that place new levies on the tuition benefits that employers provide to their workers should be repealed, educators and business representatives told Congress last week."
- The McKnight Foundation advertises its Black Doctoral Fellowship Program in the Arts and Sciences, Mathematics and Engineering.
- "Princeton University," reports the "Ideas" column, "has completed the first year of a three-year project aimed at improving the university's relations with the parents of students and involving them in the life of the university in much the same way alumni have been involved in the past."

- An advertisement for "innovative approaches utilizing hypnosis and hypnotic communication in professional practice" carries this note: *Tax deduction:* An income tax deduction is allowed for educational expenses (including tuition, travel, meals, and lodging) undertaken to maintain and improve professional skills."
- The regular "Gazette" section headline reports that "U. of Washington and U. of Pennsylvania Get IBM Computer-Equipment Grants."

The common thread would seem to be the action and interaction among government agencies, private business, and the philanthropic sector—including a reminder of the private as well as public interests of philanthropic institutions. The list also illustrates the fearful complexity of the system and the challenges to people within it to make it work.

CULTURE

Culture and the arts are not much simpler:

London, August 14 (AP)—Last minute donations by a British fund and a son of the late billionaire John Paul Getty appear to have saved a treasured painting from leaving Britain for the J. Paul Getty Museum in California.

The 14th-century work, *The Crucifixion of Jesus*, attributed to the Sienese master Duccio di Buoninsegna, was scheduled to leave Thursday unless $2.36 million was raised to match the price of the Getty Museum. The work has been in Britain since 1854.

So much for a painting? What is the son of the Getty fortune doing—bidding against his late father? ("I think it's widely known the family relationship was not as warm as it might have been," according to the director of the National Arts Collections Fund.) Why did the picture go to Britain from Siena 130 years ago—because no one was around to pay to keep it there? Are we in some kind of bidding war with Britain? With everybody?

A recent story about Patrick Hayes, the "cultural impressario" of Washington, DC, described Mr. Hayes's efforts to bring Washington up from the level of a "cultural wasteland" as he had found it when he established the Hayes Concert Bureau in 1947. He is also considered the founder of the Washington Performing Arts Society in 1966, an organization that presents a full season at the Kennedy Center, while sponsoring over 700 free concerts in schools each year.

The Getty Museum competes with a museum in Britain; Washington, DC competes with other cities; all are seeking to escape the charge of being a "wasteland." Those who have been arguing for a national industrial policy should know that there are advocates of a national arts policy; there is a new council that is intended to play a role for the arts equivalent to that of the Foreign Policy Association and the world affairs councils.

The painter Lee Krasner, who died in June 1984, widow of the late Jackson Pollock, left funds in her estate to establish a public museum in the house and studio that she and her husband occupied in East Hampton on Long Island. The museum would display works by Pollock and Krasner as well as provide funds for study and research on the work of other Long Island artists.

The Pushcart Foundation, in cooperation with The Literature Program of the National Endowment of the Arts, advertised recently in the *New York Times Book Review Section* its "Writer's Choice," "a monthly listing of the best in contemporary literature as selected by today's outstanding writers."

In the arts, as in science, education, and health, the philanthropic presence comes mixed with marketplace and government influences and pressures.

We have democratized the arts in recent decades, investing in a wide variety of efforts to make the arts more accessible to the general public. Outreach efforts often extend overseas: Citibank recently sponsored an Asian tour of the New York Philharmonic that met with intercultural controversy in Indonesia along the way. (Should a host government have the right to dictate to a visiting American orchestra the content of a concert program?)

Hardin's Law applies to philanthropy, too: *You can never do merely one thing.*

Why ask for such trouble? Why do people—individuals, foundations, corporations, even government agencies, in a sense—continue to volunteer? Why do people stick their necks out voluntarily in a society that will just as readily punish and ridicule them as it will praise and reward them for doing so?

Are we less respectful and more skeptical about volunteers than we used to be? Are the psychic rewards that people so often talk about diminishing? (The question of volunteers and professionals is discussed again in the section "Philanthropy as a Vocation.")

Further Preliminary Conclusions

The most serious problem facing the sector is not its lack of compassion, but its lack of community. There seems to me to be a deficiency in interest as well as of understanding of the system as a whole. That is itself understandable, given its extraordinary complexity. But if the result is a system so fragmented that its professional cadres are concerned only about their narrow field of interest and activity, the system as a whole becomes vulnerable to alternative solutions.

We are not philanthropic about philanthropy: We are too tightly bound to our own self-interest. We act as if we believe that in philanthropy, too, as in the marketplace, an invisible hand will guide our individual activities toward a common end.

Basic questions of tax policy toward philanthropy are perhaps the only questions that result in collective action and concern. We know little and talk too little about the values that we might share—whether the terms of *compassion* and *community* that I've used here are truly descriptive, for example, or whether they are merely euphemisms for other words that don't carry much impact any more.

My own convictions on the importance of philanthropic tradition are fairly strong. I have confidence in the marketplace and in government to provide many of the important things in life and in American society, but I am persuaded that philanthropy is simply essential to the survival of this

country as a free, open, and democratic society. The interaction among the sectors helps to offset and limit the im-
perfections of each.

I say something more on this subject in a separate discussion on values elsewhere in this book ("Philanthropy and
Its Discontents"). I mention it here because I believe that
getting this far means going further. My commentary, questions, and opinions are certainly different from yours; what
I hope this overview accomplishes is to bring your ideas to
bear on what has been said. That will make this a joint effort
to improve upon what both of us understand.

Chester Barnard brought out the dimensions of organization and system that we must hold firmly in mind as we
think about the philanthropic tradition and our places within
it. In *The Functions of the Executive* (still in print since publication in 1938), he wrote: "This general executive process
is not intellectual in its important aspect; it is aesthetic and
moral."

Philanthropy as a Vocation

> He who dedicates himself to the duration of
> his life, to the house he builds, to the dignity
> of mankind, dedicates himself to the earth and
> reaps from it the harvest which sows its seed
> and sustains the world again and again.
>
> *Albert Camus*
> The Rebel

vocation
The action on the part of God of calling a person to exercise
some special function, especially of a spiritual nature, or
to fill a certain position; divine influence or guidance towards a definite (esp. religious) career; the fact of being so
called or directed towards a special work in life; natural
tendency to, or fitness for, such work . . . 1426, "by choice
& by ellecioun And also by Vocation. . . ." *(Oxford English
Dictionary)*

Although Max Weber spoke of *"politics* as a vocation," he
posed a question that we can ask of ourselves in thinking
about *"philanthropy* as a vocation:"

Do you live *for* philanthropy, or do you live *off* philanthropy?

71

The religious origins of the term raise another interesting point: the church as an institution is said to be "called" to its work, as individuals are called to play a special role within it.

Are nonprofit organizations different from other kinds of organizations by virtue of the causes they serve? To borrow the wonderful title of Dennis Young's book, *If Not for Profit, for What?*

Are you "called" to your work? Is the organization you work for "called" in some way to serve the cause it has chosen?

> Mark Cuseta is addicted to baseball. It takes up the majority of his free time and just about all of his concern from March to September. It is his hobby, his desire. His love. And, as a result, his baseball organization—the Bayside Yankees—is propelled by him.
>
> The people closest to me think I'm crazy," said Cuseta, who this year probably will spend more than $8000 of his own money to finance the team. "But I'm not married and don't have any children. Some people like to go scuba diving . . . or take their money and buy a red Ferrari. Baseball is what I like. . . ." (*Newsday,* August 8, 1984)

Mr. Cuseta lives "for" baseball; he does not live "off" it.

"The wave of the future isn't checkbook philanthropy," says Jerry C. Welsh, an American Express marketing executive, in a *Wall Street Journal* article (June 21, 1984) on changes in corporate philanthropy. "It's a marriage of corporate marketing and social responsibility."

Mr. Welsh seems to live neither for nor off philanthropy, but seems to derive satisfaction—and motivation—from the opportunity to serve his company's interests and the public interest at the same time.

Some people risk their health and their lives throughout their careers working in dangerous circumstances for low salaries and little recognition. The Irish priest in the South Bronx and the relief worker in Rwanda run great risks routinely; unlike the daring engineers who fight oil fires in the North Sea, or even astronauts and test pilots, those doing charitable work as a career are usually paid little or nothing extra as "hardship" or "hazard pay."

The diversity of organizational purpose reflected in Independent Sector has been commented on frequently. Less comment has been made about the great diversity of people who represent the member organizations and institutions. Too little has been done to examine the differences in motivation and style of those who are volunteers and those who are paid professionals.

Professional philanthropy can be a good job, with all the economic benefits associated with mainstream, for-profit activity. Mine was such a job, and most of those who work in corporate contributions would say the same about their salaries and other benefits. Employees of some of the endowed, independent foundations would show roughly similar patterns of compensation. Executive compensation among the larger nonprofit organizations, though not comparable to the salaries of top executives of business corporations and professional firms, is still generous by most standards. College and university presidents and some other upper-echelon administrators are sometimes provided housing and other perquisites. Medical practitioners in some specialties are probably the best paid professionals in academic life, even though their professional base is not private practice but a teaching hospital.

For many others, working in philanthropy carries with it acceptance of lower pay and lesser benefits, very little firm economic security, and less attractive working conditions. (Less than what? Less than those of most people working in for-profit and public sectors doing work of equivalent expertise and responsibility.)

> Three editors fired by consumer advocate Ralph Nader's organization have filed charges of unfair labor practices against him, claiming he fired them primarily for trying to form a union. . . . Nader says he sees no reason for union activity within his or similar organizations. "I don't think there is a role for unions in small nonprofit 'cause' organizations any more than . . . within a monastery. . . ." (*Washington Post National Weekly*, July 9, 1984)

In 1983, there was a record-long strike of employees of nonprofit hospitals in New York, institutions that are presumably outside the category mentioned by Nader of "small, nonprofit 'cause' organizations." There have also been strikes of hospital workers in voluntary hospitals, including those assigned to emergency room duty.

What are the "worker rights" of those employed in the nonprofit, voluntary sector? Do some "causes" have special claim on employees that is greater than that expected of people in other areas and organizations within the sector?

The public assumption would seem to me to be that people who are employed in the independent sector—on the "donee" side, at least—are expected to "make some sacrifice" for their work. They are expected to be less well rewarded than people in the private sector because they are expected to live *for* philanthropy even if in some sense they live *off* it.

Such professionals are assumed to benefit in important if intangible ways. College professors are thought to derive important personal satisfaction from the work itself, as artists and clergy are expected to do. There are also thought to be other benefits such as greater professional autonomy, and a more relaxed and pleasant way of life. There is the social esteem that comes from such careers, from being a bit different and implicitly a bit morally superior to others whose objectives and satisfactions are measured solely in material terms.

And there is the satisfaction that is assumed to come from service to the cause, from doing something important for others.

If there are discernible trends in all this, they include the rise of the importance of nonmaterial rewards in private and public sector work; this reflects to some extent the decline of public esteem for those in the independent sector. That factor, in turn, increases the importance of material rewards in the independent sector.

> I believe the struggle for self-fulfillment in today's world is the leading edge of a genuine cultural revolution. It is moving our industrial civilization toward a new phase of human experience. . . . (p. xx)

On traditional demands for material well-being, seekers of self-fulfillment now impose new demands for intangibles—creativity, leisure, pleasure, participation, community, adventure, vitality, stimulation, tender loving care. To the efficiency of technological society they wish to add joy of living. They seek to satisfy both the body *and* the spirit, which is asking a great deal from the human condition. (p. 10)

Daniel Yankelovich, who wrote the lines just quoted in his book, *The New Rules*, proposes "an ethic of commitment." Max Weber, in *Politics as a Vocation*, spoke of "an ethic of ultimate ends" and "an ethic of responsibility."

"An ethic of ultimate ends" raises the question of using any means at all to achieve the goal; the "ethic of responsibility" raises the question of putting procedure before purpose. The "ethic of commitment" seems much closer to the ethic of responsibility: "The commitment may be to people, institutions, objects, beliefs, ideas, places, nature, projects, experiences, adventures and callings. . . ." It moves toward "closer and deeper personal relationships" and toward "sacred/expressive" values before instrumental ones.

The well known longitudinal study of American "lifestyles" by Arnold Mitchell, published under the title *The Nine American Lifestyles*, suggests a modest change rather than a cultural revolution. It puts the bulk of the American people in two categories, "Belongers" and "Achievers," both of which are committed to the system as it is without radical change. Those most concerned with social issues—the Societally Conscious—are a small fraction (eight percent of the adult population), and the most mature, best balanced group, the "Integrateds," represent only two percent. Achievers seem to be those who set the national style, if it makes sense to say there is such a thing. This group represents "the driving and driven people who have 'built' the system and are now at the helm . . . they are a diverse, gifted, hard-working, self-reliant, successful, and happy group." Some of these people, along with the narrowly focused members of the Societally Conscious group, move toward the greater maturity of the so-called Integrateds. This group, small as it is, is growing, and in the author's opinion "a major surge in numbers is possible" in the 1990s "as impressive models of Integrated individuals surface, spurring the conscious switch-over of many people on the brink of that critical psychological advance" (p. 221).

These samplings of the abundant literature on American values and habits are important to the independent sector. American lifestyles have much to say about the propensity to contribute money and service voluntarily in the public interest. Yankelovich concludes that our society has moved from an "ethic of self-denial" to something that combines a far greater tolerance of diversity and places a much higher value on personal expression and enjoyment.

The "societally conscious lifestyle" comes closest to describing us and the people with whom we work. The Societally Conscious are more concerned with social issues than with themselves. They include conservationists and leaders of consumer movements. They are people who "try to lead lives that conserve, protect, heal," but they include those who have adopted single-issue strategies and are often "aggressively confrontational." Some are those who withdraw from confrontation "to lives of voluntary simplicity."

These are the "demographics" of the Societally Conscious group described by Arnold Mitchell, a profile you might hold up against the people you know in the independent sector:

> • Excellent education: Fifty-eight percent have graduated from college or attended graduate school (sample average: 21 percent). Only 15 percent have not gone beyond high school (sample average: 52 percent).
> • Liberal politics: Fifty-seven percent declared themselves Independents (sample: 35 percent) and 53 percent liberals (sample: 23 percent).
> • Intellectual jobs: Fifty-nine percent are employed in professional or technical occupations (sample: 18 percent).
> • Affluence: Half had household incomes of over $25,000 in 1979 (sample: 36 percent), and their average income was $27,200 (sample: $18,000).
> • Census regions: Almost a third of the group lives in New England or the Pacific states (sample: 21 percent).

They shun the South (23 percent vs. 32 percent for sample). (p. 138)

These are the attitudes of this group, as Mitchell's surveys have revealed them:

- Believe woman's place is in the home: Societally Conscious (S.C.) 3 percent, sample 30 percent.
- Agree that women with small children can work and still be good mothers: S.C. 72 percent, sample 55 percent.
- Believe marijuana should be legalized: S.C. 39 percent, sample 28 percent.
- Think unmarried sex is wrong: S.C. 15 percent, sample 39 percent.
- Believe air pollution is a major worldwide danger: S.C. 91 percent, sample 81 percent.
- Agree too much is spent on protecting the environment: S.C. 13 percent, sample 34 percent.
- Believe industrial growth should be limited: S.C. 58 percent, sample 48 percent.
- Agree too much is spent on military armaments: S.C. 38 percent, sample 27 percent.
- Have a good deal of confidence in elected officials: S.C. 19 percent, sample 30 percent.
- Have a good deal of confidence in company leaders: S.C. 16 percent, sample 31 percent.
- Have a good deal of confidence in military leaders: S.C. 66 percent, sample 54 percent.
- Agree the energy crisis is real and not the concoction of interested groups: S.C. 66 percent, sample 54 percent. (Pp. 139–40)

Mitchell comments:

Despite these differences from the norms, the Societally Conscious do not view themselves as rebelling against things. The rebellious groups are those that strikingly mistrust people and feel left out; the Societally Conscious, in contrast, apparently feel they have a say in things, although they may not agree with the majority. Everything suggests that the group is impassioned, knowledgeable, and effective.

Is Mitchell talking about us? I think he is. If that is the case, and those of us in the independent sector do fit the general picture of the "Societally Conscious" minority as presented in that summary, it should raise some disturbing questions for us.

To what extent, for example, are "Societally Conscious" liberals open to points of view held by "Societally Conscious" conservatives? (The SC liberal majority would, presumably, identify with People for the American Way in its challenge to Moral Majority; does this confrontation have the best qualities of public discourse or is it a "dialogue of the deaf?") Is one point of view more societally conscious than the other?

To what extent are these "impassioned, knowledgeable, effective" people—*us*, remember—imposing their values and attitudes on those less well-informed, less well-educated, less committed to particular solutions or points of view?

But the most difficult question, it seems to me, is certainly this one: To what extent are the professionals in the independent sector becoming alienated from the volunteers?

Alienation can take the form of the professional simply out-distancing the volunteers. The professional may well be better educated in his or her field, often has greater specialized knowledge. Mitchell's profile suggests that the professional may also be guided by values that are not widely shared within his or her own organization. In one case that can be conscious if unspoken: The volunteer in effect defers to the professional's grasp of the situation, even though he or she may not agree with it.

In another case there may be growing separation of values and only the professionals are aware of it—and yet they move ahead anyway. "I know that the membership doesn't think this way, but I know it's right and so that's the way we're going to proceed."

This is, I suspect, a different sort of problem for the administrator of a medical center or research foundation than it is for a public policy organization. The expectations of professionals and volunteers differ in different parts of the sector. Protocols of communication with members and habits of democracy vary greatly.

In thinking about the vital voluntary dimension of the independent sector, however, I worry most about the growing lack of mutual understanding and deep sense of common values between those of us who are professionals and those who are volunteers.

A hospital volunteer has given her Fridays for many years to the hospital thrift shop. She has become convinced that the development staff of the hospital are overpaid and excessively impressed by their own importance. "The paid staff work for the volunteers," she says; "we don't work for them."

A volunteer who works at a botanical garden says that she resents being given the scut work, relegated to it by paid staff. "That isn't what I volunteered for," she says.

Right or wrong, accurate impression or misperception, those kinds of comments are warning signals.

More ominous, of course, are the comments that denigrate the competence, dedication, and value of the volunteers. "If it weren't for the alumni I'd love alumni work." A certain amount of that kind of talk—and I've spoken my share—is exasperation and not cynicism, and shouldn't be taken seriously. But all of us have also detected at times a different and more troubling tone of contempt in such remarks.

The "societally conscious" volunteers I have known are persistent and hard-working; most of them seek no special recognition for their voluntary efforts. They live *for* their cause. Well-educated, well-established, effective people expect to be treated accordingly. They will not accept arrogance on the part of professionals. The "societally conscious" professionals, on the other hand, are sometimes so committed to their cause that they disdain those of lesser commitment. Some are people guided by an ethic of ultimate ends, and they will cynically manipulate volunteers whenever they are persuaded it will advance their cause.

Professionals work with others' resources. They are surrogates or agents. Volunteers give their own resources, whether these be time, skill, or money. Volunteers act in an original, direct, first-order philanthropic way. To be an agent is to be engaged in second-order participation.

On the other hand, some volunteers minimize the importance of job security to professionals, and imply that those who live off philanthropy are less worthy than those who have other means on which to live. Some professionals let themselves become so dependent on their jobs—emotionally as well as financially—that they are unable to know when they are acting for the organization or for themselves.

In organizational relationships there is a "zone of indifference" (described in Barnard's wonderful book, *The Functions of the Executive*) in which routine things are kept routine, when instructions are carried out without challenge. Life goes smoothly when communication falls within the zone of indifference. Life becomes fractious when the zone of indifference narrows; calling attention to one's own importance in the system has the inevitable result of prompting others to reflect on theirs. Organizational life with a narrow zone of indifference can become intolerable. In my experience, *societally conscious people are people with a narrow zone of indifference.*

Another kind of hazard in the professional–volunteer relationship is a consequence of the very shared values and strong sense of community that most of us work hard to encourage. People working together closely, not for their own personal benefit but for a cause, are people who develop strong personal bonds. Yet in terms of organizational values, such ties are beneficial only up to a point. Good organization, especially in large organizations, requires what have been called "adequate minimal relationships." Family love (as Boulding remarked in *The Organizational Revolution*) is appropriate in families, and the "family" metaphor carried loosely into other kinds of human organizations can be harmful—to the members as well as to the organization. Professionals and volunteers are not brothers and sisters; there are more stringent limitations on organizational loyalties than there are on kinship.

The sociologist Philip Selznick (in *Leadership in Administration*) once contrasted "organizations" with "institutions." An organization is a group brought together to accomplish a particular task by common, coordinated effort; its members are recruited on the basis of the contribution they can make to the task; the members are, therefore, *ex-*

pendable: As other skills are needed, members can be replaced.

An institution, on the other hand, is an organization with a memory, with a past and a future; the relationship among the members has become "infused with value," and the members are not "expendable" in the same sense at all. The organization that calls upon its members for a total commitment and that attempts to build close, personal relationships and a common dedication will find it difficult to pass judgment on a member who falters, fails, or even disrupts the group in its work.

Bruce Mazlish's study of "revolutionary ascetics"—of Cromwell, Robespierre, Lenin, and Mao—identifies a personality type of organizational leadership that has few "libidinal" ties of friendship and love. It is a commitment to purpose that excludes normal relationships. Everyone except the leader is expendable. The leader accepts his or her inexpendability without reluctance; the cause will fail without him or her.

Such extremes of commitment to the ethic of ultimate ends are fortunately rare, but my guess is that the personality type is most likely to be found, whenever it shows up, among the societally conscious.

The threat from revolutionary asceticism is not great, but the biographies of many of the greatest figures in the philanthropic tradition make it clear that reform and change are most often associated with unwavering commitment, persistence, dedication, and single-mindedness. John Howard, Dorothea Dix, and Martin Luther King are among the more admirable examples.

A more serious threat is "professionalism" itself. Those who live off philanthropy sometimes want to improve their standing in the community, if only to be taken more seriously by those whom they seek to persuade. Improved standing can come from title, but to be president or executive director of a small and impoverished organization seems to carry little weight. The quality of commitment, serious though it may be, often lacks the charismatic quality that makes a Gandhi or a Mother Theresa so powerfully attractive.

To be paid to work for a nonprofit, voluntary organization may carry no special status at all; in some cases it may be taken as a sign of inability to succeed in more challenging and competitive work.

To be a "professional," however, in the full sense of that word, is to lay claim to a place of some honor and distinction in our society, in spite of careless usage and in spite of the serious criticism of professional behavior, practice, and values. An important new book, *The Reflective Practitioner* by Donald Schön, deals with "how professionals think in action"—and opens with a chapter on "The Crisis of Confidence in Professional Knowledge." Schön questions whether knowledge—and especially technical knowledge approached analytically—is an appropriate base for the *professional*, in contrast with the *scientist*. The new model of professionalism is borrowed from science: "The systematic knowledge base of a profession is thought to have four essential properties. It is specialized, firmly bounded, scientific, and standardized," according to Schon's summary of the position (p. 23). In some professions, such as medicine, this emphasis on specialized, scientific knowledge marks a trend toward "technical rationality," the domination of professional practice by scientific values.

In philanthropy this trend is most evident in efforts to make philanthropy a policy science and to apply such tools as cost-benefit analysis, quantification, and computer modeling. Most economists have approached philanthropic questions in this way for years. The concern that Schön and others express seems not only to result from a fear of "quantomania," but from the removal of other values from consideration. (It is significant, I think, that this thoughtful new book about "reflective practice" was recommended to me by the dean of a leading medical school.)

However, as Schön points out, philanthropy is not considered a "major profession" like medicine or a "near-major" profession like engineering; it is a "minor profession," along with those such as social work, education, librarianship, or town planning. The minor professions are said to lack intellectual rigor and depend almost entirely for their ideas on the academic disciplines of the arts and sciences. Most important, they pursue *"ambiguous ends."*

Philanthropy does not have clear and agreed-upon purposes, nor does it have firm intellectual foundations; it is susceptible to attack from political scientists about its purposes, and in the most fundamental way from economists of widely divergent ideological persuasions. Philanthropy is a tradition, first and foremost, and subject like all traditions to attenuation by neglect as well as to erosion by criticism. It is true of philanthropic as well as other traditions that they "are frequently embroiled in conflicts of values, goals, purposes, and interests" (Schön, p. 17). Such conflicts increase the vulnerability to as well as the likelihood of criticism.

The literature that deals with the philanthropic relationship emphasizes the priority of the giver and the receiver, the setting in which many of these conflicts arise. Very little attention is given to the role of the professional as agent or to the subtle but important changes in attitudes and values that occur when professionals speak and act for volunteers. Fund-raising professionals have studied more intensively than anyone else the motivations for giving, but most of us know precious little about the psychological changes that take place between an appeal made by a person in his or her own behalf, by a volunteer in behalf of that person, and by a professional in behalf of a volunteer in behalf of that person. We know even less about the psychological changes that take place when appeals are made by direct mail, sometimes "personalized," sometimes with the fullest bureaucratic anonymity.

As we moved from the simplicity of the direct face-to-face relationship to the characteristic behavior of large organizations and mass communication, the qualities of professionalism changed drastically. In what way can the philanthropic professional be said to have "clients"? Who is the client? If the client is the ultimate recipient, then what is the professional's relationship to the prospective contributor? In what way do professionals in large organizations have "autonomy" as the traditional professional is thought to have it? The medical practitioner's professional opinion presumably does not change whether the professional is teaching in a classroom; or working in a professional clinic, hospital, or MASH unit. There is no question who the client is, and there is usually little question of what the professional's responsibility is in the relationship.

"Clientage" (there is such a word) is presumably the relationship seen from the vantage point of the client rather than from the perspective of the professional. The professional offers knowledge of a special and esoteric kind with certain implied guarantees of trustworthiness. The quality of the service is also expected to be the same regardless of the social standing, ethnic background, or ability to pay. Professionalism has fallen under attack because of lapses from that high standard. Is that, too, a problem for us?

Professionals in philanthropy face other problems. What is the place of *ambition* in our work? It seems to be rarely spoken of. Our ambition is assumed to be directed primarily to the cause we serve, rather than primarily to ourselves. Some comment has been made about the relative lack of opportunity for people on the contributions side to rise professionally; the career ladder is very short. Grantmaking foundations with very large endowments sometimes have very small professional staffs. Corporate contributions professionals are by definition working outside the mainstream of their companies' business interests; if they win promotion, they are often promoted out of the contributions area, back into the corporate mainstream.

Those employed in volunteer-based organizations are often in small professional staffs with not more than a step or two between the lowest and highest ranks. There is some lateral movement from one organization to another, but few organizations offer much opportunity for advancement.

How, then, does ambition manifest itself in the independent sector? Presumably the energies are turned toward program goals, and professional satisfaction is to be found and ambition rewarded in the progress made toward those goals.

Do we now begin to talk about the differences among work

in this sector, work in the private sector, and work for government? The conventions of behavior are different; they must be, if the goals of power, wealth, and recognition that are expected to motivate people to further effort and achievement in the other two sectors are thought not to apply in the same way here.

That, it seems to me, is the root issue of Ralph Nader's labor union and of the question of strikes and slowdowns in hospitals. The line between managerial/professional/technical and office/secretarial/clerical and their expectations of treatment becomes unclear in the independent sector. Some people welcome such ambiguity; it often seems to lead to discord and unhappiness. Who within the paid staff of a nonprofit, voluntary organization is living *for* the cause and who may be said to be living *off* it?

The "revolutionary ascetic" mentioned earlier is a person who believes his or her personal ambition to be exactly congruent with the advancement of his or her cause. The two proceed together; separated, neither will survive.

The "philanthropic ascetic" rejects those things that appear to detract from or to demean the cause. There is a single-mindedness about the importance of the cause itself; only lip-service is paid to competing causes. Some philanthropic professionals appear to have fashioned their lives in such a shape, denying themselves income that they might be able to use—without challenge or criticism—for their own comfort or convenience, in order to apply even more available resources to the work that must be done.

We are dealing with a force that does not fit well with the narrower versions of self-interest, especially when self-interest is expected to reveal itself as desire for material benefit. This is, I think, an example of "rational noneconomic behavior," behavior of an almost garden-variety familiarity in the independent sector. Clean air, metaphysics, or adoption services can be even more powerful than an extra week of vacation, a new car, or even a personal computer (or a rock concert, suntan, or advanced degree).

The search for self-fulfillment may lead ever more people toward work that combines material reward and spiritual satisfaction. If so, the boundary between work in the marketplace and government and work in the independent sector may become even more blurred.

John D. Rockefeller presented a philosophy of business philanthropy that asserted the creation of honorable and honest work for people to be the highest sort of contribution a person could make. That aspiration for business has not been shared by many people in business; many if not most people outside business would not accept Rockefeller's philosophy as representative of the thinking of business leaders generally—and perhaps not even representative of Rockefeller's own views.

Economic work is necessary, and self-interest is said to be what motivates and guides it. It isn't necessary for other values to enter in. Take it from the horse's mouth:

> By preferring the support of domestic to that of foreign industry, [every individual] intends his own security; and by directing that industry in such a manner as its produce may be of the greatest value, he intends only his own gain, and he is in this, as in many other cases, led by an invisible hand to promote an end which was no part of his intention. Nor is it always the worse for society that it was no part of it. By pursuing his own interest he frequently promotes that of the society more effectually than when he really intends to promote it. I have never known much good done by those who affected to trade for the public good. It is an affectation, indeed, not very common among merchants, and very few words need be employed in dissuading them from it. (Adam Smith, *The Wealth of Nations*, Book IV, Chapter 2)

Smith believed that the businessman was better qualified to judge his interests than any government could be. In his other book, *The Theory of Moral Sentiments*, he makes this view universal:

> Every man, as the Stoics used to say, is first and principally recommended to his own care; and every man is certainly, in every respect, fitter and abler to take care of himself than of any other person. (Part VI, Section II, Chapter 1)

The reason for asking the question is to turn it around:

To what extent is any man better able to take care of another than that person is able to take care of himself?

On a scale emerging from such questions, people in the tobacco industry would tend to fall at one end and people in philanthropy would tend to be at the other. The social esteem accorded to those in the philanthropic activity would compensate for lower salaries, perhaps; those in the tobacco industry would assuage their lower self-esteem with higher salaries.

Do such thoughts lead us into the trap of thinking that people who create wealth are somehow morally less worthy of our esteem than those who dispense it?

Or do we believe that the work we do is morally "cleaner" than the work of most other people? Mine may not be much of a job and I may not do it very well, but I'm closer to heaven than they are with their efficiency and their profits because the *goal* of my work reflects a higher aspiration than theirs. They're serving themselves; I'm serving humankind. ("Writers can be guilty of every kind of human conceit but one, the conceit of social workers: 'We are all here on earth to help others; what on earth the others are here for, I don't know.' " (W. H. Auden, quoted by Noel Timms in *Social Work Values*).

If that is the case, helping people to help themselves is the best goal at which to aim, and creating jobs for people can claim a high place in the social order.

Not all jobs are alike, however, and certainly not in any moral sense: Producing wheat for sale to the public is not the same as producing cigarettes for sale to the public. An "externality" of producing and selling cigarettes is the unintended effect that some customers may develop cancer because they have been persuaded to smoke cigarettes. The advocates of "safe energy" (one of the demands of the "economic bill of rights" reprinted elsewhere in this essay) seek to reduce to the minimum possible the externalities associated with all commercial sources of energy.

To what extent do the unintended harmful consequences

of economic activity bring moral discredit to the people engaged in it?

Or, to shift direction once more, to what extent does the structure of the philanthropic relationship result in abuses of power by the professional who wields it?

There is the power implicit in making grant judgments, and there is an overtone of arbitrariness about the grantmaker's discretion. The more discretion, the more personal judgment, the more possibility for abuse. There is an implicit understanding that applicants for grants are sincere in their intentions to carry out the work they propose to do; there is an implicit understanding that the grantmaker will be guided by his or her own guidelines and will act fairly within them. Doubts and anxieties about the discretionary power lead to calls by not-for-profit organizations' spokespersons for more precise constraints upon it. Grantmakers, on the other hand, tend to narrow their guidelines and to make them ever more precise: Artfully designed guidelines will protect grantmakers from ever having to make a decision on their own.

J. Irwin Miller, a gentle person, and Irving Kristol, an acerbic one, each spoke to meetings of philanthropic professionals about what Kristol called "the sin of pride." It is virtue by association. It is not simply the arrogance so often criticized among grantmakers; it is the self-righteousness and sanctimoniousness that is common if not rampant throughout the sector, on both sides of the table. It tends to inflate the moral worth of those engaged in philanthropy and to deflate the moral worth of those engaged in other forms of work, especially work that is explicitly self-interested.

If we are to examine our own motives and understand their complexity more clearly, we should ponder long and hard Weber's distinction between living *for* what we do and living *off* it.

Philanthropy and its Discontents

> Do all that you can to seem good, for that can
> be infinitely useful. But since false opinions do
> not last, it will be difficult to seem good for
> very long, if you are really not.
>
> *Francesco Guicciardini*
> Maxims and Reflections

The best philanthropy, the help that does the most good
and the least harm, the help that nourishes civilization at
its very root, that most widely disseminates health, righteousness, and happiness, is not what is usually called charity. It is, in my judgment, the investment of effort or time
or money, carefully considered with relation to *the power
of employing people at a remunerative wage*, to expand and
develop the resources at hand, and to give opportunity for
progress and healthful labor where it did not exist before.
*No mere money-giving is comparable to this in its lasting and
beneficial results.*

　　If, as I am accustomed to think, that statement is a correct one, how vast indeed is the philanthropic field! It may

be urged that the daily vocation of life is one thing, and the work of philanthropy quite another. I have no sympathy with this notion. The man who plans to do all his giving on Sunday is a poor prop for the institutions of the country.

The excuse for referring so often to the busy man of affairs is that his help is most needed. I know of men who have followed out this large plan of developing work, not as a temporary matter, but as a matter of permanent principle. These men have taken up doubtful enterprises and carried them through to success often at great risk, and in the face of great skepticism, *not as a matter only of personal profit*, but in the larger spirit of general uplift. (John D. Rockefeller, *Random Reminiscences of Men and Events*, p. 93. Emphasis added.)

Rockefeller's little book is filled with such advice, expressed with simple clarity. If, as Maimonides said and as most people seem to believe, the highest and finest form of charity is to take another man into your business, to give him honest work so that he can sustain himself, one might agree that "The man will be most successful who confers the greatest service on the world."

I stood (until February 1987) in some broken line relationship to John D. Rockefeller. The Standard Oil Company he created was divided into 34 parts in 1911, one of which was Standard Oil Company of New Jersey, the company that became known as Exxon Corporation in 1972 and that provides the funds for the work of the Exxon Education Foundation.

"If the people of the world can be educated to help themselves," he wrote, "we strike at the root of many of the evils of the world" (p. 98). By 1908, when Rockefeller wrote those words, he had contributed most of the $35 million that helped to establish the University of Chicago.

It is my belief that the principal cause for the economic differences between people is their difference in personality, and that *it is only as we can assist in the wider distribution of those qualities which go to make up a strong personality* that we can assist in the wider distribution of wealth. Under normal conditions the man who is strong in body, in mind, in character, and in will need never suffer want. But these qualities can never be developed in a man unless by his own efforts, and *the most that any other can do for him is, as I have said, to help him to help himself.* (P. 100. Emphasis added.)

Many have believed that education is the means by which such qualities of "personality" are developed. Others have argued for the tenets of religion, for the nurturing support of the family, for the character-building qualities of competitive sports. Others speak of "cultural values"; the British economist P. T. Bauer argues that the uneven development of Third World countries is more than anything else the result of the different weight and importance put on economic achievement and efficiency. No amount of central planning, says Bauer, will overcome those profound cultural differences.

I think Bauer and Rockefeller would agree: What is most needed in poor countries is a change in their character, in their "personality" as Rockefeller put it, in the value they put on economic performance.

Neither of the major political parties in the United States would disagree with the premise that the most important thing any society can do is to have a strong private-sector economy that will provide work for substantially everyone. The emphasis is different, and exaggerated in the rhetoric of a presidential campaign year, but the basic premises are accepted by both parties.

It is not simply a matter of the distribution of goods: It does matter how they are produced as well as distributed. As Rockefeller said, "The only thing which is of lasting benefit to a man is that which he does for himself. *Money which comes to him without effort on his part is seldom a benefit and often a curse"* (P. 98. Emphasis added.). If self-worth is a value of fundamental importance, self-help is essential. "If we can help people to help themselves, then there is a permanent blessing conferred."

The discontent of modern philanthropy is revealed in what appears to be a widespread uncertainty about, perhaps even dissatisfaction with, ideas such as those expressed by

Rockefeller. It is heresy to some to put a high value on the search for gain and profits. Economic work is less noble than intellectual or creative effort, for one thing, and capitalism is destructive of the finer values.

We are concerned, wrote Herbert Marcuse,

> with sensitivity and sensibility, creative imagination and play, becoming forces of transformation. As such they would guide, for example, the total reconstruction of our cities and the countryside; the restoration of nature after the elimination of the violence and the destructiveness of capitalist industrialization; the creation of internal and external spaces for privacy, individual autonomy, tranquillity; the elimination of noise, of captive audiences, of enforced togetherness, of pollution, of ugliness. These are not—and I cannot emphasize this strongly enough—snobbish and romantic demands. Biologists today have emphasized that these are organic needs for the human organism, and that their arrest, their perversion and destruction by capitalist society, actually mutilates the human organism, not only in a figurative way, but in a very real and literal sense.
>
> I believe that it is only in such a universe that man can be truly freed, and human relationships between free beings established. I believe that such a universe guided also Marx's concept of socialism, and that these aesthetic needs and goals must from the beginning be present in the reconstruction of society, and not only in the end or in the far future. . . .

Quite apart from the work itself and who provides it, Rockefeller believed that there must be strong individual motivation and involvement or that the person's very character and integrity would suffer. To speak of a job as a right means that employment will be provided regardless of the person's "will" to sustain her- or himself.

Two conclusions, in passing:

1. Socialist societies by definition are organized in such a way that the state assumes primary responsibility for the well-being of individuals and for the well-being of the culture as well. Socialism seems to be a form of political organization that claims to obviate the need for voluntary philanthropy.

2. A socialist society changes the terms of how self-worth and individual dignity are achieved. They are not *earned* by the work of individuals, as Rockefeller assumed was necessary; they are a blessing of the state.

I have belabored this point because I believe that it is the principal point of contention among us. Those who believe that even private philanthropy undercuts the will to work and vitiates the necessity for each person to stand on his or her own feet are, I expect, largely absent from the deliberations of Independent Sector.

The tension that might exist is between those who see voluntary philanthropy as the means to an end in which the state assumes far greater responsibility for meeting individual needs—toward what I have called "socialism" earlier—and those who believe that voluntary philanthropy is a social value worth preserving in its own right; that neither compassion nor community will ever be adequately served either by the marketplace or by government.

I adapted the title of this essay from Sigmund Freud's *Civilization and Its Discontents.* I might have borrowed another title from him: *The Future of an Illusion.* Some believe that human nature at its core makes philanthropy illusory, as Freud believed religion to be; philanthropy is an example of what in Marxist terms is called "false consciousness," an ideological sleight-of-hand that tries to put a benevolent face on an exploitative system.

One very serious charge that is levied against the philanthropic tradition from within is the charge that it has abandoned its original role of helping the poor and turned its resources toward subsidizing the pleasures and diversions of the rich.* Others argue that the shift away from "welfare" in philanthropy has simply reflected the vast increase of government programs in that field.

---

*One would not think so, given the relatively small proportion of gifts to the arts, but it raises another interesting question: How do the purposes of giving differ between giving by the rich and giving by the poor? Research indicates that the poor put religion and health before art; is that true of the rich? Or do the rich also give to art because they have more money to give?

There has also been a different sort of emphasis shift: the expansion of public policy activities in the independent sector. One strategy sees the primary work of philanthropy as influencing the ideas that will ultimately take form in legislation. Whether the legislation addresses the problems of the poor or the support of the arts, it is legislation and the government funding that comes with it that is at stake.

Another change in strategy is vividly reflected in the membership of Independent Sector: the proliferation of single-issue organizations, some of which tend to be very closely attached to partisan political activity.

As practitioners, most of our energies are engaged in improving our knowledge of how to perform our particular jobs. What is at issue in philanthropy, however, are the most important issues facing our society and the world. Behind what we do are assumptions about what is good for individuals and how their interests can best be balanced with those of society.

We don't often talk about it, partly because we're preoccupied with other things and partly because it sounds dangerously presumptuous, but *we are engaged in the struggle for man's soul.*

That is one reason I find the reminiscences of John D. Rockefeller so engaging: There wasn't any question in his mind that *that* is what human effort is supposed to be about, whether in economic activity or in the support of education.

Values in Conflict

It is in this context that one should reflect on the statements of the Organizing Committee Report that shaped the role and work of Independent Sector when it came into being almost five years ago. It wasn't the Organizing Committee's goal to stir discussion and controversy; its goal was to express common purpose:

> Without denying the endless diversity and pluralism of the sector, the Committee felt strongly impelled to identify and state certain values which any such organization should seek to foster including:

commitment beyond self
worth and dignity of the individual
individual responsibility
tolerance
freedom
justice
responsibilities of citizenship

To "enhance" these values, the Committee said, Independent Sector might "expand the diversity of personal options"; it would most certainly reflect the tradition of voluntary association, and it would be "a seedbed for new ideas, new art forms, etc.," and a setting for experimentation. Collectively, the sector produces alternatives to government action; it also "reduces powerlessness and helps promote empowerment" and gives people generally a greater voice in public affairs. Functioning well, the sector makes for more "enlightened" voters, who will in turn be more demanding of government performance and more responsible about allocating scarce resources.

The result combines the views of John D. Rockefeller and Herbert Marcuse; that is, it combines values that are often incompatible and always difficult to balance.

There are a couple of possibilities for the future of Independent Sector that come to mind under the circumstances: Leave things as they are, with profound differences of philosophy glossed over in a spirit of cooperation, and let Independent Sector as an organization concentrate on specific tasks of research or public education; or, make Independent Sector a continuing seminar on the issues that arise out of values that often conflict. Some will argue that doing the second will prevent us from doing the first, and that we will bog down in debate while someone else decides the future of philanthropy. Some will argue that focusing on the first and ignoring the second almost guarantees the wasting away of the real values of philanthropy and their replacement by values as expressed by tax policy.

My bias is clearly in favor of organized inquiry into the values, principles, and purposes of philanthropy, as well as efforts to better understand how our system works. The future of philanthropy depends on its self-renewal, in John Gardner's sense of that term. Self-renewal does not come about by rote repetition of past practice; it comes about by giving new life to ideas gone stale or ideas never really quite understood in the first place. It accepts that the good things in life are often the source of distress and confusion:

> Conflict of goods is the heart of our problems. Love clashes with honor, order with freedom, art with friendship, justice with prudence, kindness with honesty—and not just in the rare, melodramatic cases of major decisions, but in the constant, quiet grind of everyday living. Somehow we manage to balance their claims by bargain, compromise, sublimation, partial combination, and sacrifice. (Mary Midgley, *Beast and Man*, p. 191)

For example, the Organizing Committee applauds innovation and experimentation in the arts. At what cost? How does one reconcile the conflict between a commitment to the music of Mozart and a commitment to the music of John Cage? We choose between them, of course, but we can also solve such problems by allocating money for both.

"We must always remember," wrote Rockefeller, "that there is not enough money for the work of human uplift and that there never can be. How vitally important it is, therefore, that the expenditure should go as far as possible and be used with the greatest intelligence!" (P. 100). Yet earlier in the same chapter, Rockefeller said that "we can well afford to ask the ablest men to devote more of their time, thought, and money to the public well-being. I am not so presumptuous as to define exactly what this betterment work should consist of" (p. 90).

The philanthropic tradition is pluralistic. In this sense, philanthropy shares the character of the marketplace. It is assumed that not only does no single source have all the answers, no single source is even interested in all the questions.

It is a commonplace to speak of the United States as "a pluralistic society," but what we mean by it is different from the way it is used by others. A Polish writer's recent discussion of pluralism dealt only in terms of the decentralization of government; the positive contributions of the private and nonprofit sectors don't seem to occur to him as expressions of a healthy plurality of competing and cooperating values and interests.

Some who advocate our kind of pluralism see virtue in alternatives to almost everything. Our conception of politics is broader than government.

> The main postulates of pluralism are these: (a) Society consists essentially of a variety of groups organized around what they perceive to be their particular "interests." (b) In order to promote and defend their interests, groups use their resources to influence public officials and politicians, hoping thereby to shape public laws, decisions, and policies. (c) Conflict and competition among groups is restrained by a tacit consensus among the groups that they will observe the "rules of the game" as embodied in the relevant constitutional and public laws. (d) If group politics is to be kept within socially desirable limits, public officials and group leaders must accept a "politics of negotiation" in which bargaining and compromise are the primary forms of political action and the substantive determinants of public policies. (Sheldon S. Wolin, "The American Pluralist Conception of Politics," p. 227)

The author goes on to say that "toleration is the value that seems more appropriate [than compromise] as the primary value" of pluralism. Pluralism in the modern world grew first out of a claim for religious toleration, but John Locke "lumped conscience and property under the same rubric" and gave rights to economic association that were originally sought for spiritual association. Adam Smith then argued that competition among small churches would have the same benefits as competition among small businesses: "The unseen hand could be made to work for the cause of political order as well as for economic well-being."

Wolin is not at all sanguine about the future of an American society dominated by political pluralism.

> If the society as a whole faces a future of lessening expectations, scarcer resources, and painful decisions, it will be no easy task to persuade highly organized groups to accept

the so-called "hard choices." Why should they, when for
over 200 years they have been encouraged to practice a politics based on each group seeking its own advantage and,
above all, to do so while mindful of the cynical knowledge
that all hard choices are not equally hard for all groups or
classes, that unequal power of some groups makes it inevitable that the choices will be framed to reflect that power? (P. 258)

Wolin cites political scientists who formerly advanced the
pluralist tradition who now believe that "we need . . . an authority above the selfish squabbles of interest groups. . ."—
powerful enough to keep the most powerful interest groups
in line.

Pluralism has also discredited the idea that, except for national defense, there are no common values that, as a col-
lectivity, we can develop and share. There are only common
means we can use to further individual, group, organizational, and class ends.

Two comments: First, the philanthropic tradition offers
common values that we can and do develop and share. Second, the common means we can call upon make it possible
to develop the common values.

American pluralism also seems to me to be more complex
than Wolin describes it. His main emphasis is on economic
interest groups contending for political influence. The pluralism of the independent sector is not simply the innocuous
and marginal sibling of a powerful system of interest groups.
Some of the most effective interest groups seem to represent
no economic interest at all, at least in the usual sense. When
they are most convincing, their persuasive power derives
from a position that seems to rise above narrow economic
self-interest. The independent sector is more important in its
influence, because of the persuasiveness of its moral position,
than the discussions and analyses of political scientists and
economists would lead us to believe.

The independent sector provides abundant illustration of
the indirect economic and political power of not-for-profit
organizations. The "powerless" in our society prove to have

power, influence, and effectiveness greater than our stereotyped conceptions of them permit.

Insiders and Outsiders

It is worth concluding this chapter with comment on the protocols of admission to the places of influence in the independent sector.

For Independent Sector itself, I understand, some of the most sensitive issues are those of membership. The question of membership raises questions of sectoral balance—how many donors and how many donees—but it also raises all those difficult questions of what constitutes the public interest. The admission of one organization will nullify the possibility of another organization seeking membership. The independent sector organizations that are most strongly ideological are at times like the discordant membership of international organizations. They devote great energy to trying to exclude their opponents from the hall. In more parochial terms, it is like the informal organization of ethnic rivalry: "I wouldn't be caught dead being a member of anything *he* belongs to" (or any of the variations on that theme).

Apart from the formalities of membership in this particular organization, I wish I knew more about how new ideas emerge and new voices are heard. My impression is that we need to know much more about the processes of social reform: who first perceives a need, who begins to articulate the problem, how organizations form and gain support, how alliances are made, how influence begins to be commanded—or how it is pre-empted or co-opted by other leaders, already established.

Some minority leaders, for example, now take the position, as I understand it, that it is government that is most responsive to their needs. The philanthropic community has itself become an Establishment, locked into dominant organizations that have no interest in sharing their power, influence, or resources.

Other critics argue that the Establishment has abandoned the historic commitment to the poor for an indulgent emphasis on the avocational interests of the rich. There has been a shift from assistance to the poor (a responsibility abandoned to the government) to support for the arts and other cultural interest that are beyond the enjoyment of the poor.

How do the outsiders gain acceptance? Which outsiders?

The process today is probably not different in principle from the past. The dramatic changes are found in the sophistication of the means used to gain attention and influence. "Consciousness raising" is a way of life in a pluralistic democracy like ours. (There is, however, a law of emotional gravity that works here, too: What goes up must come down. Raising consciousness is not the same as keeping it there.) Each new agenda item tends to diminish or even to eliminate an item that had won a place on the earlier agenda.

Who decides who will be replaced? Which insiders must go?

It is in the independent sector that the voices that shape social policy are first heard. That has long been the case—it was clergymen and female volunteers and "people of means and influence" who led the fight against slavery and child labor and for decent treatment of the mentally ill and lepers. More recently, it has been in the independent sector that the conservation movement was transformed into the environmental movement. The environmental movement has had enormous economic impact, often on precisely those economic interest groups within business and labor who saw their interests affected adversely. Ask the tobacco industry about the power of the independent sector; ask the liquor industry.

My personal inference from all this is that not-for-profit organizations have begun to form coalitions around shared values that are beginning to replace the traditional political parties. Independent Sector as a "trans-ideological" organization will soon find itself confronted by ideological competitors. The independent sector may in fact become a competition between two powerful sets of ideas such as those exemplified by the Moral Majority and People for the American Way. The power of the appeal around social philosophies may well prove to be more powerful than that of "interests" as political scientists have defined them in the past. Democrats and Republicans are scattered along with independents and the adherents of minor parties all across those two organizations. People are more likely to vote their single-issue ideological coalition than their political affiliation.

One of the fundamental institutions within the independent sector is the church, and lively debate has recently emerged about the proper demarcation between the jurisdictions of the church and of the state.

Few if any among the single-issue organizations are likely to yield their claims to priority because their priorities threaten the philanthropic system as a whole. It is not in the character of single-issue organizations to accept martyrdom for their ideas in behalf of a common good: Martyrdom is fine, but only in behalf of the idea that they believe to be central.

The most serious threat to the independent sector may, then, prove to be not its weakness, but its strength; not its irrelevance, but its centrality; not its prudent compromise and toleration, but its diffuse but fearful force of conviction.

Conclusion

It seems that one thing we need for our task is a certain courage, a courage in following out the course of our thoughts where it leads us, a mental courage, about which common experience allows us to say definitely that it is infinitely less widely diffused than physical courage is.

Gabriel Marcel
The Mystery of Being

Philanthropy in Education

Private voluntary giving will not increase unless there is better and firmer understanding of its importance to our society and the people in it. That understanding is not the product of a how-to course; it is not the result of rote learning from a textbook; it will not follow directly from classroom exhortation or from unreflective experience. I hope that the philanthropic tradition might come to be thought of as a familiar topic of the formal education of Americans, tied in some cases to the out-of-classroom student experience of giving and raising money and volunteering and becoming involved in the tradition as a dynamic process.

Such an education should deal with fund raising and giving as part of a single process. More of us might then better understand the psychological quirks that make that relationship so difficult at times. The linkage of research, teaching, practice, and experience has not yet been achieved for most people—including those of us who are paid to be involved in it.

Public education will not advance until professional education does. Professional education will not advance until philanthropy begins to permeate the undergraduate curriculum—especially those basic courses known as general education. While research proceeds in its plodding, unorganized way, philanthropy must earn its place in the discussions among students and faculty members. It has to be talked about on the campus as a continuing and pervasive influence in the society, contending for attention with other unresolved issues: nuclear weapons, homosexuality, ethnic conflict, Marxism in the Third World, deconstruction in literary criticism, the place of religion in American politics, and so on.

Conversation interacts with learning in the classroom and research in the library; it doesn't always lead to action, but it should always seek understanding. More not-for-profit organizations with an established base on the campus should seek to become more directly involved in the campus dialogue about philanthropy. There is a natural link between courses in sociology and psychology as well as politics and economics and the activities of the philanthropic organizations. Many of these organizations play an important role in providing forums for debate of all sorts of issues; most of them have close ties with faculty members in those fields and in other departments; all of them have a continuing interest in engaging students as volunteers.

- The first responsibility is to help professionals in philanthropy to become better educated in their own tradition.
- The second responsibility is to encourage research and the dissemination of the results of that research.
- A third responsibility—and all these have to go on concurrently—is to encourage the publication of teaching materials: more histories like Robert Bremner's *American Philanthropy*, more anthologies like Brian O'Connell's *America's Voluntary Spirit*, and more analysis like James Douglas's *Why Charity?*

Knowing that some views of society are unsympathetic or even hostile to the philanthropic tradition, we need to know what those arguments are. Independent Sector's task of advancing the tradition must go beyond cheering it on.

None of this noble work will proceed without money—or at least, no widespread effort will occur. The surprising fact is that the independent sector has failed to invest in the study of itself. Scholars are likely to work in fields where resources are available to support their work. Marginal journals and esoteric articles require subsidy. These facts are known to all of us in the field, yet few of us invest in advancing the understanding of the philanthropic tradition.

We are our own bottleneck.

The Future of the Tradition

His whole life was scented by the memory of those fruitful beliefs of which it was possible to sacrifice the letter without giving up the spirit. You have benefitted from this inner struggle of your father: you were able to observe in him that wonderful hour of psychological development when one can still feel the moral sap of the old beliefs without being constrained by its chains upon science. Without realizing we owe whatever is left of our worth. We live by a shadow, sir, by the lingering scent of an empty perfume jar. After us, people will live by the shadow of a shadow; I fear sometimes that it may prove somewhat ephemeral. (Ernest Renan, giving the welcoming reply for the Academie française to M. Cherbuliez upon the latter's installation in that body in 1882, speaking of the new member's intellectual indebtedness to his father and his father's world.*

Renan was speaking of the fading power of religion, especially among intellectuals, in the Europe of his day. The trend has continued. The religious traditions of Judaism and Christianity have lost their power to inspire and challenge

---

*The quotation was first drawn to my attention in an interview with Will Durant for *Newsday;* my colleague John Marcus, professor of history at Hofstra University, tracked down the text and citation above.

the sophisticated humanists of western Europe. Until about a decade ago, the religious tradition was replaced by a new Marxist tradition; it too is being abandoned, along with existentialism. Utopian visions (and even Dystopian ones) succeeding themselves in an endless and frustrated search for social perfection.

Nietzsche noisily announced the death of God, but the death of the religious tradition in Europe came, as Eliot predicted, "not with a bang, but a whimper." Traditions attenuate: They wilter, fade, weaken, diminish. They are not overthrown in revolution; they are abandoned.

The philanthropic tradition is deeply rooted in religion in America. Religion is the most powerful motive force behind individual charity. Religion indirectly influences corporations and foundations just as it more openly and directly influences political parties.

There is a danger that threatens philanthropy, then, if religion weakens in this country as it has in Europe. The new secular society of modern Europe has broken free of the domination of the church. In the process, they have put their faith in the state to meet the needs that had been met by religious charity. Philanthropy as a private and voluntary act of individuals and churches has been replaced by legislated programs of state agencies. Philanthropy was never a stated target of revolution; it was merely a victim along with its religious sponsor. Unlike the situation in Europe, however, there never has been a state church in this country.

In a secular society striving to preserve religion, like ours, there is a tendency to make the philanthropic dimension the exclusive preserve of the religious or the secular.

There is then the danger: that partisan politics begins to divide the religious and the secular, with private philanthropy on the former side and public altruism on the latter.

It is not simply a matter of competing claims for best representing America's most distinctive virtue. The conclusion to the essay on "Philanthropy and Its Discontents" in this book makes the point that "the independent sector is more important than we realize." The philanthropic tradition is not just acts of benevolence; it is also a powerful lever of social change. It is the voice of discontent and dissatisfaction as well as the expression of nurture and encouragement.

It is often in the independent sector that the voices that shape social policy are first heard. Another, more positive aspect of the independent sector was pointed out to me by John Simon (who in turn was prompted to think about it by his former colleague at Yale, George Silver). Philanthropy surfaces needs that are met by the marketplace—new pharmaceuticals and chemicals, for example, and even new uses of technology.

The choice would appear to be between two futures. In one, philanthropy fades away along with religion, and the state becomes the dominant influence. The independent sector becomes inconsequential. The other choice is a future in which the independent sector becomes increasingly political, whether dominated by religious or secular ideology. Desire to reshape the community when it takes legislative form often overwhelms concerns of compassion; the massive scale of development sometimes drives out relief.

There is a third future that is most like the present and recent past: It accepts the complexities and contradictions of the tradition and maintains some balance between the demands of compassion and community.

Will we continue to withstand the pressures?

The International Dimension

I have left out thus far the consideration of who should be included in our philanthropic activity. How wide a net do we cast? Where does our responsibility stop?

A charitable act requires more than one person; helping yourself, the ancients discovered, is not charity. (Have you noticed the proliferation of advertising based on buying products and services because we "deserve" them? That ain't charity.)

Put the question in the language of economist Morris Silver: Are we willing to include *genetic strangers?*

We work outward from our own immediate responsibilities. Individuals contribute to their local church and volunteer fire department; corporations contribute to community hospitals that serve their employees; community foundations are designed to keep their attention largely on local needs.

How have we managed to persuade ourselves to provide technical assistance to agricultural cooperatives in Ghana, or scholarships for poor Peruvians, or food relief to Thai refugees? Why have we been willing to share our resources with "genetic strangers" in remote parts of the world—strangers who threaten our peace and security far less directly than do richer and better developed countries.

Let me borrow again from St. Thomas Aquinas; as we think about international philanthropy it would be useful to bear in mind the "ten points of enquiry" into almsgiving that he set out to examine:

1. is almsgiving an act of charity?
2. the different kinds of almsgiving;
3. which are the more important, spiritual or corporal alms?
4. does corporal almsgiving have a spiritual effect?
5. is giving alms a matter of obligation?
6. do we have to give material alms even if it means depriving ourselves of what is necessary?
7. can we give as alms what has been unjustly acquired?
8. whose function is it to give?
9. to whom should they be given?
10. how should we give them? (Pp. 237–73)

There is a religious motivation of long standing and great power of serving God by helping those at a distance as well as by helping those nearer to us. A tiny fraction of our total resources is involved; it is even a tiny fraction of the small fraction that we commit to philanthropy.

That is another answer: We can afford it. Could we afford more?

A friend of mine is persuaded that Americans will expand their philanthropic horizons abroad only when they know more about the world and better understand its interdependence. The first task is one of public education; the first task of international education is therefore domestic; we must first enlighten Americans about the needs of the world and about what we might be able to do to help people cope with them.

It is wishful thinking at best and pernicious at worst to argue that there is a strong case to be made for the national political or economic interest to increase philanthropic support to the poorest countries of the world. Self-interest of the political kind will not increase food shipments to starving Ethiopian children when the Ethiopian government is pro-Soviet and anti-American as well as oppressive in its own right. And, although there may be scarce minerals yet to be discovered, still hidden someplace beneath those parched sands, most of the poorest countries remain that way because they promise neither short-term nor long-term return on investment.

The poor people of the poor countries are not a threat to us; they can command no tribute. (That is not always the case among our own poor, who are relatively much better off, much more likely to rise up in a "revolution of rising expectations.") It is better to recognize that philanthropy that seeks to help the poor will be rewarded perhaps in heaven; it won't garner many benefits here on earth.

Our increased sense of interdependence will, of course, encourage more philanthropic support of such things as international educational exchanges, especially with those countries that are prospective allies and customers. It will stimulate us to invest more of our resources in the study of foreign language and foreign cultures—we have begun to realize that we are engaged in a struggle of ideas with people we know too little about, people who really are important to our welfare and security.

The main contribution we have come to make to the countries of the Third World has been our "know-how." Missionaries as well as non-religious relief and development organizations devote their primary energies to helping people learn how to help themselves. That help ranges from technical assistance (that includes technical training so that the project can continue after the technical assistants have departed) to education in community development and even political action.

American private voluntary organizations have become a powerful presence in the developing countries of the world; in many cases they actively oppose official policy and offer (or ally themselves with) an alternative to what the host government provides. In many cases, American philanthropic organizations oppose United States policy, sometimes in alliance with local governments considered hostile or unfriendly by the White House and the State Department. They are often at loggerheads with one another on ideological grounds, and ideology is sometimes the dominant style of thought: dogmatic, simplistic, single-minded.

Consciously or not, we are spreading the threatening American doctrine of pluralism abroad, often in societies that have permitted only certain voices to be heard on issues of importance. Some governments attempt to seal themselves off from all ideas they consider alien and hence threatening. No government that I can think of takes uninvited criticism from outsiders with very good grace.

There is growing reason to expect more defensive action against the increasingly "activist" and overtly political—but private and voluntary—organizations working abroad. To the extent that that kind of confrontation occurs and American lives are put in jeopardy and even lost, the federal government will intervene.

Another consequence of any such confrontation is that non-political relief and development activity will also be cut back or made more difficult. It is difficult enough already to negotiate a technical assistance agreement with a Central American government when the project will be funded both privately and with funds from the Agency for International Development.

The same hard choice is involved abroad that we face at home: The more influential the sector in shaping political and economic policy, the more pressure there will be to impose controls and restrictions. We should do everything we can to preserve the independence of the independent sector.

That may mean that in time some organizations will have to express themselves with greater restraint and act more discreetly.

Where you or I would be cautious; others among us might be bold. Where you or I would be aggressive, others among us might be prudent.

That is another reason we have so much to talk about.

Assessment

The Introduction said that this essay would examine some of the assumptions about philanthropy and the independent sector. That much has been accomplished, I think. The Introduction also said that the main purpose of the paper would be to search for common themes. I am less confident that I have succeeded in bringing them out.

There is more attention to "compassion" than to "community," for example. There is an important *dialectical* tension—perhaps most poignantly illustrated when we debate the trade-offs between relief and development—that we can never finally resolve. That tension also appears in the relationship between givers and receivers, between dependency and autonomy.

One fundamental bridging idea between compassion and community—that of stewardship—isn't even discussed. Any Independent Sector statement about fostering values should include stewardship explicitly. (It is implicit in "effective sector management," but that ducks the question raised by the religious tradition of stewardship—where the idea originated.)

Stewardship suggests professional responsibility—and that should be a common theme of the continuing deliberations of Independent Sector. Reflection in and about practice, to borrow Donald Schön's language, will reveal that there are wide differences among us in the way we understand the "roles, rules, and relations" of our field. It may be that we should think in terms of several forms of professionalism rather than in terms of a single ideal.

As long as we *presume* to act in behalf of others, however, we solicit their trust and respect—and we should examine carefully whether we deserve it.

There may be some structural changes under way: still more innovations in generating fee income; closer interaction between the main business and the philanthropic giving of corporations; more "mixed economy" combinations of government, private business, and not-for-profit elements. I won't bother to speculate about the future of tax policy: That could cause short-term upheaval as well as long-term shifts of responsibility among the sectors and among corporations, foundations, and individuals.

The scale of our activity may cause qualitative changes that are inevitable and both necessary and harmful. Efficiency in generating new income may be achieved at such a cost of depersonalization and alienation that it crushes the "commitment beyond self" as well as the "worth and dignity of the individual." We would do well to reflect on the "iron laws of organization" that Kenneth Boulding formulated almost 25 years ago. (It is Boulding's recent opinion that *scale* is the most important variable in organization: Being too big or too small has more impact on the character of an organization than anything else.)

These questions do not leap out from the outline of the philanthropic tradition that appears in the Introduction. Perhaps that outline will have to be expanded. Someday it should be possible, however, to construct an encyclopedic summary of philanthropy, as Mortimer Adler has done with his "Syntopicon" and the *Encyclopedia Britannica*.

I mention that because the new *Britannica* overlooks philanthropy, as far as I can tell, although an earlier edition—the eleventh—dealt with it quite adequately.

That's the way it goes: One day you take it for granted, and the next day it's gone.

Bibliography

AQUINAS, ST. THOMAS. *Summa Theologiae*. Vol. 34, *Charity*. New York and London: McGraw-Hill; Eyre and Spottiswoode, 1975.

BARNARD, CHESTER I. *The Functions of the Executive*. 1938. Reprint. Cambridge, MA: Harvard University Press, 1968.

BAUER, P. T. *Equality, the Third World, and Economic Delusion*. Cambridge, MA: Harvard University Press, 1981.

BOULDING, KENNETH E. *The Economy of Love and Fear*. Belmont, CA: Wadsworth Publishing Company, 1973. Revised edition, *A Preface to Grants Economics*. New York: Praeger, 1981.

BOULDING, KENNETH E. *The Organizational Revolution*. 1953. Reprint. Chicago: Quadrangle Books, 1968.

BOWLES, SAMUEL; GORDON, DAVID M.; AND WEISSKOPF, THOMAS. *Beyond the Wasteland*. New York: Anchor/Doubleday, 1984.

BREMMER, ROBERT. *American Philanthropy*, 2nd ed. Chicago: University of Chicago Press, 1988.

BUNYAN, JOHN. *The Pilgrim's Progress*. 1678. Reprint. Roger Sharrock, ed. Oxford: Oxford University Press, 1975.

CALABRESI, GUIDO; BOBBITT, PHILIP. *Tragic Choices*. New York: Norton, 1978.

DANBY, HERBERT, TRANS. *The Mishnah*. Oxford: Oxford University Press, 1933.

DOUGLAS, JAMES. *Why Charity?: The Case for a Third Sector*. Beverly Hills, CA: Sage Publications, 1983.

FREUD, SIGMUND. *Civilization and Its Discontents*. trans. Strachey, James, New York: W. W. Norton, 1962.

FREUD, SIGMUND. *The Future of an Illusion*. Robson-Scott, W. D., trans.; Strachey, James, ed. New York: Doubleday, 1964.

GALL, JOHN. *Systemantics*. New York: Pocket Books, 1977.

GARDNER, JOHN. *Self-Renewal*. 1963. Rev. ed. New York: Harper & Row, 1963.

GEERTZ, CLIFFORD. *Local Knowledge*. New York: Basic Books, 1983.

GOODMAN, JOHN C. "Poverty and Welfare." In Moore, John H., ed., *To Promote Prosperity*. The Hoover Institution, 1984.

JAMES, WILLIAM. *The Varieties of Religious Experience*. The Gifford Lectures of 1901–1902. New York: Longmans, Green & Co., 1902.

KEMPIS, THOMAS À. *The Imitation of Christ*. New York: Sheed and Ward, 1960.

KITMAN, MARVIN. "Corporate Ax on Public TV." *Newsday*. Long Island, New York, August 28, 1984.

LOCH, CHARLES S. *How to Help Cases of Distress*. 5th ed. London: Charity Organization Society, 1895.

LUKES, STEVEN. "Types of Individualism." In *Dictionary of the History of Ideas*, vol. 2. New York: Charles Scriber's Sons, 1973.

MARCUSE, HERBERT. "Society as a Work of Art." In Arblaster, Anthony and Lukes, Steven, eds., *The Good Society*. New York: Harper & Row, 1971.

MAZLISH, BRUCE. *The Revolutionary Ascetic*. New York: Basic Books, 1976.

McCARTHY, KATHLEEN. *Noblesse Oblige: Charity and Cultural Philanthropy in Chicago, 1849–1929*. Chicago: University of Chicago Press, 1982.

MIDGLEY, MARY. *Beast and Man*. Ithaca, NY: Cornell University Press, 1978. Quoted in Timms: *Social Work Values*.

MITCHELL, ARNOLD. *The Nine American Lifestyles*. New York: Macmillan, 1983.

NEAL, WILLIAM. *The Difficult Sayings of Jesus*. Eeerdmaus, 1975.

O'CONNELL, BRIAN, ED. *America's Voluntary Spirit*. New York: Foundation Center, 1983.

PERL, PETER. "Say It Ain't So, Ralph." Washington, DC: *Washington Post National Weekly*, July 1984.

ROCKEFELLER, JOHN D. *Random Reminiscences of Men and Events*. Tarrytown, NY: Sleepy Hollow Press and Rockefeller Archive Center, 1984. (Reproduction of a series of articles from the monthly, *The World's Work* (Doubleday, Page & Co.), 1908–1909.)

SCHÖN, DONALD A. *The Reflective Practitioner*. New York: Basic Books, 1983.

SELZNICK, PHILIP. *Leadership in Administration*. New York: Harper & Row, 1957.

SHERRILL, ROBERT. *Military Justice Is to Justice as Military Music Is to Music*. New York: Harper & Row, 1970.

SHILS, EDWARD. *Tradition.* Chicago: University of Chicago Press, 1981.

SILVER, MORRIS. *Affluence, Altruism, and Atrophy.* New York: New York University Press, 1980.

SMITH, ADAM. *The Theory of Moral Sentiments.* 1853. Reprint. Indianapolis, IN: Liberty Classics, 1976.

SMITH, ADAM. *The Wealth of Nations.* New York: Random House Modern Library, 1937.

SPIEGEL, HENRY W. *The Growth of Economic Thought.* Englewood Cliffs, NJ: Prentice-Hall, 1971, p. 577.

TAYLOR, JEREMY. *The Rules and Exercises of Holy Living and Holy Dying.* 1650, 1651. Reprint, 2 vols. in 1. London: John Henry Parker, 1849.

THOMPSON, DENNIS. *The Democratic Citizen.* Cambridge, England: Cambridge University Press, 1970, p. 67.

TIMMS, NOEL. *Social Work Values.* London: Routledge and Kegan Paul, 1983.

TITMUSS, RICHARD. *The Gift Relationship.* London: George Allen and Unwin, 1970.

WEAVER, RICHARD. *Ideas Have Consequences.* Chicago: University of Chicago Press, 1948.

WEBER, MAX. "Politics as a Vocation." In Gerth, H. H.; Mills, C. Wright, eds. and trans., *From Max Weber: Essay in Sociology.* 1946. Reprint. Oxford: Oxford University Press, 1962.

WIENER, PHILIP P. [AND OTHERS]. *Dictionary of the History of Ideas.* New York: Charles Scribner's Sons, 1968.

WOLIN, SHELDON S. "The American Pluralist Conception of Politics." In Caplan, Arthur; Callahan, Daniel, eds. *Ethics in Hard Times.* New York: Plenum Press, 1981.

YANKELOVICH, DANIEL. *New Rules.* New York: Random House, 1981.

YOUNG, DENNIS. *If Not for Profit, for What?* Lexington, MA: Lexington Books: D. C. Heath and Company, 1983.

PART II

Essays and Reflections

Introduction

Part I of this book, "Major Challenges to Philanthropy," was written in one sustained burst during August of 1984. When I agreed in February 1986 to convert it into a "real book," it was my hope to make use of the other writing that was so much a part of my life at Exxon Education Foundation. Much of that writing was done in preparation for speeches and lectures, and it is from a selection of those that these essays and reflections are drawn.

The selection process attempts to draw from these pieces aspects of the philanthropic tradition that are inadequately presented in Part I. The pieces vary greatly in length, but collectively they are intended to convey again the scope, variety, and complexity of American philanthropy in action.

The essay by Virginia A. Hodgkinson of Independent Sector concisely reports on the rapid expansion of scholarly and applied research in philanthropy, as well as on some of the encouraging new developments in philanthropic education.

Philanthropy as Moral Discourse

This essay explores the making of the philanthropic agenda and some of the ways voluntary initiatives influence public policy as well as social values.

If thought makes free, so does the moral sentiment. The mixtures of spiritual chemistry refuse to be analyzed. Yet we can see that with the perception of truth is joined the desire that it shall prevail. That affection is essential to will. Moreover, when a strong will appears, it usually results from a certain unity of organization, as if the whole energy of the body and mind flowed in one direction. . . . Whoever has had experience of the moral sentiment cannot choose but believe in its unlimited power. . . .

But insight is not will, nor is affection will. Perception is cold, and goodness dies in wishes; as Voltaire said, 'tis the misfortune of worthy people that they are cowards; "un des plus grands malheurs des honnêtes gens c'est qu'ils sont des lâches." There must be a fusion of these two to generate the energy of will. . . .

The one serious and formidable thing in nature is a will. Society is servile from want of will, and therefore the world wants saviours and religions. One way is right to go: the hero sees it, and moves on that aim, and has the world under him for root and support. He is to others as the world. His appropriation is honor; his dissent, infamy. The glance of his eye has the force of sunbeams. A personal influence towers up in memory only worthy, and we gladly forget numbers, money, climate, gravitation, and the rest of Fate.[1]

Emerson understood that benevolence is not enough. For kindly feeling to become beneficent, for good will to become action, requires a coalescence of insight and affection—of recognition of a problem and a concern for those affected—fused "to generate the energy of will." Emerson argues that ordinary people are immobilized by cowardice: they are brought to action by persons of will and purpose. Those of strong will are the catalyst of the spiritual chemistry that makes up the moral sentiment. Without leaders, without direction and focused purpose, most of us would remain stuck in our doubt and confusion in the face of the great moral demands of life.

The organization of efforts to make things better, or to make them less bad, is philanthropy. It begins with perception: someone has to *see* suffering and to recognize it for what it is. That requires imagination—not simply the sensitivity of the observing novelist or anthropologist, but imagination linked to moral sentiment, moral sentiment linked to action. To these is added organization. The Good Samaritan, coming to the aid of a stranger in need at some risk to himself, is acting as an individual. It is the transformation of moral sentiment and imagination into collective action that has shaped the core of the philanthropic tradition.

The thesis of this essay is that it is within the philanthropic tradition that the moral agenda of society is put forward. Philanthropy's contribution to moral discourse is as critic of the other institutions of society—even, on occasion, as critic of itself.

Robert H. Walker, in *Reform in America,* describes a cycle of reform. The first phase is a time of discovery, of recognition that something is wrong, marked by competing definitions of what the problem is. A second phase is completed by competing proposals for change. The first cycle takes place as voluntary initiatives of private citizens; the second is marked by movement of those new insights into public policy. To cite one of Walker's paradigm cases: slavery becomes an indigestible knot in the stomach, and abolition brings temporary relief; the negative achievement of abolition eventually inspires hope that there is a fuller pattern of citizenship not yet achieved; legislation begins to redefine the qualifications of citizenship. Voluntary initiatives lead eventually to reform of the law.[2]

The moral sentiment is not, of course, confined to the philanthropic sector. Politicians and government officials sometimes interpret their roles and responsibilities in order to enhance the social consequences of their actions—as happened so often during the 18th and 19th centuries, when merchants aligned themselves with religious leaders to create communities, to build schools and hospitals, churches and markets.

Notions of enlightened and humane government are based on empirical evidence as well as on theory; notions of socially responsible business corporations are supported by fact as well as by ideology. But the case has been well made by James Douglas in *Why Charity?* that the operations of the marketplace are theoretically indifferent to public goods and that the acts of government must be categorical rather than responsive to individual needs. These inherent constraints on the first two sectors create opportunities for the third— indeed, require the third.[3] The rhetorical role of philanthropy is to point out the deficiencies of social institutions—whether those deficiencies occur by design or by default. What is different about the philanthropic tradition of the West, then, most extensively manifest in the United States, is that the genius of organization has amplified the sporadic actions of

individuals into a loose system, a tradition of moral sentiment in action, a moral sector parallel to that of the political
and economic. Law protects these private initiatives for the
public good; tax policy encourages them.

Within the third sector are two kinds of activity: initiatives that respond to recognition that things have gone wrong
and people are suffering, and initiatives that propose opportunities to enhance the quality of life. The definition of
philanthropy that emerged in the late 19th and early 20th
centuries links the two: it defines the purposes of philanthropy as those of identifying the causes of human suffering
and social misery and developing strategies to eliminate
them, Philanthropy as moral discourse has since deferred
somewhat to the demands of social science. Moral claims are
validated or rejected by survey research, on the one hand,
or reduced to echoes of ideology by analysis, on the other.
Skepticism has been brought to bear systematically on the
claims and methods of beneficence.

The case against philanthropy is not necessarily misan-
thropic, but it often exhibits harshness. Emerson himself, in
"Self-Reliance," complained

> . . . do not tell me, as a good man did today, of my obligation
> to put all poor men in good situations. Are they *my* poor?
> I tell thee, thou foolish philanthropist, that I begrudge the
> dollar, the dime, the cent, I give to such men as do not
> belong to me and to whom I do not belong . . . your mis-
> cellaneous popular charities; the education at college of
> fools; the building of meeting-houses to the vain end to
> which many now stand; alms to sots; and the thousandfold
> Relief Societies;—though I confess with shame that I some-
> times succumb and give the dollar, it is a wicked dollar
> which by and by I shall have the manhood to withhold.[4]

There is a widely held point of view that true social betterment on a large scale cannot come about by voluntary
action. "Charity must be coerced," as economist Barbara
Bergmann once put it. Voluntary action must be superseded
by the obligations of citizenship. Benevolence requires beneficence to have meaning; privileges dependent on voluntary
action must be followed by rights, by enforceable claims.

Voluntary action is too often undermined by free riders; free riders will contribute their share only when compelled to do so. This point of view also contends that in a democracy the resources for social good should be gathered by the state through taxation and allocated through established processes by representatives and agents of the commonweal.

Recent political developments in the United States, however, have given weight to contrary arguments. It is complained that dependence on public solutions to social problems—as reflected in the programs of the New Deal and the Great Society—leads to state interventions that imperil freedom and drain a diminished treasury. Western European welfare states have begun to back away from social commitments taken for granted in the recent past. The competition of the new international marketplace has encouraged philosophies of public welfare that identify enlightened charity with job creation. As Maimonides declared 750 years ago, the highest form of charity is to help a person become self-supporting. It is still a beguiling notion: public welfare drains the treasury; job creation fills it up. Welfare increases taxes; job creation increases profits. George Gilder has even argued that it is altruism that inspires the marketplace: those who take economic risks do so not out of self-interest only, but out of an understanding that their actions will benefit others as well.

In the wake of welfare state's decline, there are also increasing signs that western Europe and Japan are encouraging a larger and more active private philanthropic practice to make up for some of the reductions in public spending for social goods. These nations now borrow eagerly from the American experience. The Japanese are busily establishing foundations and organizing corporate philanthropy; British and French universities are turning to business corporations and even to alumni for financial support.

Although attracted by the possibility of offsetting public expenditures by private giving, these countries have not yet discovered that it is in the voluntary and nonprofit third sector that the moral agenda of government is given form. Emerson's four elements of insight, affection, will, and leadership, empowered by organization, assert the claims, even though Emerson himself opposed them:

> If an angry bigot assumes the bountiful cause of Abolition, and comes to me with his last news from Barbadoes, why should I not say to him, "Go love thy infant; love thy wood-chopper: be good-natured and modest; have that grace; and never varnish your hard, uncharitable ambition with this incredible tenderness for black folk a thousand miles off."[5]

It is out of the competing rhetoric that the moral vision of some people becomes the moral standard of the nation as a whole. Nor does the process end there: it is the function of philanthropy as moral discourse to point out the gaps between the ideal and the actual—whether it be in terms of civil rights, the claims of the poor and defenseless, or the protection of the natural environment.

The high aspiration of philanthropy is inseparable from low technique. Egoism is on the same scale as altruism, and cannot be wholly removed from it. The sublime in the philanthropic tradition is often deflated by the mundane. Giving money is inseparably linked to raising money. Raising money often requires appeals to emotion rather than clean, objective, logical demonstration. As scholars and artists find to their dismay, merit is not always self-evident to prospective patrons. There is a widespread inability to remain inspired to do good while using guile and pressure to make doing good possible.

The evidence for my thesis is to be found in particular cases, and they lie conveniently at hand. It is helpful to imagine what it would mean to have to deal with these cases *without* a third sector, leaving them exclusively to the agencies of government and marketplace. What would America be, in theory, without its philanthropic tradition?

1. *International human rights.* A popular singer named Paul Simon performed at a benefit concert in Zimbabwe recently with a group of South African musicians. Simon has also recorded a new album, "Graceland," described by him in *U.S. News and World Report* as rooted in "black music on the other side of the Atlantic." Simon says that "I knew

'Graceland' had political implications and just hoped that the music would be interpreted as a positive statement insofar as the black peoples of South Africa were concerned."[6]

Beyond the commercial recording and concert, the so-called benefit—at which those in attendance share in entertainment contributed by performers—or other social gatherings where the excess of income over expense is donated to charity, is designed to raise funds for the cause and at the same time to call broader public attention.

These two concerts were part of an international philanthropic endeavor, a kind of secular missionary activity. Popular culture exploits its appeal to recruit new followers to the cause of human rights. There is also an appeal to an ill-defined sense of solidarity, a joining of hands across borders and across racial and ethnic lines to give participants a sense of strength and momentum. Beneficent interventions of this kind—to help the poor of the world, to bring down the racist government of South Africa—are often applauded by those who find other forms of cultural imperialism unacceptable.

The antiapartheid movement in the United States has been sustained almost entirely by philanthropic effort. It is unusual in not being primarily dependent on ethnic ties, as is the effort to relieve the oppression of Jews in the Soviet Union or to support rebellion in Northern Ireland, to cite two more typical examples. The American opposition to apartheid gathers its support in this country from those who are most strongly committed to the advancement of civil rights.

Certain styles of moral discourse seem to be effective and appealing to some groups. Common patterns of behavior and perceived analogies appear over time among diverse and previously unrelated causes. These sometimes lead to the formation of coalitions along ideological lines. The emergence of social movements out of this process is only dimly understood and is too little studied by philanthropic practitioners.

Those engaged in philanthropic practice give little evidence of being concerned about philanthropic theory. The function of philanthropy as moral discourse remains hidden. For example, one moral issue that is seldom publicly faced by supporters of rebellion in Northern Ireland or resistance to apartheid in South Africa is that of offering money and moral support without sharing directly in the mortal risks entailed.

A major failure of much philanthropic activity intended as *moral* action is that it thus often appears to be empty symbolism, obscuring rather than sharpening the moral issues. The search for rhetorical impact requires suppression of detail and complexity. In the heat of the struggle there is little time or sympathy for structured moral discourse, especially among those whose philanthropic role may mask political ambitions or the search for financial gain.

Moral discourse in philanthropy should be—but seldom is—candid about its own persuasive devices. The ethics of rhetoric is given less attention than are the moral objectives to be won by rhetorical means. Ends are thus commonly and uncritically used to justify means. Action overwhelms reflection. (And Emerson asks, "If malice and vanity wear the coat of philanthropy, shall that pass?")

Because philanthropic intervention in behalf of others has its greatest consequences for those helped rather than for those helping, the ethic of responsibility is also weak. Those whose philanthropy is based on moral absolutes find themselves mired in inconsistency in a world where good and evil are so haphazardly distributed and so difficult to disentangle.

• A small child from the Philippines is brought to Washington for surgery to correct severe congenital deformities of the hands and feet. The surgery is performed by professional medical staff members who have volunteered their services, and performed in a religiously affiliated hospital that donated its facilities. This act of mercy is the work of the Washington chapter of an organization called Operation Smile, "founded in 1982 to improve medical treatment of children of other countries."[7]

Religion accounts for almost half of the private giving in America, and churches and other religiously inspired organizations enlist the efforts of tens of millions of volunteers. Religious organization is behind large numbers of day-care centers and homes for the elderly and infirm, and religious denominations founded many, if not most, hospitals and colleges. Religious values based directly on biblical injunctions continue to color philanthropic activity.

It is a common American practice, originating in Christian universalism and made possible by the nation's relative affluence, to make its medical resources available to citizens of other countries, as in the case of Operation Smile. This practice calls us to rise above the commonplace that "charity begins at home," at least while absorbing substantial costs in the treatment of a child from a foreign country, despite the fact that very large numbers of American children lack medical care for which their need is presumably as great as that of the child from the Philippines.

Operation Smile and other organizations argue for a universal beneficence, sustained most generously by Americans until such time as other, less advantaged nations acquire medical resources of equal quality. Yet, "Thy love afar is spite at home," Emerson argued. Many would still agree.

2. *Domestic poverty.* A. M. Rosenthal, who wrote a book about the Kitty Genovese case in 1964 (in which a woman was attacked and murdered while 38 people watched from different vantage points without taking action to help), now sees himself as "the 39th witness."

"Almost every day of my life," he writes in a *New York Times* column, "I see a body sprawled on the sidewalk. . . . Some show signs of life; others are totally still. I assume they are all alive but I never stop to find out or even bend over to see if I could possibly be of some help."[8]

The familiarity in large cities in the United States of the "people wrapped in cardboard," those "bag ladies shuffling in the night streets to keep warm," is acute and distressing. Rosenthal's failure to do anything about their plight leads him to classify himself among those moral cowards who failed to come to the help of Kitty Genovese. He is angry— at himself and "at the cops and the hospital people for not taking them somewhere they can be taken care of."

Social history suggests that few of us are able to accept all people in distress as equally deserving of our assistance. (Recall Emerson's derisory reference to "alms for sots.")

Some people seem to be in greater need than others, to be more deserving of help.

• Howard University was recently the scene of a "mock tribunal" to "dispel the myths of the homeless." According to a report in the *Washington Post*, homeless men and women told about their experiences in shelters and how they came to be homeless in the first place.

> The room fell silent as David Hamilton Jones, 47, came forward on crutches. Jones said he once worked as an electrical engineer for companies that contracted with the federal government. For him, health problems that kept him from working caused financial problems, and he found it difficult to find a place to live. He told the audience he wants to work. "I'm not looking for a handout."[9]

In modern societies, *needs* have come to be defined increasingly as *rights*. The moral rhetoric seeks to persuade us that rights are not only political, but economic and even cultural. A central moral issue of philanthropy, then, is the way in which we choose, establish, and affirm such rights. One approach is for philanthropic voices to bring pressure to bear on the public authorities. Roman Catholic Bishop John R. McGann, of the Diocese of Rockville Centre in New York, argues in a *New York Times* essay that "affordable housing is a basic human right."[10] The bishop urges an end to the curtailment of federal funds for the housing of the elderly and the handicapped, "in light of the grave moral responsibility of government to be deeply involved in such a critical need of its citizenry."

The antipoverty activist Mitch Snyder recently concluded a hunger strike that successfully preserved a public building as a shelter for the homeless in Washington. The hunger strike is by now a familiar device to win public sympathy for a cause and also to bring public pressure to bear on officials. Personal witness of this kind, in its many familiar variations in recent times, is an essential ingredient of American philanthropic discourse.

• Charles Hyder, self-identified by his sign "Fasting Physicist," had lost 160 pounds (of an original 310 at the starting

point six months earlier) when he received a message from
Mikhail Gorbachev:

> Your spiritual strength is needed to continue the struggle
> for preventing a nuclear catastrophe. For that reason, we
> urge you to stop your hunger strike.[11]

In the rhetoric of philanthropy, basic needs come before
less urgent ones. Corporal alms often come before spiritual
alms, as Thomas Aquinas said many centuries ago. The
elderly, the handicapped, and small children presumably
have a more pressing claim on philanthropic resources than
does the unemployed electrical engineer. Still, the engineer's
need may be more easily met and dealt with, while those
other claims seem endless.

There is no national assessment of the philanthropic effort
as a whole, no "National Philanthropic Policy" established
by Congress. We have only a gross calculation of how much
money is contributed and to which areas of concern it is directed. We have, of late, estimates of the numbers of volunteers and rough breakdowns of what they do. National
philanthropic priorities change depending on media cover-
age, economic conditions, and prevailing ideological winds.
How then do we choose among the myriad of opportunities
to do good?

One quandary of philanthropy is the priority given to
needs near at hand when there is suffering elsewhere. One
answer is to balance them: the sponsors of the United States
portion of the Live Aid concert later organized Hands across
America. The former fundraising effort was aimed at the
plight of starving people in Africa, the latter at the plight of
those in poverty in this country.

As Guido Calabresi and Philip Bobbitt have pointed out,
some public choices have tragic side effects.[12] Calabresi analyzed, for example, the method of allocation of kidney dialysis
machines. The number of machines available was determined
to be significantly smaller than the life-dependent demands
on them. A first-order solution is to limit categorically those
who are eligible to have access to the machines (by age group,
for example). A second-order solution is to provide more ma-

chines; implicit in this second-order solution is a further reallocation that directs more medical resources to those suffering from kidney disease and less to those suffering from other diseases.

Those who cannot face the consequences of first-order choices turn to second-order choices, but discourse about the moral implications of second-order choices tends to be ignored by those whose entry into the matter is an agonizing first-order emergency. As Calabresi points out, some first-order solutions are morally intolerable, even though equally tragic second-order consequences may follow if we avoid them.

Philanthropy as moral discourse is cacaphonic. Those who believe that philanthropy represents a sector (as politics and economics are sectors) often indulge the babel of claims it as if it were guided by a Smithian invisible hand. The philanthropic marketplace is a triumph of free enterprise, scarcely restrained by the gentle guidance of the IRS. Anyone captured by a moral cause can organize and seek to enlist others to serve the same cause.

• The evangelical preacher and faith healer Oral Roberts, an early exponent of the electronic church, captured national attention by announcing that he would be dead within a year if he was not successful in raising $8 million to relieve financial pressures on the medical center he founded in Oklahoma. According to the evangelical Protestant monthly *Christianity Today:*

> "I desperately need you to come into *agreement* with me concerning my life being extended beyond March," states a fund-raising letter signed by Roberts. "God said, 'I want you to use the ORU medical school to put My medical presence on earth. I want you to get this going in one year or I will call you home!' " Roberts said he received this message last March. . . .
>
> Calvin College communications professor Quentin Schultze, a student of Christian fund raising, criticized Roberts's latest appeal, saying it reflects poorly on Christian organizations. But he added: "You've got to see it in the context of a man who has a tremendous amount of pressure

on him. He's at the top of an organization that has to bring
in millions of dollars each year to keep things going. . . ."

Critics say Roberts's approach to raising funds, even if
sincere, constitutes a kind of moral blackmail. . . .[13]

Philanthropy as moral discourse is most often couched in
terms that reflect immediate personal experience:

• Sammy Davis Jr., the entertainer and motion picture
actor, almost died of liver disease. According to an interview
in *Newsday*, Davis now believes that because he has survived
his illness he has a responsibility to help others similarly
afflicted. Davis expresses the common experience of a calling
to philanthropic action:

"Maybe that's one reason I have survived. . . . I think
I was put here to do more than sing 'Bojangles' and
'Candyman.' "[14]

• A man named David Tilman was the subject of a recent
newspaper profile in the *Daily Progress* of Charlottesville. The
reporter expressed admiration for Tilman's capacity for voluntary service to the Boy Scouts and as a member of the
volunteer fire department and rescue squad while at the same
time holding down a full-time job with the telephone company. "I just figure the Boy Scout work is more important
. . . so I go with that. That's one reason I quit the National
Guard (after 22 years of service), was because of the Boy
Scouts."[15]

The newspaper profile was one of a series on "Piedmont
People," a familiar journalistic device to lend support to
philanthropic work as a community service. Our democratic
populism wants us to believe that ordinary people participate
in the moral discourse of philanthropy as much as powerful
organizations or famous personalities.

The strong will and sense of purpose that Emerson wrote
about is transformed by moral aspiration. As Emerson saw
so clearly, the moral sentiment can be foolish as well as
practical, fraudulent as well as self-sacrificing. We must
judge them all. Our answer to the claims of the helpless and
the moral arguments of those who come to their aid is a measure of our civility, our humanity, and our good sense.

NOTES

The examples I have chosen reflect my recent parochial reading habits as a former resident of New York now resident in Virginia, but the kinds of evidence offered here will be found in the newspapers of every American community.

1. "Fate" in *The Conduct of Life*, in *Emerson: Essays and Letters*, ed. Joel Porte (New York: Library of America, 1983), pp. 956–57.

2. Robert H. Walker, *Reform in America: The Continuing Frontier* (Lexington: University Press of Kentucky, 1985), introd. and part 2.

3. James Douglas, *Why Charity? The Case for a Third Sector* (Sage Publications, 1983).

4. Emerson. "Self-Reliance," pp. 262–63.

5. Emerson. "Self-Reliance," p. 263.

6. "A Songwriter's South African Odyssey" (conversation with Alvin P. Sarnoff), *U.S. News and World Report*, March 2, 1987, p. 74.

7. "Operation Smile: Medical Help over Miles," *Washington Post*, Feb. 23, 1987, Section 4, p. 1.

8. A. M. Rosenthal, "The 39th Witness," *New York Times* (Long Island ed.), Feb. 12, 1987, Section 1, p. 31.

9. "Dispelling the Myths of the Homeless," *Washington Post*, Feb. 15, 1987, p. B3.

10. "Affordable Housing is a Basic Human Right," *New York Times* (Long Island Edition), January 25, 1987, Section 4, p. 25.

11. "Personalities," *Washington Post*, Feb. 28, 1987. Mr. Hyder's hunger strike was still under way as this was written.

12. Guido Calabresi and Philip Bobbitt, *Tragic Choices* (New York: Norton, 1978).

13. "Did Oral Roberts Go Too Far?" *Christianity Today*, Feb. 20, 1987, Vol. 31, pp. 43–45.

14. "People," *Newsday*, June 18, 1985.

15. Lawrence Hardy, "Search for David Tillman Could Lead Number of Places," *Daily Progress*, Feb. 22, 1987.

Virtue and Its Consequences

By most criteria, philanthropy is a virtue. Or *charity* is surely a virtue—or at least most of the time. This essay argues that the study of virtue will enrich our understanding of philanthropy and of the problematic of beneficence.

This is an exercise in exploratory discourse. It comes at a time when the social and political environment is rich with references to the Constitution and its history. It also comes, for me personally, not long after I had the privilege to lecture at Monticello. Being here in this place in the company of the members of the American Philosophical Society thus links me in some sense with Jefferson, Franklin, and the makers of the Constitution.

Their mode of discourse was also exploratory. They had to be open to ideas if they were to bring unity from their diversity. Others, less exploratory in their approach to discourse, would have failed. Only ideologues, such as those whom Eric Hoffer labeled true believers, would enter upon

This essay is adapted from remarks presented at the annual meeting of the American Philosophical Society, Philadelphia, April 25, 1987.

the shaping of a constitution knowing all the answers beforehand. And so I enter upon this modest discussion of virtue
with exploratory intent, hoping that my own understanding
will be improved, and that others might wish to share in a
joint venture of inquiry.

Among other things, exploratory discourse reflects our
awareness that the consequences of our actions, including
our best intentioned actions, are often problematic. That is
what is implied in the title of these remarks: that the consequences of acts of benevolence toward others may or may
not result in benefit to them. It is perhaps the human condition. As the German ethologist Wolfgang Winckler wrote
15 years ago, "Man is a creature whose will is greater than
his ability and whose ability is greater than his sense of
duty."[1] Given the resulting uncertainties, it is not surprising
that so much attention through the ages has been given to
the formation of the moral values of the young. The young
human animal must be tamed and domesticated, like any
other exuberant creature, but then also civilized—capable of
self-restraint, capable of political judgment, capable of public
discourse.

Thus, presidents and other notable public figures are held
up as exemplars of the good life. They are usually assumed
to be exemplars of private morality as well as public virtue.
Even when the gap is widest between those two dimensions
of the life of a political leader's behavior we still do not argue
in favor of a life that deliberately and systematically indulges
personal vice while cultivating an image of public virtue. Instead, we cultivate a sophisticated tolerance of lapses from
virtue—which implies that we know what virtue is, what vice
is, and what it is reasonable to expect as a norm of human
social behavior in our culture. A recent *Washington Post* study
concluded that middle Americans normally thought of as
"conservative, patriotic and Republican" had become dis-
illusioned. When asked about the qualities they sought in a
president, about half emphasized competence: qualities of
intelligence and experience; and the other half virtue: qualities of character.[2] In a recent lecture at Monticello, presidential adviser Brent Scowcroft listed three aspects of pres-

idential character: courage—the willingness to stick with decisions once made; the ability to pick good people, and "to know when to listen to them"; and judgment, a quality Scowcroft considers more important in a president than great intelligence.[3]

In the years since presidents' tax returns have been made public, people have had reason to mock the modest charitable donations of some recent incumbents. One attribute we expect to find in presidents—as character models—is generosity.

My present interests range over philanthropy, political and social thought, and the American presidency, but virtue and vice appear everywhere in our culture, and this discussion could draw on phenomena from other areas of modern life. Given today's ethical realities, what should we attempt to teach young people today about virtue, about vice as well as virtue, or—to put it in less burdened language—what should we attempt to convey to them about the good life? We seem to say that we want young people to be people of good character; that being of good character implies, among other things, being benevolent and generous—actively involved in initiatives for the public good. Our focus, however, is most often on the benefits to young people, and we take for granted that our voluntary efforts will be beneficial to the poor, the oppressed, the hungry, and the homeless. We fail to point out that it is difficult to do good.

Bertrand Russell's *Education and the Good Life* appeared in May 1926; by the end of that year it had been reprinted seven times. The book was an optimistic report of the effectiveness of new insights from psychology in shaping character. "Think what it would mean," he wrote: "health, freedom, happiness, kindness, intelligence, all nearly universal. In one generation, if we chose, we could bring the millenium. [*sic*]"[4]

Russell believed that science had achieved a level of understanding of human behavior sufficient to shape the human personality into civilized forms. The insights of psychology would make "the education of character" possible. Russell's confidence has disturbing overtones 60 years later. Much has happened to make us think that the consequences in practice of such social and educational benevolence are often questionable at best. The worst extremes of modern totalitarianism were yet to be revealed when Russell wrote that book; George Orwell's *1984* was yet to be written. Mass education to shape human character according to a predetermined image of what constitutes virtue and the good life has come to represent the most evil distortions of utopian thought rather than the culmination of human wisdom. Konrad Lorenz, another German ethologist, expressed a commonplace when he said that "Knowledge is power and man has achieved great power over his environment. He has not, however, gained the same power over himself and his own behavior. This has resulted in a very dangerous state of affairs."[5] Whether we like it or not, we seem to be faced with the education of vast numbers of young people, and their education requires education of character as well as instruction in knowledge.

An example of the problem is education in the philanthropic tradition—education in the values of voluntary public service, voluntary association for public rather than private ends, education in altruistic values intended to balance education in egoistic ones. It is a tradition in which most Americans take great pride. It is the virtue of individual Americans that has become the most distinctive virtue of American society as a whole. The purpose of this paper is to focus on the need for education for voluntary action for the public good—organized philanthropy. The question is whether thinking about philanthropy in terms of the ethics of virtue provides an effective educational framework.

It is useful to remember that the origins of the term *virtue* are closely akin to words meaning *custom* or *usage*. Yet, as Walter Lippmann wrote in *A Preface to Morals*, virtuous actions are "those actions men cannot be expected to do."[6] That is, virtue can stand for no more than what a particular society accepts as the norm of behavior, unless one adds the moral dimension of conscience, as Lippmann does: "For virtue is that kind of conduct esteemed by God, or public opinion, or that less immediate part of a man's personality which he calls his conscience."[7]

Philanthropy is usually thought to be a moral virtue, to fall within a definition such as that offered by David Hume in *An Inquiry Concerning the Principles of Morals* (1751): "The epithets *sociable, good-natured, humane, merciful, grateful, friendly, generous, beneficent,* or their equivalents, are known in all languages, and universally express the highest merit which human nature is capable of attaining."[8]

Virtue has other characteristics: as John Dewey pointed out, virtuous action must also reveal "wholeheartedness, persistence, and sincerity."[9]

The philanthropic tradition develops in two main streams: that of charity—acts of mercy to relieve the suffering of the innocent and helpless; and that of philanthropy—acts of community to improve the quality of life. The idea of charity is essentially religious; the idea of philanthropy is essentially secular.

The history of the idea of virtue may also be said to develop in two main streams of thought: the classical and religious tradition of moral behavior, and the Renaissance and Enlightenment traditions of virtue as excellence, as "manliness." The former stream is the one that would see charity as a moral virtue; the latter might look upon philanthropy as the display of wealth appropriate to a person of high social standing.[10] The Enlightenment view tends to look upon virtue as rational self-interest, to the point that Rousseau could argue that virtue "was no more than love of self." However, virtue takes on a third dimension, in addition to morality and self-esteem: that of "a defiant political slogan."[11]

"[T]he principle of all virtue," Lippmann declared, "is to transcend the immediacy of desire and to live for ends which are transpersonal."[12] In the tradition of voluntary giving, almsgiving has long been criticized as "throwing money at the problem," as responding impulsively but not thoughtfully. Modern philanthropy, in contrast, is characterized by some scholars as the systematic effort to uncover the root causes of social problems and to devise strategies for their solution. Philanthropy in this form is then above "the immediacy of desire" and beyond the self-interested claims of the self to the transpersonal.

The three streams of philanthropy as moral virtue, personal excellence, and political protest continue to be mixed in our tradition. They do not mix well. For example, grand philanthropic gestures of mercy toward the poor cause uncomfortable feelings in many people who think that one should follow the Lord's instruction and do one's giving in secret. The very idea of doing good in order to enhance one's social standing seems egoistic rather than altruistic and thus contrary to the essential nature of beneficence. The motivation as well as the outcome is judged. To what extent, one must ask, are such attitudes simply the reflection of cultural norms and to what extent are they the product of universal values? One persistent thread of almsgiving throughout history insists on protecting the dignity of the recipient. It recognizes that the philanthropic relationship is asymmetric, a relationship of dominance and dependence. In a society that places a high value on individual autonomy, to be dependent on the voluntary generosity of another is to be put in a demeaning position. So strongly is this felt that some argue against philanthropy as a virtue: Philanthropy is instead an artifact of a culture that has failed to meet basic human needs. This recent quotation is typical of this point of view when cast in religious terms:

> The logic of Jesus' Golden Rule and of Moses' and Jesus' commandment to love thy neighbor as thyself admit of no other conclusion, for private and church charity have proven, beyond the shadow of a doubt, that they are incapable of preventing the suffering and death of innocent travelers along life's highway. Only government, funded by our taxes, *whether relinquished willingly or unwillingly,* can do the job. That's the reality.[13] (Emphasis added.)

Views of human nature emerge that imply that we can be expected to do good spontaneously, without self-interest, or that contend that we will not do good unless our self-interest is also advanced in the process. The focus of attention in all this, of course, is on the giver rather than on the recipient. But philanthropy—especially in that form of it called charity—is usually thought of as a virtue, as a habit of doing good. To assert that someone "does good" for others presumably means that those others are better off. The doer of good is also thought to be better off after the fact for having done good in the first place, even thought the end result may be measured by increased happiness offsetting decreased resources.

To speak of virtue and its consequences is also intended to imply that the consequences are problematic. We do not know when we set out to do good to or for another whether that will in fact be the result of our action. To act voluntarily for the good of another is to enter the realm of unintended harmful consequences as well as intended benevolent ones. The virtue of prudence, according to theologian Josef Pieper, is "the ability [the determination?] to see what is truly there"—presumably the philanthropic virtue of highest priority.[14]

With Russell, our society seems to believe that young people should be nourished in the tradition of voluntary action for the public good. This morning's *Philadelphia Inquirer* has a feature article about Haverford College's honor code: "A college where trust is the rule."[15] The University of Virginia also has an honor code, and students charged by other students with violations are in turn judged by their peers. Two points are implied in such reports: that trust is essential to healthy community life, and trust in contemporary society is less evident than it should be. The economic importance of trust was pointed out some years ago by Kenneth Arrow[16]; the political importance of trust is forced upon us whenever there are allegations that trust has been violated in or near the White House.

Voluntary action for the public good takes many forms. We usually think of "philanthropy" only in the dimension of voluntary giving, and give too little weight to philanthropy as moral discourse. For example, Amy Carter, daughter of the former president, was arrested and tried (and later acquitted) of action at the University of Massachusetts to prevent recruitment efforts by the Central Intelligence Agency. Students at the University of Virginia disrupted a meeting of the Board of Visitors to protest University investments in corporations doing business in South Africa.

Civil disobedience and even revolution have thus often been thought to be a virtue—the virtue of political courage—whether directed against public policy or private interest. Philanthropic activity—voluntary initiative for the public good—is the mechanism by which many Americans use their First Amendment rights to reform American society. Such efforts often require demonstration of the virtues of courage and charity, hope and justice. The much-debated virtue of prudence—practice of the virtue of knowing the truth of the consequences of one's acts before committing them—may be lacking. Hence the problematic nature of philanthropy, a qualified virtue as all of them are.

The study of virtue is useful, it seems to me. It is even unavoidable if we are to be concerned about the moral as well as the political and economic heritage we pass on. There has been much talk about "the need for values" in education, a notion as simplistic as Russell's 60 years ago, assuming that there is agreement about what constitutes the good life and the good society. There has been increasing talk about character, also a useful notion if we go back to Aristotle and see that character is not the simple summing of individual virtues. The idea of philanthropy as a virtue helps us to see that no single virtue is sufficient, although it may have claim to being the virtue that best expresses our humanity.

The study of virtue is undermined by its conceptual ambiguity, which is one reason why scholars have largely abandoned it in recent years. Virtue is also difficult to talk about because it carries with it 19th century notions of oppressive perfectionism and original sin.

The study of virtue also reveals that it is problematic. Its outcomes are uncertain. Philanthropy is an example of a virtue that is judged not only in terms of its motivations, but of its consequences.

NOTES

1. Wolfgang Wickler, *The Biology of the Ten Commandments*, McGraw-Hill, 1972, p. 1.
2. "GOP Stronghold Reflects Voters' Growing Disillusionment," *The Washington Post*, April 22, 1987.

3. Miller Center of Public Affairs, University of Virginia, April 14, 1987.

4. Bertrand Russell, *Education and the Good Life*, Boni and Liveright, 1926, p. 316.

5. Wickler, loc. cit.

6. Walter Lippmann, *A Preface to Morals*, Macmillan, 1929, p. 222.

7. Ibid.

8. David Hume, *An Inquiry Concerning the Principles of Morals*, Bobbs-Merrill, 1957, p. 9.

9. John Dewey and James H. Tufts, *Ethics*, Henry Holt, 1909, pp. 403–405.

10. Jerrold E. Seigel, "*Virtu* in and Since the Renaissance," in *Dictionary of the History of Ideas*, Scribners, 1973, vol. 4, pp. 476–486.

11. Carol Blum, "Virtue," in *Blackwell Companion to the Enlightenment*, Blackwell (forthcoming).

12. Ibid.

13. John C. Cort, "Christ and Neighbor," *New Oxford Review*, May 1987, p. 21.

14. Gilbert Leilaender, *The Theory and Practice of Virtue*, University of Notre Dame Press, 1984, p. 22.

15. Huntly Collins, "A college where trust is the rule," *The Philadelphia Inquirer*, April 25, 1987.

16. Kenneth Arrow, *The Limits of Organization*, Norton, 1974.

A Dialogue
Between
the Head and
the Heart

These reflections on reason and emotion in philanthropy are inspired by Thomas Jefferson's famous letter to Maria Cosway.

My theme is philanthropy and liberal education. My text is a letter-essay that Thomas Jefferson once wrote that goes by the title, "A Dialogue Between My Head and My Heart."[1] It is an essay on friendship, charity, the human condition, and the methods and values of science and morals. The letter was written to a married British woman whom Jefferson had met in Paris (and for whom he developed a strong but platonic affection), on the occasion of her departure for America. Jef-

This essay is adapted from a "Conversation at Monticello" sponsored by the White Burkett Miller Center of Public Affairs at the University of Virginia, September 12, 1985.

141

ferson was so moved by their parting that he returned to his apartment and wrote the long letter that same evening.

The body of the letter is in the literary form of a dialogue between Head and Heart, first as an exchange about the joy of friendship and the pain of separation. Jefferson then speaks of the "divided empire" of the self, the dialectic between reason and emotion, between self-interest and altruism, in each of us.

Friendship is at issue because of Jefferson's distress at the departure of his friend. His head tells him that the principle to follow is to avoid becoming entangled with others, with "their follies and their misfortunes," and to play it safe. Don't rush into new relationships; recognize beforehand the anguish they may cause, and cultivate instead the pleasures of privacy and contemplation. In a miserable world, the best course is to avoid adding misery to it.

Jefferson's heart responds that because the world is full of sorrow, it is only sensible to share our burdens: "For assuredly nobody will care for him who cares for nobody." In fact, the balance will tip the other way: ". . . thanks to a benevolent arrangement of things, the greater part of life is sunshine."

Although Jefferson attributes to the Head the hegemony over the world of nature, he claims for the Heart the human virtues of sympathy, love, justice; of benevolence, gratitude, and friendship. The methods and values of science include calculation, and calculation in the form of self-interest in human affairs is a misapplication of science. Morality is too important, he says, "to be risked on the incertain combinations of the head"; the foundation of morality requires "the mechanism of the heart."

There is, on balance, in Jefferson's view, a long-term wisdom in the reliance on the human affections rather than on human cleverness. Jefferson implies that the concessions that the head makes to the heart are the source of some of our most important moral victories. (Although he doesn't make the point, I suspect that Jefferson would agree that the discipline imposed by the head on the heart often saves us from doing harm in our rush to do good. I will return to that later.)

Beyond friendship, in our less personal relations in society at large, Jefferson counsels against the misleading influence of narrow self-interest. The head leads us astray when it intrudes in the affairs of the heart. He illustrates his theme with two examples, the first that of a weary soldier seeking a lift on the back of Jefferson's carriage. Jefferson's self-interest advises against it: His head argues that there will be other soldiers further on; eventually we'll put too much of a burden on the horses. Jefferson rides on, but his conscience gets the better of him: It may not be possible to help everyone, his heart pleads, but we ought to help those we can. The logic of compassion wins out, but too late, because when Jefferson turns back to find the soldier, the soldier has taken another road.

The second illustration is not one of voluntary service, but of voluntary giving. Jefferson's head tells him that a woman seeking alms is in fact a drunkard who will only waste his charity in the taverns. Jefferson's heart again belatedly overrules his head, but this time he is able to seek out the woman and learn the truth about her. She was not a drunkard, after all, but a woman seeking charity to place her child in school.

Jefferson recognizes that there are consequences to these actions of the heart: "We have no rose without it's [*sic*] thorn; no pleasure without alloy." There are risks to be run, which implies that pain may well be incurred in the search for happiness. But that is better than lonely isolation, better than the security of the contemplative life that his head advises him to choose: "Let the sublimated philosopher grasp visionary happiness while pursuing phantoms dressed in the garb of truth! Their supreme wisdom is supreme folly . . ."

The dialogue between the head and the heart is a metaphor for the study of the philanthropic tradition. Jefferson's letter serves as a useful point of departure. Jefferson himself was a man of strong and developed reason as well as powerful and courageous commitment, presumably a model of the educated person, sensitive to human values, aware of human failings, pragmatic and visionary.

The philanthropic tradition is a setting in which to study

the divided empire. We all have learned how our self-interest works, and we could quickly add to Jefferson's reasons for not picking up the soldier on the road: Not only will others be demanding the same help; the next thing you know they'll all want to sit up front with us.

Jefferson's example of the woman seeking alms makes us aware of the ancient moral problem of *desert:* Jefferson gave the woman help because she proved *not* to be a drunkard. Would he have helped her if his first impression had been accurate, had he detected the tell-tale odor on her breath? Today, we might simply evade the issue by contending that drunkenness is a disease, not a vice, and the woman deserves our help because she is sick. And that might then prompt us to ask ourselves—our hearts asking our heads—is there any-one out there who *doesn't* deserve our help?

The issue of the deserving poor and needy of our contem-porary society has been debated at length in recent years. It continues to be a controversial issue of public policy. The complexities of the problem are by now familiar: Inspired by our hearts, we have followed our heads and turned the mentally ill out of institutions and into the streets. The con-sensus seems to be that such people shouldn't be made to live in the streets. At the same time, we have come to know that public shelters and institutions are often dangerous, heartless places. The morally right thing to do, it would seem, would be to find decent homes that will take these people in. Decent homes, presumably, like yours and mine . . .

In Santa Cruz, California, according to newspaper reports, able-bodied young people are found in considerable numbers claiming food, shelter, and freedom of action as the rights and protections belonging to the modern vagabond. They are neither seeking nor interested in employment.

Should we consider the mentally ill on the streets of New York and the idle dropouts on the streets of Santa Cruz equal in their claims on us?

In choosing one's friends, Jefferson said, one should ex-ercise careful judgment. Friendship should not be based on externals or self-interest: "I receive no one into my esteem until they are worthy of it." Did Jefferson apply a test of worthiness to his acts of charity? He apparently took the soldier's plea at its face value; the soldier was worthy simply by virtue of being a soldier on duty. The woman seeking alms, on the other hand, required a test to determine that she was worthy of his assistance. Had she turned out to be a drunkard after all, she would have failed the test. Whether one should make judgments about the moral worth of those seeking aid is one of the recurrent issues of the philanthropic tradition, livelier today perhaps even than it was in Jefferson's time.

Friendship is not the basis for charity, for voluntary giving and service. Acts of philanthropy reach out to total strangers, often in distant places, usually without the ability to screen out the unworthy or otherwise unqualified. Nothing could be more familiar to Americans today, for example, than the drawn faces and swollen bellies of starving children in Africa, yet presumably few of us are personally acquainted with any of them. Our hearts tell us only that we *must* act to help them—even though are heads cannot tell us why.

That African appeal has touched millions of people, perhaps unprecedented numbers around the world. It has enlisted the efforts of people usually identified not with the relief of suffering, but with the manufacture of pleasure and self-indulgence. The rock musicians and other entertainers who produced the "We Are the World" and "Live Aid" fundraising extravaganzas were not more expert about the Ethiopian crisis than the readers of daily newspapers. They were able to condemn the situation as morally intolerable and to use their extraordinary promotional skills and technologies to raise large amounts of money very quickly—yet without any expertise at all in using that money to effect the changes they felt were necessary.

The dialogue between the Head and Heart over what we should do when faced with a human tragedy such as the famine in Ethiopia warns us of the limits of our emotion. The tens of millions of dollars raised by the rock concerts and records are not quickly and easily converted into food for the hungry. Rock stars prove to know little about the logistics of food aid, and seem to have only just recently discovered that Ethiopia is the center of a terrible civil war. We have learned to our dismay that some Ethiopians are willing to starve other Ethiopians for political ends. To seek to bring food for the innocent through that maze of ancient animosity may call for the cleverness of con men as well as for the patient commitment of saints.

Closer to home, and with no Russians to point a finger at, our failures to deal humanely and effectively with the homeless, even when we are inclined to respond to them, are instructive in teaching us that it is difficult to be enlightened and humane. Such failures seem to lead some people to conclude that the effort should not be made in the first place. As a nation, our head is telling us that we are better advised to ignore the "follies and the misfortunes" of others, and to make ourselves comfortable in our studies (or television rooms).

The purpose of liberal education is to bring some semblance of *detente* if not harmony to the divided empire of the human mind and spirit. To study the habits of the heart is to study the consequences of friendship and charity, of high aspiration and low technique, to reflect on knowing when to mind one's business and when not to, on wanting to do good and knowing how.

To study the tradition and practice of philanthropy is to confront liberal education at its best: in the education of the public citizen and the private person, in the continuing education of the Head *and* the Heart.

NOTE

1. Merrill D. Peterson, ed., *Thomas Jefferson: Writings*, The Library of America, 1984, pp. 866–877.

Hofstra's Most Distinctive Virtue

Voluntary service to those in need of our personal help more than our money, help to those who need time and understanding, is at the core of the philanthropic tradition. Sometimes, new dimensions of service emerge spontaneously and anonymously in a community, out of the fabric of institutional life. That is what happened at Hofstra University—and continues there.

One of the shortest careers in government service ended yesterday with the resignation of Dr. Eileen Gardner from the Department of Education.

Dr. Gardner joined the Department a week ago. During that week it became known that she had written a paper for the Heritage Foundation in 1983 in which she argued that

Adapted from remarks presented at Hofstra University's 50th anniversary ceremonies in Hempstead, New York, 1985.

"spending on education for the handicapped had 'selfishly drained resources from the normal school population and most probably weakened the quality of teaching.' "

Dr. Gardner defended her position by explaining that " 'what happens to a person in life, the circumstances a person is born into, the race, the handicapping conditions, the sex—those circumstances are there to help the person grow toward spiritual perfection.' "

The setting of these remarks is Hofstra's 50th anniversary; a panel on "evaluating philanthropy." We are talking about the relationship of philanthropy to education, but I want to come back to the case of Dr. Gardner. First, a brief effort at definition:

One working definition of philanthropy reflected in this panel is the familiar one of philanthropy as rational, large-scale giving by foundations and individuals to enhance the quality of life in the community, and the extension of that grantmaking activity to corporations.

My preferred, broader definition includes giving for *charitable* purposes—acts of mercy to relieve suffering, to provide assistance to those unable to fend for themselves in meeting the ordinary daily challenges of life.

This broader definition also includes voluntary *service* and voluntary *association*—philanthropy is more than almsgiving, more than grantmaking.

The history of the philanthropic tradition in this broader sense is "the social history of the moral imagination":

- How some individuals have developed new concepts and ideas for improving the conditions of life for the society and for other individuals
- How groups have organized around compelling ideas to improve the public good
- How resources have been marshalled to accomplish those ends

That is, (1) the intellectuals who conceived of the application of the ideas of social science to the solutions of social problems (2) used the mechanism of the philanthropic foundation to engage the interest and effort of others to advance their ideas, (3) supported by the wealth made available to them voluntarily by such people as John D. Rockefeller.

The story at a more local and personal level can be seen in one strong thread running through the history of Hofstra University. As far as I know, it is an unwritten history. I speak of the history of Hofstra's commitment to disabled students.

When I first came to Hofstra a dozen years ago, I found an organized, sophisticated, sensitive, institutionalized commitment to the education of the disabled. I even found a mimeographed guide, prepared by students, on "Everything You Always Wanted to Know About the Handicapped but Were Afraid to Ask."

The new residence halls on the new north campus on Mitchell Field had been designed with a concern for access by disabled students.

My son remarked that when he came here as a student four years ago he was uneasy in the presence of the physically disabled. He was uncertain about how to behave, as we all have been. In a very short time he became "used to" the presence and activity of disabled students. Living and working with the physically disabled at Hofstra is a natural part of life on this campus. It is more a part of the life of Hofstra than of any other campus where I have studied or worked.

There is more to it than social accommodation. Many of the disabled students need help from others, sometimes on an extensive and continuing basis. That help is provided by family members to some extent, but often by other students—students who themselves have no visible disabilities. Some of the most extraordinary acts of devotion and understanding that I've ever seen are routinely evident on this campus.

The students benefit, of course. A friend of mine who has taught psychiatry at Johns Hopkins for many years describes this kind of philanthropic activity as "a prescription for mental health" for those who engage in it.

The charitable and philanthropic acts that are evident in Hofstra's philanthropic tradition of concern for the disabled reveal "the social history of the moral imagination" in very concrete ways. It is a tradition that has a powerful and enduring impact on many students, whose lives and values are changed by the experience. Yet some students are not touched by it in the same way. Why?

And few students, I suspect, learn anything about why this tradition developed as it has on *this* campus and not on most others; about the individuals whose moral vision founded the tradition, which became persuasive and compelling to others; how the resources for these activities were found; how the activities were organized and institutionalized—made collectively binding on the allocation of some resources—and which aspects of concern for the disabled still remain beyond the scope of what is available even here.

There was a freshman seminar at Gettysburg College a year or so ago on the theme of "social justice and individual responsibility." There might be a similar course at Hofstra, or one on "the social history of the moral imagination" and how it is manifest in small communities like college campuses.

My purpose is to raise the question of where the philanthropic tradition belongs in the general education of undergraduates. My own inclination is to put the burden on the history department, but recently a political scientist and I talked about the role of interest groups; "one-way transfers of exchangeables" have become known as *grants economics*. The social psychology of the relations of dominance and dependence, as well as the psychology of helping behavior and the philosophical question of the limits of altruism also come to mind, along with the legal questions of rights and the allocation of medical resources. Someone told me that more than half of the student semester credit hours at Hofstra are in undergraduate courses in business; historians of corporate philanthropy make it clear that business leaders come in all shapes and sizes, and that some of them are acutely sensitive to the moral dimension of economic activity. And, of course, the religious roots of charity are clearly central to these ideas—they are even determining in the thought of people like Eileen Gardner. (The shock effect of her remarks should not obscure the point she seeks to make about how we should understand the human condition.)

Hofstra students are mainstream Americans. Perhaps in one small but important way their lives have been deepened and enriched by their experience here—their experience with disabled students *outside* the classroom. Whether their intellectual development *inside* the classroom has helped them to grasp the distinctiveness of the philanthropic tradition, and make of it a guide of their subsequent behavior, is not clear to me. And if it is not true of a place like Hofstra where the practice of philanthropy is everywhere in evidence, is it likely to be raised in the consciousness of students at "less enlightened" institutions?

The anonymous heroes of Hofstra's most distinctive virtue—its enlightened and sensitive and continuing commitment to the disabled—should be the source of a larger contribution to the education of Hofstra students. Those who have made Hofstra a morally better and finer place have done something extraordinary.

Why it is still thought of as "extraordinary," and why it should rather become a matter of the ordinary course of life everywhere, is a topic in the "social history of the moral imagination."

It is something worthy of attention in the liberal education of all undergraduates.

In celebrating its 50th anniversary, Hofstra is engaged in an exercise of reflection and self-assessment. The student who spoke at the opening convocation proudly referred to Hofstra's accounting program as being rated seventh in the country by the leading accounting firms. The other evening I attended the induction ceremony of the history honor society on campus, and I spoke with conviction of the high intellectual quality of that department. Hofstra has an important and difficult commitment to selectivity in admissions, and it has always had an unusual depth of talent in its faculty. It has an excellent library; as a frequent user of it, I join the applause for the steps already taken toward its *second* millionth volume.

Yet if I were to point to the characteristic of Hofstra that is its proudest achievement, one for which I can claim no personal credit or notable contribution, it would be this sensitive concern for those whose response needs only the opportunity that others must provide. On this single point, Hofstra need defer to no other place. And this single point may be enough to justify its future as well as its past.

Philanthropy in Action

The Social Philosophy and Policy Conference (SPPC) was the first time that professional philosophers had convened for a comprehensive discussion of philanthropy. My purpose was to present some of the situations and problems that confront philanthropy in action that could be illuminated by moral philosophy.

The Ethiopian Famine Relief Effort

Few things have more effectively captured the public sentiment in recent decades than the televised news reports about the Ethiopian famine first broadcast in the United States in 1984. The images dramatized suffering on a large scale among innocent people, particularly among defenseless children. The reports themselves indicated that literally millions of lives were in jeopardy, and that beyond immediate death by starvation there was also the prospect of large

This essay is adapted from remarks presented at the Social Philosophy and Policy conference on Private Philanthropy and the Public Good (held in New York City in October, 1985). Reprinted with the permission of the Social Philosophy and Policy Center of Bowling Green State University.

numbers of people mentally and physically maimed for life by lack of protein.

The surrounding conditions were shown to be almost unbelievably harsh: large numbers of people crowded into refugee camps—or, even worse, unable to get into those camps at all. Thousands of people were reported to have died en route to the relief centers.

The political environment was also one of civil disorder. A government that described itself as Marxist-Leninist was engaged in drastic social and economic reform, including relocation of large numbers of people. A civil war between the central government in Addis Ababa and the secessionist rebel forces in Eritrea greatly complicated the situation. Public resources were diverted to weapons and warfare rather than to relief efforts, and the central government attempted to block relief shipments to rebel territory as part of its military strategy.

The neighboring countries of the Sudan and Somalia, also suffering severely from the drought, were drawn into the Ethiopian crisis. Somalia has been engaged in sporadic warfare with the government of Ethiopia for some years; the two sides have exchanged international sponsors (the U.S. and USSR). Sudan, divided by ethnic conflict north and south, proclaimed a policy of sanctuary for refugees fleeing from Ethiopia, even though its own resources to assist the refugees were critically needed by its own people.

The philanthropic constant in this situation might for present purposes be identified as the international relief community, led largely by American private voluntary organizations (PVOs), but also including international agencies such as the UN refugee commission and other private agencies such as the French organization called Doctors Without Borders. The PVO community had warned of the impending crisis long before it became headline television news. A few American agencies were already in Ethiopia when the news story broke in the United States, even though the Ethiopian government's relations with the United States were at the lowest diplomatic level.

The Ethiopian crisis continues—deaths are estimated at

2,000 a day after a year of exceptional international effort—
although the attention given to the crisis by the media has
diminished sharply and shifted to other issues (most notably
South Africa). What are some of the questions that have occurred in the course of the philanthropic response to the
Ethiopian famine? Are they issues that might apply to similar
crises elsewhere in the world?

- Is civil disorder the key? Drought in other African countries (most notably Botswana) has not resulted in suffering comparable to that in Ethiopia. To what extent
  should governments be held accountable for the suffering of their people in such circumstances? Does international relief ease the political burden on a bad government in Ethiopia?
- What is the true role of the famine relief effort? The
  sums raised, although historic in terms of voluntary
  giving for relief purposes, are a small fraction of the
  sums and supplies provided by governments. Is the role
  of private philanthropy that of consciousness-raising
  rather than the actual relief of suffering?
- To what extent should these problems be dealt with by
  voluntary giving? The scale of the financial need and
  the high levels of political action necessary to stabilize
  the country and the region exceed the grasp of voluntary
  action. Does voluntary giving obscure the need for more
  drastic and costly political action?
- On what basis can governments justify assistance to
  peoples where no significant political interest or benefit
  can be served? Our political "ally" in the region is Somalia; why should we help Somalia's principal enemy?
  Ethiopia has no importance to American economic interests; why invest a billion dollars in short-term refugee relief when the problem is likely to recur and there
  will be no discernible or measurable benefit to the
  United States?
- Finally, what is the role of the news media? By extension, what are the appropriate uses of the media by
  entertainers acting as volunteers to raise money for

famine relief? What impact will fund-raising initiatives launched in behalf of Ethiopian famine relief have on large-scale fund raising for similar or even different purposes? Will international communication make international fund raising a new force in societies where private giving has been modest or non-existent?

War and Revolution in Central America

The emergence of a Sandinista-dominated Marxist government out of the revolution against the Somoza government of Nicaragua has led to a strongly negative response from the government of the United States. The Reagan administration has given active support to rebel forces in opposition to the Sandinistas. At the same time, U.S. policy has supported the government of El Salvador against rebels that reportedly receive support from Nicaragua. Similar civil and international military action, polarizing forces around extremes of left and right at the cost of moderate influences, is taking place in Honduras. Peace initiatives have been sponsored by other governments (the Contadora group) as well as by the United States (the so-called Kissinger commission), and by a wide range of private voluntary organizations.

To a much greater extent than in Ethiopia, religious groups have sought to influence public policy toward Central America—supporting Administration policy as well as opposing it. Voluntary action by church groups to provide "sanctuary" for refugees fleeing Central America has challenged immigration and refugee policy directly. Highly publicized legal action initiated against church groups has generated increased financial as well as moral support. Other religious groups that support Administration policies have raised funds for humanitarian aid for the Nicaraguan rebels—funds that the Administration has been unable to extract from Congress. (The IRS classification of some of these nonprofit organizations is not made clear in newspaper reports.)

- The essential question is the freedom of action claimed by and accorded to voluntary nonprofit organizations seeking to influence or change U.S. foreign policy—by direct action outside the United States.

- Can "humanitarian aid" be kept humanitarian in military situations? Are private contributions in fact fungible? Do they free up other funds for military purposes?
- Should boundaries be placed around the activities of church groups in foreign affairs? Is the separation of church and state jeopardized by the roles played by church groups in Central America?
- Does political action by churches and others undermine philanthropic behavior? How might we draw the line between politics and philanthropy?

Controlling Nuclear Weapons

This is the title of a new book by Robert Dahl which examines the question in terms of the trade-off between "democracy and guardianship."[1] At what point does a democracy yield its democratic processes to the decision of experts—when the consequences of error are catastrophic?

No issue is more familiar. Philosophers and others have engaged in extended discussions about it: A recent issue of *Ethics* was devoted to the topic.[2]

In terms of philanthropic action, the range of activities has spread across vast public rallies in Central Park in behalf of the nuclear freeze; teach-ins and student referenda at Brown University; the development and distribution of course materials and teacher guides by the Institute for World Order; and investment in academic research at a cluster of leading universities and research centers by the Carnegie Corporation.

Many have called for a massive effort to concentrate philanthropic resources and energies on this issue. The actual amount of funds currently allocated is probably small, in the total scheme of philanthropic giving. The numbers of people called to the debate, however, by educational and religious institutions, appears to run into the millions.

- To what extent should private voluntary organizations influence U.S. nuclear policy? To what extent should

U.S.-based organizations attempt to influence the policies of other governments?

- To what extent is direct action of the kind most dramatically illustrated by Greenpeace justified within the framework of the philanthropic tradition?
- What is the role of the media in this issue? Are philanthropic organizations accorded different editorial treatment from that given to governmental and private economic points of view?

South Africa*

Seldom has an issue become so intertwined among the three sectors. Private voluntary action has led to effective pressures on business corporations and on inter-governmental relations. Religious organizations have again played a leading role, along with civil rights groups.

South Africa appears to have drawn attention away from the Ethiopian famine as the leading issue of African affairs pressing on the public consciousness. Voluntary efforts have become linked with political as well as religious and social groups within South Africa. The principal multinational corporation effort to improve the lot of South African blacks has been led by a black American clergyman (Leon Sullivan). Business corporations and philanthropic foundations have been the principal sponsors of black South Africans studying in the United States under a program managed by the Institute for International Education. The American Chamber of Commerce in South Africa was the focal point of a South African fund-raising effort, supplemented by funds from the United States, to build a vocational school in Soweto. Colleges and universities with African studies and Afro-American studies programs have been the campus focal point for debate about the issue.

- What are the rights of private voluntary groups outside South Africa in supporting anti-apartheid protest that lead to violence and death of South Africans?

*See the following essay, "Tainted Money."

- Is the strategy of disinvestment justified by religious organizations and educational institutions if the consequences are harmful to their own financial stability?
- Should philanthropic efforts in South Africa aim at long-term reform or short-term disruption?
- Are the philanthropic interventions in support of apartheid in South Africa (Jerry Falwell) or in opposition to it (almost everyone else) examples of American cultural imperialism? How do they differ?

Lincoln Center for the Performing Arts

The arts present the most permeable boundaries among the three sectors. Not only do for-profit and not-for-profit interests co-exist with a variety of public agencies, initiatives that begin in one sector mature in another. Foundation-supported artists make recordings with for-profit recording companies; tax-exempt theaters become the home of subsidized productions that eventually become highly profitable. Individuals are supported by sales of their work, by foundation grants, and by grants from public agencies (such as the state arts councils and the National Endowment for the Arts).

Lincoln Center is a familiar and symbolic hub of such activity, but many similar institutions have been established across the country.

- Should public and philanthropic funds be used to support activities that become profit-making?
- Should philanthropic funds, by definition not-for-profit, be permitted to result in private benefit? Should distinctions be drawn among artists, producers, and others in this regard?
- Does philanthropy subsidize elite culture with public money? Should public opinion be enlisted to validate or even guide the arts when public and philanthropic monies are involved?
- Should not-for-profit philanthropic enterprises be permitted to supplement their base income with resources earned by profit-making activity?

- Should access to the arts be free? Does the right to education have a cultural counterpart in the arts?

The Homeless

The homeless and derelict populations of large cities such as New York have increased substantially in recent years. Part of the cause appears to be reduced public funds for welfare; of perhaps even greater significance has been the decision to "mainstream" large numbers of the mentally ill and others thought to be at risk in modern urban environments.

A well-publicized controversy arose in New York City in 1983 over the rights of religious organizations serving the homeless under city contracts. The Salvation Army and the Roman Catholic Church objected to requirements that, as contractors to the city, they sign statements affirming non-discrimination in employment for homosexuals. The case appears to be a classic example of the conflict of two social goods.

- Do charitable organizations have special rights under the law that exempt them from legislation deemed to be in conflict with their ability to carry out their charitable objectives?
- Does charitable assistance to the poor lead to pauperization?
- Does charitable assistance to the poor relieve families of their obligations to family members who may be retarded or otherwise found "unacceptable" or too burdensome in the home?
- Have private agencies, especially those representing specific and strong religious convictions, be permitted to intervene in the lives of the homeless with financial support from public as well as private sources? Does the combination of efforts of New York City and the Salvation Army in behalf of the homeless violate the separation of church and state?
- Does public charity acting around rules of civil service develop workers in sufficient number and professional commitment to deal with the growing population of

homeless, the mentally incompetent elderly, and those terminally ill? In the past, many if not most workers in these fields of service have been drawn to them by religious calling. Can a secular society inspire service of similar levels of self-sacrifice?

Social Philosophy and Policy

This last example deals with the thorny questions that grow out of reflection on the relationship of money and ideas, of means and influence.

The present conference is an example of private voluntary funds being used to encourage the discussion and publication of the thoughts of philosophers and others about "Private Philanthropy and the Social Good." As this essay has attempted to demonstrate, the role of private philanthropy is far broader than fund raising and grantmaking, although it appears that most academics limit their reflection on the tradition to this single dimension. Some of the examples cited here—controlling nuclear weapons, the Central American conflict, the efforts to defeat apartheid in South Africa—call to mind the extensive interaction among campus-based academics, intellectuals in publishing and media, and the alliances of secular intellectual with religious spiritual forces.

In some cases, the philanthropic objectives to be served come in conflict with the sources of support. The risks fall on *all* participants in a philanthropic venture, not simply on those whose money is involved. More than money is in the game for the participants—status, prestige, reputation, and credibility are also at risk. This is often especially true in situations that are thought to be controversial: Risk is shared by corporations who may alienate shareholders and prospective investors; by churches divided into contending factions within local congregations; by colleges and universities drawn into sometimes disruptive debates about external issues, debates that may antagonize otherwise sympathetic donors, parents, or prospective faculty members.

The larger public agenda advanced by a non-profit organization may jeopardize the original and life-giving mission of the organization itself. Funds to supplant the funds lost to higher causes seem to be in short supply. The consequences of action may be ennobling and organizationally fatal at the same time.

The self-interest of donors is often lamented; less often heard is concern about the self-interest of recipients. Philosophers who deal with social and political philosophy deal routinely with explosive material, not only in the classroom, but in their published work. Because some ideas of intellectual interest to philosophers are offensive in the larger society, it is often difficult for philosophers to find patrons or sponsors. (On occasion that is all too frequent, the threat to open philosophical discourse about issues or positions that are unpopular comes from within the academy rather than from outside. The most effective pressure on an academic may be that posed by hierarchical superiors in whom are vested powers over tenure decisions and promotion.)

Philosophers who affirm the standard of reason are also vulnerable to charges of bias, partisanship, and ideology when dealing with social issues. They may sometimes be rewarded for that same partisanship, of course, by pleasing those in the friendly camp, whether the camp is filled with internal or external allies. But discourse suffers when partisanship triumphs, when interest—political, economic, or social—seems to outweigh rational argument.

It is difficult for the non-philosophers to know how to cope with situations in which the experts—the philosophers—accuse one another of ideological distortion. In complex political situations, the facts are difficult to obtain as well as to interpret; the "data" are harder to control than in the scientific laboratory. It is much more difficult to reach agreement on public policy issues such as world hunger, political stability and peace in Central America, efforts to improve the prospects for world peace in the face of mass annihilation, and so on. Such issues raise difficult and often imprecise questions of the sort put forward here. Yet such issues cry out for the wisdom as well as the skills of those who devote their careers to thinking carefully about the social world and its values.

- To what extent does the world of philanthropy behave as a marketplace, where different styles, fashions, and ideologies compete for support? To what extent do (and should) intellectuals compromise their intellectual objectives in order to win support?
- Is the marketplace of grants materially different from the campus competition for students or the publishing competition for readers? Should different standards of behavior be expected of the participants?
- How should philosophers be paid?* ("Generously!" cried out one listener when I posed that question to another audience.) By earning their income from the sale of their work as teachers, writers, consultants, and lecturers? By subsidy from government agencies? By individual patronage? By subsidies in the form of grants from foundations and corporations? By some or all of the above?
- How should grantmakers choose among the possible investments in social philosophy and policy? Should the goal be to encourage work on issues at the fringe of reflection and speculation, or should the goal concentrate on more immediate and practical objectives?
- What are the most successful models of the subsidy of philosophy? Which models appear to be most reliable over time?
- Is the philanthropic relationship corrupting in the realm of ideas as it is sometimes alleged to be in the realm of charity and almsgiving?
- Are philosophers more to be trusted in dealing with sensitive issues of social policy than are foundation executives, corporate executives, agents of government?

Conclusion

PHILOSOPHICAL INQUIRY

The hope of this paper is that it will cause trained and experienced students of philosophy to give clarity and direction to the philosophical discussion of philanthropy, as

*See Part I, "Major Challenges to Philanthropy," page 42.

broadly defined here. What are the philosophical methods appropriate to addressing these particular questions?

Treated philosophically, the cases briefly defined here might prove to be the basis for extracting the ill-defined principles of philanthropy. They might help to bring to conscious reflection the inconsistencies, paradoxes, and contradictions between philanthropic behavior in different settings.

How do the specific questions reveal larger social issues? For example, to what extent may they be used to consider in concrete terms some of the underlying trade-offs between the short-term and long-term? They force us, I believe, to consider the political dimension of philanthropic action— the gray area between public education and consciousness raising, on the one hand, and lobbying, on the other. How might we begin to formulate a defensible distinction between philanthropy intended to improve the quality of life in the community and political action that proclaims the same high purpose?

Moving from specific examples of philanthropy in action (more fully and carefully delineated than they are sketched out here, of course), we can begin to identify the characteristics of voluntary action. It would seem from the cases themselves, for example, that there is a greater readiness for interaction among the not-for-profit, for-profit, and governmental sectors during times of crisis and times that are more normal.

Such observations might, in turn, eventually carry us to higher levels of philosophical discourse: For example, to what extent is the philanthropic dimension determinative of the social order? To what extent does philanthropy reveal the nature of society?

PHILANTHROPY IN EDUCATION

The emphasis of this essay has been on the contribution to social philosophy and policy that might result from a better understanding of philanthropy in action. The conference itself has called upon distinguished scholars to address the underlying fundamental questions raised by philanthropic values and behavior; practitioners of various sorts have approached the subject from a different perspective. The study of philanthropy should be considered in the framework of education as well as that of research, policy, and practice. How should philanthropy be approached in teaching? The illustrations of philanthropy in action that make up the second part of this book appear as grist for most of the disciplinary mills of the humanities and social sciences. I have proposed that we deal with their philanthropic dimension explicitly, within the framework of existing courses and curricula.

What are the principles of philanthropy, and how are they taught and learned? By systematic investigation in formal academic study, or by experience and the guidance of mentors in the context of voluntary service? What are the appropriate methods of philanthropy, the methods that best protect the integrity of the philanthropic relationship? Is the model of non-profit organization effective? Can voluntary initiative carry the burden of important social needs, of advancing the spheres of distributive justice? Must charity be coerced?

These questions may be appropriate to liberal education in preparation for a life of public service. They may be of considerable consequence in the general education of young Americans as citizens. They are questions, however, that go well beyond technical competence. Technical competence is also required of young people these days, as is competence in verbal and mathematical expression and reasoning, and the useful skills of dealing with others. (The skills of dealing with other people are of special importance in situations where responses are not obligatory and where self-interest is often unclear. These are common situations when people come together for public purposes.) Questions of value, purpose, morality, and meaning are raised by exploration of philanthropy in action. They are also questions of the kind that most people still think of as philosophical questions. Does philanthropy then have a proper place in the philosophical curriculum?

NOTES

1. Robert Dahl, *Controlling Nuclear Weapons*, The Frank W. Abrams Lectures, Syracuse University Press, 1985.
2. Special Issue on Ethics and Nuclear Deterrance, *Ethics*, vol. 95, no. 3, 1985.

Tainted Money: The Ethics and Rhetoric of Divestment

Returning to academic life after an absence of ten years in the world of corporate philanthropy, I was disappointed to read that "anti-apartheid students" at the University of Virginia had disrupted a closed meeting of the Board of Visitors and held an overnight vigil in the rotunda. The students reportedly demanded that the board withdraw university investments in companies doing business in South Africa or face continued disruption of its meetings.

I was disappointed, but not surprised. Reports from campuses around the country for several years have made it clear that political theater is the chosen style of discourse for advocates of divestment. I suspect it is because their "movement" has never attracted broad interest, much less strong support. To have their way they must rely on intimidation. Using such tactics does serious harm to what I believe to be

From *Change*, May–June 1987, pp. 55–60. Reprinted with the permission of the Helen Dwight Reid Educational Foundation. Published by Heldref Publications, 4000 Albemarle St., N.W., Washington, D.C. 20016. Copyright © 1987.

the university's central mission: to develop and clarify social thought and to uphold and improve public discourse.

The quality of public discourse is one aspect of my concern. The other follows from my recent experience with the ethical implications of divestment for universities as well as for corporations. My example is drawn from Harvard's decision to announce last October 3rd that it would divest $158.7 million of stocks and bonds held in nine companies. Five of those companies were oil companies, and one of the oil companies was Exxon. At the time, I was president of the Exxon Education Foundation (and continue to serve it as a consultant). Because I am also a former college president, I was asked by Exxon management for my comments and suggestions.

It is convenient at times to use Harvard and Exxon to illustrate the divestment controversy because both are symbols of great power, wealth, and responsibility. They can easily withstand the heat of controversy. I have great respect for both institutions, although I am on Exxon's side in this case and critical of Harvard. I speak only for myself, of course, in all of the opinions expressed.

- Given the fact of Harvard's divestment of Exxon's stock, should Exxon continue to make philanthropic grants to Harvard?
- Given Harvard's action, indeed, should Harvard be willing to accept philanthropic contributions from Exxon? (For the sake of argument, set aside Exxon's decision last winter to leave South Africa.) And, in recognition of the recent events at the University of Virginia, the ancient question:
- What is the role of the university in taking stands on specific public issues that have no direct bearing on the university's activities?

There are important practical as well as moral considerations involved, and it is the kind of messy problem that defies simple answers. "The spirit of liberty," as a Harvard document quotes Judge Learned Hand, "is the spirit which is not too sure it is right."[1] I am not at all sure that I am right, but then I'm not too sure that Harvard is. I am most certain that the methods of the protestors at Virginia are wrong.

Harvard announced that it would divest Exxon's stock because there was a possibility that Exxon was selling products that were being used by the South African police and military to implement the system of apartheid. In the spring of 1985 Harvard had decided that that was the bottom line: It would divest from companies whose products or services might be used in that way. Harvard had to *assume* that Exxon's products were being used by the police and military because Exxon was precluded by South African law both from refusing to sell its products to the government and from making public the details of what it sold.

Harvard was uncomfortable because of "the strong record of the five oil companies and Ford [Motor Company] in opposing apartheid and adopting progressive labor policies." Until this action, Harvard's selective divestment policy was aimed at companies that failed to take the Sullivan Principles seriously. Exxon had always earned the highest rating by Reverend Sullivan's criteria. None of that balanced the requirements of the new policy, however. Harvard praised the companies but denounced the consequences of their work. Harvard recognized that its actions might not be well understood and that "the broader community will not perceive the subtleties of this complex matter." Harvard also admitted that its action could "stigmatize the companies involved. . . ."

Harvard expressed the hope that its arguments would withstand careful scrutiny: "Consistency in the application of our policies is essential for our position to stand against repeated assaults, and we are obviously not pleased if our supporters are bruised in the process by our actions."

Those words are in a letter from Harvard to an oil company (not Exxon), which had posed the awkward question of whether Harvard intended to accept philanthropic support from a company whose stock was deemed unacceptable on moral grounds:

> In light of your favorable comments . . . and our past relationship, we must point out that part of the financial sup-

port you have received from us is generated by the earnings of our affiliate in South Africa, and this shall continue to be the case in the future. Before we consider any new commitments, in view of your strong feeling concerning the morality of [your] decision, we would appreciate knowing whether you wish us to continue our financial support.

Harvard's response followed:

... the specific answer I would like to offer is—yes, Harvard would like to continue its longstanding relationship with [your company], despite the fact that we will be disposing of our security holdings in your company over the next 12 months.

In a separate exchange, a different company posed a similar question to another university:

The question we must ask ourselves now is what we ... should do about future payments in light of the action taken by [your] university. . . .

You can understand our dilemma. We would not wish you to take money from a company you consider to be acting immorally. We would not wish to contribute to an academic institution that is seeking to use its economic power as a political weapon to compel us to follow policies that would jeopardize the jobs of our employees. We would understand, but hardly sympathize, with an action taken simply to avoid trouble.

The same question has been posed to other divesting colleges and universities and invariably has received the same response: Yes, we cannot hold your stock for moral reasons, and yes, we will be happy to continue to receive your support.

The rationale for the different perspectives has been put this way by a university president in what may become a classic text:

A business corporation exists to make a profit; a university exists to advance an ideal. Your decisions necessarily involve calculations of costs and benefits; ours, though cognizant of economic realities, can take basic moral values into greater consideration. You are constrained by statute and some sense of public image; we face the additional constraints imposed by our statement of mission and responsibility to our many disadvantaged constituencies.

Thus on issues like South Africa investment we must adhere to different standards from the ones you espouse. . . .

Another college argues that it doesn't impugn the company's motivations in doing business in South Africa and "we would hope that you would not impugn ours for dissociating ourselves from all business activities in that troubled land."

In spite of these professions of virtue and efforts to avoid appearing moralistic, it seems to me clear (a) that the colleges and universities have made South Africa a moral issue, and (b) that they see themselves in a position morally superior to that of business corporations.

In a guide to the divestment controversy published by the American Council on Education in May 1985, "the argument for divestment" was summarized this way:

Arguments for divestment are based, first, on moral grounds. Along with churches, colleges and universities are expected to reflect in their actions a concern for social values and basic human rights. Thus, responsible investment policy should preclude an investor's profit at the expense of its moral convictions.[2]

It is of such stuff that moral majorities are made. It is presumptuous for universities to take on a moral role when there is such profound division within them—both about the content of that moral role and about its tendency to impose intellectual conformity on faculty and students.

Should corporations stop making grants to Harvard and to other divesting colleges and universities? Should universities decline to accept gifts and grants from companies that fail to measure up to (changing) standards of behavior in South Africa?

When I tried to assess my own thoughts on the matter, my first reaction was to say that Harvard should refrain from seeking support as long as Harvard is caught up in basing its investment decisions on a narrow moral position. My conclusion after thinking about the question for six months remains substantially unchanged. To borrow a term used by moral philosophers, I question Harvard's *moral seriousness.* As I understand it, to be morally serious means to be prepared to accept the consequences of one's moral position. I take that to mean in this case that Harvard should deny itself the benefits of corporate philanthropy when that philanthropy is in part dependent on what Harvard has condemned as ill-gotten gains.

Less "consistency in the application of [its] policies" would mean that Harvard return to the more balanced and broader approach to investment in companies doing business in South Africa. The appearance of moral arrogance would be avoided, and both parties could return to disagreements reflecting their different perspectives.

Unlike those who think it is possible to purge investment decisions of all social values, I believe that "ethical invest-ment" is a defensible practice—if one accepts the conse-quences. If I choose not to invest in gambling casinos because I believe that kind of business to be morally corrupt, I can invest in a "cleaner" business and risk a lower rate of return on my investment. There are, in other words, not only in-dividual companies I would not invest in, there are whole industries I want no part of. If that means I cut myself off from their philanthropic support as well as investment in-come, so be it. Benevolence may not cost anything; benefi-cence does.

There are lots of reasons, good and bad, for making in-vestment decisions. Some of the reasons are cast in moral terms. The more one bases economic decisions on moral val-ues, the more difficult it will be to survive economically. I have to be prepared to accept the economic consequences of my non-economic values.

And it is a hard world out there. As Derek Bok advised his colleagues at Harvard:

> Unless we choose to live like hermits in the desert, we must all be linked in indirect and innumerable ways to the wrongs of the world—through the goods we buy, the taxes we pay, the services we use, the investments we make.[3]

The problem facing multinational business corporations in today's world is that some of them—like Exxon—often are doing business in as many as a hundred countries. On any given day, Amnesty International will be reporting on human rights violations in many of those countries, and Freedom House will have classified most of them as oppressors of free speech and democracy. (There is also the problem of residual evil from past sins: There are those who have not forgiven the Germans for Hitler, the Russians for Stalin, the Japanese for Pearl Harbor, the British for imperialism, the Americans for Viet Nam. . . .)

Doing business successfully at all in the modern world is difficult. Being ethically sensitive makes it more so. To the extent that being ethical means being consistent, a moral stand on one issue requires a similar stand on similar issues. Knowing where closure comes is difficult.

I conclude that Harvard should not accept support from companies whose stock it disqualifies on moral grounds. Harvard's argument—that there is a fundamental difference between its active role as an investor and its passive role as a recipient of grants—does not wash. Harvard does not want to launder the reputations of the morally unworthy, directly or indirectly.

What about Exxon? Exxon announced earlier this year that it was selling its interests in South Africa and the question is now moot. Exxon is presumably again qualified to be welcomed back to Harvard's portfolio. The question of Exxon's response is still worth asking, however academic it may have become in the meantime.

My conclusion is simpler about corporations than it was about the universities, although perhaps not easier to defend: Corporations should keep their relationships with colleges and universities in long-term perspective. Those who would applaud an end to corporate philanthropic support of Harvard include (a) some who hate Harvard and (b) some who hate Exxon (apart from those who hate them both for being rich and powerful). There are also those who believe that philanthropy should be doled out only to ideological allies and the well-behaved, and those who believe that corporate philanthropy corrupts the university.

The relationship between business and higher education

has served the private interests of both and the public interest as well. There are times when each party tries to take advantage of the other. On the average, however, it has been a valuable and constructive relationship, which is one of the reasons I was so disappointed with Harvard in this case.

What is "Harvard," after all? On the divestment issue I draw on two sources: Roderick M. MacDougall, Harvard's treasurer and chairman of the Corporate Committee on Social Responsibility (he shared with me the letter I've quoted earlier) and one of the most thoughtful and persuasive writers on the South Africa divestment effort, Derek Bok (his two open letters to his Harvard colleagues are masterful). The problem is that he failed to win the argument. I agree with Bok and disagree with MacDougall, and infer that they disagree with each other. It seems certain that there is deeply divided opinion on the issue at Harvard, especially in the faculty. (Was it Mary McCarthy who once defined a faculty member as "someone who thinks to the contrary?") Various forces are always at work trying to tie "Harvard" down to one moral or political position or another, and the consensus, if reached, is fragile at best.

Exxon, however, is by definition (at least to this point in time) a much more closed and disciplined organization. It doesn't encourage free-wheeling internal debate on such matters throughout its executive ranks, but assigns problems to specific people for analysis and recommendation. Although the process is more orderly than in universities, it doesn't mean that those charged with the responsibility of dealing with corporate controversies of this kind don't talk and fret and analyze them to death. Responsibility is especially burdensome when one is expected to be wise as well as smart.

Exxon certainly does not see itself as bearing the burden of moral spokesman for society. It gladly leaves that role to others. At the same time, an Exxon is not the amoral, greed-driven monster its critics make it out to be. An Exxon reflects the morality of its society and—voluntarily or under duress—accepts it. It is on such grounds that companies like Exxon have developed over the years "philosophies" of corporate social responsibility. They have gradually modified and broadened their perspective to include "communities of principle" as well as "communities of interest" (Henry Shue, *Basic Rights, Subsistence, Affluence, and U.S. Foreign Policy,* 1980).

It is within the young tradition of corporate social responsibility—say, since the 1920s—that leading corporations like Exxon accepted the Sullivan Principles. In Exxon's case, there was little business interest in South Africa, but it provided philanthropic support to help blacks in South Africa. It also played a leading role in the South African Exchange Program of the Institute of International Education. Morality—called "enlightened self-interest" to make it more palatable—has infected the economic values of business corporations, too.

The fundamental difference is that Exxon had direct moral as well as economic commitments in South Africa, and Harvard doesn't. There are no risks to the lives of Harvard's employees in South Africa, but there were to Exxon's.

In spite of divestment, Exxon should deal with Harvard in the same way it always has. It should continue to make grants and to provide other kinds of support on the merits. But the matter shouldn't be left there. Somehow, the Harvards and the Exxons should better understand how their conflicts or cooperation affect the public interest. That is unlikely to happen in the sometimes hysterical arena of campus discourse; it might happen behind the closed doors of corporate offices, where critics are too seldom made welcome.

The divestment issue raises a number of vexing problems that only true believers wish to ignore. Divestment raises the question of "tainted money," for example. Although Harvard would like to put the blame on the South African government's policies in this case, and let the oil companies merely be the victim rather than the culprit, the fact is that the oil companies may have been engaged in a business activity that Harvard found morally objectionable in its consequences. It might be all right for *them*, Harvard implied, but we have no reason to be a party to such behavior. The implication, if it holds, is that the oil companies, were they only more committed to morality and less committed to their profits, would not have to be tainted by the stain of helping apartheid inadvertently.

The term "tainted money" was coined in 1895 by a Congregational minister named Washington Gladden, an active figure in the Social Gospel movement of the time. In 1905 he led an attack on the mission arm of his denomination for accepting a gift of $100,000 from John D. Rockefeller. His language echoes over the decades: "The church which accepts the Standard Oil Company as its yokefellow can hardly hope to keep the respect of right-minded young men and women." Gladden offered this motion:

> that the officers of this board should neither invite nor solicit donations to its funds from persons whose gains have been made by methods morally reprehensible or socially injurious.[4]

If to be morally serious means accepting the consequences of one's actions and beliefs, then those who hold such views must side with Reverend Gladden. Gladden argued with easy optimism that other good Christians would come forward and provide the $100,000 if the mission board would return Rockefeller's check. The sticky part is that that often does not happen. Those who seek purity in the sources of their funds also run the risk that those they set out to help won't get that help. For Reverend Gladden, to be morally pure (as well as morally serious) meant that he must risk denying the Christian message to those in need of it. His moral posture was perhaps more important to him than his commitment to religious mission.

Episcopal Bishop Paul Moore, Jr., a contemporary Washington Gladden, was recently part of a delegation to South Africa. He met with business executives, blacks in townships, and political leaders. He was near a bomb explosion. He heard, from President Kenneth Kaunda of Zambia, "his deep fear that if South Africa were to explode, all of South Africa would be engulfed and hundreds of thousands would be killed." Even so, Bishop Moore concludes in a newsletter article for the Cathedral of St. John the Divine in New York City that such an outcome is bearable, even supportable:

> It may take a long time, more pain, but the people are will-
> ing to suffer almost anything in order to attain freedom.
> You could feel that. It was unmistakable and, in a way,
> deeper than anything I saw or heard during my visit. It was
> faith, pure faith.[5]

It may be the faith of black South Africans, but it is also
their blood; the Bishop's faith, perhaps, but not *his* blood.
Nor is it Harvard's. It could have been Exxon's, because
Exxon people were there. Nor is the blood that might be
spilled that of the "anti-apartheid students" at the University
of Virginia.

Nor is it mine.

The moral dilemma of those who seek to do good is that
they may instead do harm—in this case, terrible, irreparable
harm. Is it more damnable to risk other people's lives by
encouraging a more violent course than it is to permit continuing oppression?

I should make my position clear: I believe that it is not
in the best interest of black and colored South Africans (or
white South Africans, either) that leading American business
corporations leave that country. Disinvestment is certain to
be followed by a steady deterioration of business practice.
For all their faults, the best American business corporations—
and I include my former employer in that category—make
serious efforts to be socially responsible. Their failures are
probably no more frequent or serious than those of great universities.

To pose another question: What is the proper relationship
between donors and donees on social questions like this? If
a university comes to a different conclusion from a corporation on the best strategy to help South Africa become a
civilized nation, should that break the relationship? The divestment "movement" has pushed moderates like myself to
the limit. Others have quickly gone beyond that: "Anyone
who won't own my stock doesn't deserve my support," they
might argue. "If you won't accept the consequences of your
actions, I will."

In the Harvard–Exxon case, so much weight was put on
one aspect of Exxon's business activities in South Africa that

it outweighed all other considerations. That is questionable
in itself; it quickly brings to mind as well the thought that
later on, on another issue, Harvard might also decide to ask
for purity of result as well as nobility of intention. As Murray
Kempton pointed out (in a telling review of a book that seeks
to "rate America's corporate conscience,") "the more delicate
the calibrations, the worse the confusions in the measurement
of conscience."

There are further implications in the South Africa case.
A recent initiative would ban investment of public funds in
companies doing business in Northern Ireland. Jesse Jackson
recently added Argentina, Chile, and Peru to his list. Whose
list should we use? How long must it be?

Divestment has a further consequence, familiar to those
fortunate enough to have read Albert O. Hirschman's *Exit,
Voice and Loyalty* (Harvard, 1970). As long as you own stock,
you have voice; when you sell your stock you exit your relationship and you lose your right to speak. (A Virginia faculty
member argued that the university should keep its investments and use its shareholder position to press for disinvestment. The strategy makes sense even if you disagree—
as I do—with American business withdrawal from South
Africa.)

Whether universities should take positions on issues such
as South Africa, either rhetorically or financially, can best
be answered by voices from two of my favorite universities.
The first is that of Derek Bok:

> At bottom, this is also a dispute about the nature of the
> University itself and the ways in which it should and should
> not respond to evil in the outside world. . . . Much as I op-
> pose apartheid, I strongly believe that universities should
> not use their power to press their political and economic
> views on other organizations and individuals beyond the
> campus.[6]

That was written in 1984. In 1967, in an even more highly
charged environment, a committee of the University of Chicago issued a "Report on the University's Role in Political
and Social Action":

> The instrument of dissent and criticism is the individual faculty member or the individual student. The university is the home and sponsor of critics; it is not itself the critic. . . . In the exceptional instance, these corporate activities of the university may appear so incompatible with paramount social values as to require careful assessment of the consequences. These extraordinary instances apart, there emerges, as we see it, a heavy presumption against taking collective action or expressing opinions on the political and social issues of the day, or modifying its corporate activities to foster social or political values, however compelling or appealing they might be.[7]

In addition to the moral commitment to protect academic freedom, there is a self-interested reason to hold such views. Intruding in the affairs of others exposes one to retaliatory intrusion in one's own affairs. Is a symbolic action (especially one of dubious effectiveness) worth such risk? How often should one take the risk? What makes an instance extraordinary, exceptional?

In any event, there are other options open to anti-apartheid activists. Universities provide space and often financial and logistical support to a wide range of political organizations. Why is it necessary to force the university as an institution into an extreme and awkward position on the South African issue?

My own opinion is that the divestment "movement" has not been much of a campus movement at all. It is very narrowly based and commands token and largely uninformed support. The tactics of many divestment advocates have obscured the issues and made it difficult if not impossible for the uncommitted to sort out their ideas and come to reasonable conclusions. The discourse of pro-shanty and anti-shanty should perhaps be dismissed as the moral equivalent of panty raids. Even a good cause should not become a convenient excuse for intimidation.

The first purpose of a college education, the historian Karl Weintraub once said, is to learn to understand the complexity of things. If that purpose is loosened by slipshod argument or undermined by coercion, or if it loses place to moral fervor or political ideology, the central mission of the university will be fatally compromised.

Lift the rock of apartheid and you will not find respect for complexity. Those slugs and grubs are blind to it. They see only Truth. The moral life is for them, because it is so simple. They have smothered the spirit of liberty, or perhaps never breathed its air. The moral life is never hard for true believers. But it certainly is for the rest of us.

Where does all this leave "the rest of us?" Given the intellectual complexity of the issues, the moral urgency of a situation steadily becoming more ominous, the pressing need to keep our wits about us, how should we proceed? The divestment effort may have succeeded in so undermining the U.S. business presence in South Africa that we have already lost the constructive influence symbolized by the Sullivan Principles. Xerox has now left, in a decision that its chairman says pleases no one. Eastman Kodak, which tried to keep its products out of South Africa, finds that it couldn't achieve that without going out of business everywhere. Economic pressures seem not to have worked in South Africa, although it is possible that they have permanently changed—damaged, in my view—the relationship of for-profit and not-for-profit organizations in the United States. A college trustee who worked for ten years to persuade his college to divest feels mildly triumphant. He believes his efforts have been a positive contribution to reform in South Africa. Colleges using their economic power to urge their moral convictions on society is, in his view, smart politics. What else, he might ask, can a college do? What else can American college students do? If they can't use their pressure on trustees to divest, what can they do? The situation in South Africa *is* one of those exceptional, extraordinary instances the people at Chicago were talking about, isn't it?

Where do we turn for help? Harold Macmillan once said that the purpose of an education is to prepare one to know when someone else is talking rot. The literature of higher education is filled these days with appeals to improve "thinking skills," to develop "critical thinking." In another time there was a different word for it: casuistry. Casuistry, according to one theological dictionary, is "the application of moral principles to particular situations or to individual circumstances." In another theological dictionary "it refers to any form of argument, usually about moral or legal issues, that employs subtle distinctions and twisted logic in order to justify some act that would generally be considered disreputable." This delightful short essay actually argues in favor of resuscitating casuistry at its best, "the attempt to formulate expert opinion about the existence and stringency of moral obligations in typical situations where some general precept would seem to require interpretation due to circumstances."

The controversy over the right of Reverend Charles Curran to teach theology at Catholic University offers another illustration. Curran argues for precisely the kind of careful, fair, open discourse that I do. If a recent lecture at the University of Virginia is any indication, he tries very hard not to let himself be swept up as a folk hero. He does not want to abandon his commitment to discourse in order to offset the organizational power of his Vatican critics. Curran believes that the church has a moral responsibility to influence political and economic issues. The set of issues he addresses is as thorny and complex and painful as South Africa. Yet, in speaking of abortion, Curran deplores "single-issue politics," the reduction of complexity to simplicity.

Divestment is single-issue politics. A relationship based on the broad economic and social performance of a company is reduced to a single aspect of its activities in a single country. The position seems to me exactly analogous to that of the pro-life opponents of abortion. The congressman is told that all of his votes on other issues don't equal his one vote on this one. This matter is so important that all other matters must yield to it.

Single-issue advocacy has the ring of passion to it, the moral voice that in the church is called prophetic. (To borrow a perceptive remark, a prophet is someone to admire but not someone you'd want to work for.) Prophets are critics of society, and many people now believe that the central mission of the university is to be a critic of society. The collective voice of the institution is louder and more intimidating than the voice of a single protestor or a handful. Divestment advocates add leverage to their case by enlisting the university as an institutional investor, which amplifies its leverage by bringing pressure on the corporation. The hope is that the leverage becomes so great that it causes the South African government to change its policies.

But, it is argued, the passion of the prophet is needed when human beings are degraded as they are in South Africa. We must transmute that passion into political power. That's what prophecy is all about. That's what the social mission of the university is all about.

In a world of prophets, which one to follow? Isn't that the question? How does one choose between Jerry Falwell and Bishop Moore, between Washington Gladden and John D. Rockefeller, between Archbishop Tutu and Helen Susman? If it is on the basis of "faith, pure faith," as Bishop Moore would have it, then choice may be even more difficult. In the university, modern tradition has it, the difficulty of discriminating between good thought and bad is so demanding that the quality of thought itself claims primacy.

Universities, I conclude, must turn from prophets to moral philosophers. Moral philosophers must turn from talking to one another to talking to—even occasionally listening to—the rest of us.

NOTES

1. Harvard University Corporation Committee on Shareholder Responsibility, "CCSR Statement on Investment Policy," *Minerva*, vol. 24, nos. 2–3, 1986, p. 270.

2. American Council on Education, *Perspective: College Sanctions on South African Investments*, 1985, p. 33.

3. Derek Bok, "An Open Letter to the Harvard Community," *Minerva*, op. cit., pp. 248–249.

4. Washington Gladden, "Tainted Money," in *The New Idolatry*, McClure Phillips, 1905.

5. Paul Moore, Jr., "Danger and Hope: Images of South Africa," from the newsletter of the Cathedral of St. John the Divine, New York, n.d., p. 6.

6. Derek Bok, op. cit., p. 254.

7. University of Chicago, "Report on the University's Role in Political and Social Action," *Minerva,* op. cit., pp. 277–278.

The Ethics of Corporate Grantmaking

Ethical Confusion

Some years ago, a group of colleagues at Washington University published a collection of articles and essays on *Ethics and Standards in American Business.*[1] Although most of the contributors taught in the business school, one was a distinguished philosopher, Albert William Levi. Levi wrote about "ethical confusion in the business community," and in the process talked at length with a number of business executives. He summarized the views that he gleaned from those conversations in these paradigm statements:

> A. Ethics is ethics and business is business. Profits are one thing and moral squeamishness is another. You have to make a choice.
> B. I'm a businessman and I try to be ethical, but when others in my field cut corners morally, I don't see how I can stay in business if I don't follow suit.
> C. Morality is terribly vague, it seems to me. The churches say one thing, the bosses of my company another,

This essay is an Occasional Paper of the Council on Foundations, derived from a Council seminar in Philadelphia, April 1987. Reprinted by permission of the Council on Foundations.

and I guess the government even something different. Who's right?

D. Business as a whole *is* ethical. Of course you'll always find a few crooks, but they're built that way. They'd cheat whatever they worked at.

E. If a man follows the Gospel he can't go wrong. Too many business executives have let the basic religious truths out of their sight. That's the trouble.

Levi then summarizes these positions:

A says: Ethics and business are by nature incompatible. B says: In competitive activity the morally lowest necessarily sets the standard. C says: Morality is a matter of "knowledge," and with plural answers, there is no way to choose between them. D says: Immorality is a defect of personal character. It will always exist. E says: Morality means following the rule of religion.

Levi concluded that these statements "indicate the doubts and uncertainties, the confusions and inconsistencies which pervade the thinking" of the business community on ethical matters.

A similar ethical confusion seems to characterize corporate grantmaking. Grantmakers confess to "doubts and uncertainties," and some indicate that ethical matters arise more frequently than in the past.

Corporate grantmakers, if interviewed by a philosopher working on an essay on the ethics of corporate grantmaking, might well show a pattern similar to that sketched out by A. W. Levi.

A. The first question to answer is, What's in it for us if we make the grant?

B. The second question is, Do we *have* to make the grant? What's the competition doing? Will they make us look bad?

C. The whole process of grantmaking is so *arbitrary,* anyway. You can make a case for almost any grant.

D. The average of corporate grantmaking is quite high— higher than the average of business practice in other functional areas, probably. The exceptions prove the rule.

E. The underlying thrust of corporate philanthropy derives from Judeo-Christian ethics. That's the tradition we
have to keep turning back to, and those are the values that
should guide our grantmaking.

Part of the confusion results, I think, from what various
writers refer to (including Peter Drucker, who has shown an
unerring instinct for emergent trends in business) as the *tur-
bulence* of the marketplace. When conditions are turbulent,
it is difficult to know the direction of events.

In the case of corporate grantmaking, things have sud-
denly become unstable, after a decade and a half of relative
calm and moderate growth (roughly from 1970 to the mid-
1980s). It is possible to offer three plausible interpretations
about what is taking place in the environment of corporate
philanthropy:

• This is a period of slump; corporations are readjusting
to new competitive factors, severe reorganization and restructuring, and downward pressures on earnings and profits.
Grantmaking is bound to reflect cost-cutting and staff reductions elsewhere in the corporation. As things settle down
again and begin to improve, corporate philanthropy will recover, too.

• This is a period of rethinking philanthropy along with
everything else. Grantmaking has to serve corporate purposes
first. As Jerry Welsh of American Express argued several
years ago, the future is in cause-related marketing; "checkbook philanthropy" is a thing of the past.

• This is the first stage of a long period of decline. Business
social philosophy has changed. Competitive forces no longer
permit management to turn its attention to an array of social
problems that don't directly affect business performance. A
greatly diminished core will remain, but it will be the least
that corporations can get away with.

There is, in other words, some reason for doubt and uncertainty about trends in corporate grantmaking. In general,
it is not yet clear whether American business will come forward with a statement of a new philosophical consensus, as
it did forty years ago, or whether echoes of an abandoned

philosophy will continue to be heard while a new way of doing business takes over in fact. I don't often these days hear statements like this one from corporate leaders:

> During the forty years of my business career, I have observed a slow but steady transition in the attitude of corporate management from one of more or less exclusive preoccupation with self-interest, to one of self-interest tempered with a broadening sense of social consciousness. (Frank W. Abrams, former chairman of Standard Oil Company of New Jersey, in his testimony in the *A. P. Smith* case, 1952.)[2]

When we hear such statements now, we doubt that it reflects a consensus of business leadership as it did in Abrams' time.

In fact, most people believe that there has been a rapid shift backwards, towards a "more or less exclusive preoccupation with self-interest." Many of those charged with grantmaking are thus reshaping their work to this narrowing sense of social consciousness. The rationale for corporate philanthropy has always been presented in terms of "enlightened self-interest," a self-interest that justifies grantmaking in terms of long-range and indirect benefits. During the first several decades of corporate grantmaking—say, from 1870 until World War I—insistence on *direct* benefit excluded corporate grants for public purposes; the argument for indirect benefits over the long term carried the day—it even became part of corporate law.

Corporate law does not *require* corporate philanthropy, of course. Corporate philanthropy is still a voluntary decision of management, influenced by tradition and peer pressure but not controlled by them. Rather than abandon philanthropy altogether, the emphasis is on increasing the corporate benefits from making grants. Philanthropic budgets decrease in size, and grantmaking priorities are reordered.

During a period of corporate affluence, the nonprofit sector can expect to share the gain; in a period of cost-cutting and layoffs, the nonprofit sector can expect to share the pain.

It is not surprising that grantmaking executives appear

to be uncertain about how to behave. Hedging is as popular in grantmaking as it is in the stock market. It is a climate in which ethical uncertainty is bound to increase—and ethical performance is likely to deteriorate unless there is a conscious effort to rectify the balance. Business ethics courses become popular, as do books on business ethics, when news stories and editorials on ethical *failures* in business become more frequent. Such has been the case in the recent past. (The major capital campaign to endow ethical studies at Harvard Business School is not in celebration of high ethical standards in the marketplace.)[3] Although the stock market has taken the worst of it, large corporations have been ethically embarrassed as well. Corporate training programs are beginning to add courses and seminars in ethics. Bristol-Myers has a new program at Dartmouth, for example.[4] The current wave of interest is just beginning.

When people are unable to follow a clearly drawn path of behavior, some show an innate sense of direction and others stray or wander about in confusion. If their past behavior has been that of following instructions rather than understanding how the map was drawn, such people may find themselves quickly lost. They won't know which instruction to follow, which one to abandon, which new direction to explore.

Others, those who show that "innate sense of direction," may have achieved an understanding of map making. Take their map away from them, and they know how to read the stars and the angle of leaves and the moss on trees and all those other skills and arts that the Boy Scouts tried to instill.

The difference between map reading and map making, between following instructions and exercising your judgment, may be the simplest way to bring out an important distinction between "morality" and "ethics." Moral behavior can be thought of as the behavior imposed on us by our parents and the other influences charged with domesticating us. We are expected to follow the rules whether we understand them or not. Ethical behavior, by contrast, means the capacity to make judgments, to apply principles in specific situations, to interpret rather than imitate. A person of very limited intelligence can follow clear and explicit rules. It requires a higher form of intelligence to exercise judgment and autonomy.

I agree with those who believe that ethical maturity begins in childhood. Moral values are best taught at that time. Some philosophers and psychologists contend that many of the abstractions of ethics can be reduced to simple situations that children can deal with and even begin to understand. Require a child to make his bed in the morning. It becomes a habit, if repeated often enough. Explain why: "On balance, neatness is better than disorder, and over time you will find that a remade bed is more comfortable to sleep in." That suggests that good behavior pays, and that a modest investment of energy now will be repaid with a modest benefit of comfort later on. More important, the child may begin to learn that if he makes the bed his mother won't have to. (It is in such modest ways that consideration of others begins.)[5]

To believe that morality is best acquired in childhood raises a question of the utility of ethical education later in life. Many people believe that college is too late—that courses in business ethics at the level of the professional school come too late to make a difference. If that view is correct, why bother with corporate training in ethics?

First, even those who are morally sensitive and well-disciplined benefit from the review of principles and the discussion of cases. Second, the ethical implications of new practices may not be self-evident, and discussion will bring that out. Third, the process itself will strengthen the moral dimension of the corporate structure. Fourth, even those without a reliable moral compass can benefit from a reliable map of the territory.

In the face of uncertainty, the greatest anxiety is felt by those whose personal habits are rule-bound, or who work in a corporate setting that leaves little to individual judgment (or both). At one level of the organization there may be great insistence on following the rules to the letter; at another level there may be rich rewards for those who know what to do when the rules no longer apply—or, more commonly, when the rules remain but no longer mean what they meant before.

Following rules often leads to bad results because the meaning of the rules has changed while the form has remained the same. Letting rules determine behavior is also often seen as praiseworthy in a junior executive and as a weakness in a senior executive.

The way out of ethical confusion will not be found in rules. We have entered a period where we may be called upon to fashion a new ethics, a new understanding of the consensus concerning what is ethical and unethical. The sources of ethics and morality are to be found in custom and usage as those reflect the externalized values of the community and the internalized values of individual behavior. We can expect ethical norms to change as community values change, reminding ourselves that values don't change monolithically or uniformly. "Openness" and "accountability" were more generally applauded in the 1970s than in the 1980s. The "tolerance" praised in some circles as sensitive consideration of the rights of others may be considered by others to be the reflection of an empty and spineless relativism.[6] And, if tolerance of other people's values has increased in many ways, there is much resistance in some others. Most religious leaders argue that religious values should permeate our lives, and not be relegated to ritual observance on weekends. Many corporate leaders consider the influence of organized religion out of place in the business corporation, and worry about personal values supplanting corporate ones.

To address the complex and uneasy relationship of religious and secular values in corporate philanthropy would require another essay. The matter is extremely sensitive as well as complicated. Even so, religion and philanthropy are so interwoven in the American tradition that I am convinced the tensions should be discussed and clarified rather than avoided and ignored.

The question here is whether the values of corporate grant-making are changing, putting more emphasis on the benefits to the donor and less on the needs of the recipient. If they are, is that an *ethical* issue? For example, when someone advocates that grants to nonprofit organizations be used as a means of increasing corporate profits, one of the questions that must be asked is whether that is an ethical matter as well as an operational and organizational change. It may be argued that it is a different strategy to achieve the same ends—or that it is simply adding a second end to the first one, or making the whole process more efficient. If it is an *ethical* change, what do we mean by that? If the answer is given that the result will be more money flowing through nonprofits to increasing numbers of people in need, that will reflect one approach to ethics. If the answer is given that the moral rules of philanthropy and the practices of marketing are incompatible, that will reflect another approach. A third approach may be that we have to balance rules and results in the way that is most "responsible."

Almost all ethical problems are complex, not simple. Many problems have an ethical dimension, and in some cases the ethical consideration will govern the solution—the ethical aspect will determine the choice among the available alternatives.

But it is wise to remember that not all problems are ethical problems, and that the ethical consideration should not always be conclusive. Leaping to ethical conclusions is as risky as leaping to financial or manufacturing conclusions. On the other hand, more business problems arise from neglecting the ethical dimension than from putting too much emphasis on it.

Thinking About Ethics

Grantmakers make grants or reject them, or recommend to others that grants be made or not. Grantmakers are *agents*, actors, and making a grant is an act. Grantmakers as well as others often ask whether a grant *should* be made or not; some grants are not automatic (although many are: consider matching gifts, for example). Asking that sort of question involves a *spectator* or *commentator*. It is a level of reflection one step higher than that involved in the act itself.

At a third level there is a different sort of question that is asked, and this is what *philosophers* do (amateurs and capital-P philosophers alike). According to the British moral philosopher Bernard Mayo (from whom I borrow this analysis), moral philosophers ask:

- *Why do we do what is right?*
- *Why should we do what is right?*
- *How do we know what is right?*

Mayo adds a fourth question to these "three fundamental questions" for moral philosophy, and adds a fourth:[7]

- *What do we mean by 'right'?*

To which I will add a fifth, of fundamental importance to corporate grantmaking (that we will come back to later):

- *Who do we mean by 'we'?*

We could also add, in parentheses after "right" in each of those questions: "(*or wrong*)."

I would also add, adapting a suggestion from a philosopher who is a writer and corporate consultant on business ethics, three other questions that are particularly germane to corporate grantmakers: A grant is thought to be:

- Good (or bad) *for whom?*
- Good (or bad) *when?*
- Good (or bad) *by what standard?*[8]

For example, "Will a grant to a private voluntary agency engaged in development in Central America be helpful to that organization?" is one way of asking the first question. A different way of asking the question would be to ask, "Will we be criticized for making a grant in a country where we have very little business interest?" The question of whether the grant will help the people most directly affected by it in Central America may never be asked at all. The question of timing may be crucial. A grant for a chemistry laboratory may not be considered timely if the donor is a chemical company being sued for illness following the use of a toxic chemical. The third question—by what standard—might come up with a grant for research that includes pressure to redirect the research away from the original objective. That would be thought to violate an accepted grantmaking practice. (Are corporate strings on research support any different from government strings? What do we mean by "strings," anyway?)

In thinking about notions of good and bad, right and wrong, students of law have been more persistent in studying the underside of their domain than have moral philosophers. Criminology is a fat and affluent field. There are not only books about it, there are courses, even degrees. I know of no courses or degrees in immorality.

I have a great many books about ethics and morality. I have very few that confront the *un*ethical and *im*moral as their main theme. There are some important exceptions, of course: Ronald Milo has published a book entitled *Immorality*.[9] Sissela Bok has written a bestseller with the title *Lying*.[10] There is a reawakened interest among moral philosophers in Aristotle's notion of *akrasia*—"weakness of will"—the failure to behave morally even when we know the right thing to do.[11]

This is as good a time as any to point out that ethics and morality can mean (a) theory and practice, or (b) the externally imposed and the internalized.[12] "The two words, once fully synonymous . . . have now so divided their functions that neither is superfluous . . . *ethics* is the science of morals, and *morals* are the practice of ethics."[13] The distinctions are useful to philosophers, but in my opinion common usage now considers the two terms to be interchangeable.

(This digression may also be a good time to argue that references to "business ethics" are misleading; ethical problems characteristic of life in large complex organizations do not differ in important ways among business corporations, government agencies, universities, even religious organizations. It is moral life *in the organization* that is the common factor.)

Thinking About the Unethical

We might find it fruitful to study what lies under the rock of ethics as well as that which basks in the sunshine of our approval. The handiest guide to the set of problems that plague us will be found in J. Barton Bowyer's book *Cheating*.[14] Shortly after it was published in 1982, I made reference to it in a talk to college and university development officers.

Since I believe that people who raise money are engaged in an inextricable relationship with those who give it away, it should also be apposite here. (The relationship between fundraisers and grantmakers is to be the subject of another essay.)

Bowyer provides a summary table that is suggestive of what he has discerned to be "the structure of deception":[15]

The Structure of Deception
(with process defined)

DECEPTION
(distorting reality)

DISSIMULATION (Hiding the Real)	SIMULATION (Showing the False)
MASKING	MIMICKING
Conceals one's own Charcs* Matches another's Charcs	Copies another's Charcs*
(To Eliminate an Old Pattern or Blend It With a Background Pattern.)	(To Recreate an Old Pattern, Imitating It.)
REPACKAGING	INVENTING
Adds New Charcs Subtracts Old Charcs	Creates New Charcs
(To Modify an Old Pattern by Matching Another.)	(To Create a New Pattern.)
DAZZLING	DECOYING
Obscures Old Charcs Adds Alternative Charcs	Creates Alternative
(To Build an Old Pattern, Reducing Its Certainty.)	(To Give an Additional Alternative Pattern, Increasing Its Certainty.)

*Charcs: Characteristic Spectrum

From *Cheating*, by J. Barton Bowyer, copyright 1982 by St. Martin's Press, Inc., New York. Reprinted by permission.

Cheating is to ethics as crime is to law.

I am not here concerned with the illegal aspects of grantmaking (which are probably most often those associated with using foundations in self-dealing abuses of the tax law). In fact, I am most interested in the gray areas of behavior where it is often difficult to know the right way to behave, the right thing to do, the right rule or principle to apply.

I have not re-read Bowyer's book to see whether there are examples in it drawn from charity and philanthropy, from fundraising or grantmaking. Most of the examples seem to be drawn from military strategy, politics, and business. But it is instructive to think about "cheating" in the context of the ethics of everyday life. It is especially useful to keep in mind the terms of art proposed by Bowyer: *hiding the real; showing the false.*

I use some of these techniques—but not all—every time I face an opponent on the tennis court. Ruses are employed in every sport: Faking permeates every move in basketball; trap plays and hand-offs are used in football (where the quick kick was once popular). Baseball is filled with stratagems, ploys, and gambits: stealing bases, pick-off plays, the pitcher's deceiving changes of pace.

When we speak as we did earlier of how morality is taught to children, we should remind ourselves how much of it is learned in sports—playing by the rules. One might have said *playing by the ruses.* The arts of deception are part of sports, even though they are not required by the rulebooks. Deception is useful to victory, perhaps even essential when the physical skills are evenly balanced.

Having been sensitized to the feminine perspective, I must also mention that children learn much from other forms of play than sports, not overtly competitive, and without written rules. *Fantasy*—the delights of pretending, of dressing up, of deceiving oneself as well as one's friends. Misapplied, the harmless deceptions of childhood fun in sports and fantasy can become pathological in adults.[16]

"Hiding the real" and "showing the false" are so much a part of some aspects of our behavior that an important judgment involves deciding which rules and norms apply in each situation. Their misapplication in our personal lives is what Eric Berne's *Games People Play*[17] was about—and the terrible problems that usually follow from applying the wrong rules or playing the wrong game. Watergate and the Iran-Contra scandals are variations on a familiar political theme of deception: that one can cheat and still be moral if the cause is just.

Those whose professional tools are words have reason to be uneasy about the ethics of persuasion. (Those whose professional tools are numbers are equally uneasy about the ethics of statistics.) Corporate grantmaking takes place in a world that uses persuasive language (and statistics) all the time. The deceits of language used in fundraising brochures and in corporate annual reports are alarmingly similar.

Beneath the surface of fundraising and grantmaking language is the social dynamic of power and influence. The philanthropic relationship is usually asymmetric: in its cruder forms, it appeals to the cupidity of the one and to the vanity of the other. It is an environment in which cheating can be commonplace and yet unrecognized as such.

Bowyer concludes his book with this observation:

> Nature may not cheat but man does—to be human is to cheat and be cheated.

Bowyer has also come to a conclusion about *some* people:

> The clever mind, prepared or not, can be cheated more easily than the simple. The avaricious mind will cheat itself. The wise mind, here prepared, taking "consiglio," [advice] will at least know the rules of the game.[18]

Virtues and Vices

We don't often reflect enough on the relevance of cheating to ethics. We have also lost touch with the immensely useful traditional ways of talking about moral behavior—that part of ethics that focuses on the study of virtue. The words themselves appear to be a major obstacle. On the one hand, the word *virtue,* for many people, calls to mind puritanical religious values, narrowness, priggishness, sexual repression, and the hypocrisy of the Victorian age. On the other hand, virtue represents for them a goal of perfection, which a corporate colleague finds to be "both unrealistic and personally destructive."

Although some corporate grantmakers find as I do that using traditional ethical language and concepts is helpful, some others do not find it so. I have found to my chagrin that it is easy to be misunderstood if virtue-language is brought into a conversation about ethics. At the same time I agree with Bernard Williams, whose *Ethics and the Limits of Philosophy* is immensely readable as well as challenging:

> The word "virtue" has for the most part acquired comic or otherwise undesirable associations, and few use it now except philosophers, but there is no other word that serves as well, and it has to be used in moral philosophy.[19]

What I want to talk about is a *pattern* of behavior in situations that encourages us to praise some behavior as ethical and to criticize other behavior as unethical. The notion of a pattern of behavior suggests persistence, predictability, the "conventions" that make up the conventional:

> Conventions embody expectations; they impose limitations; they result in liberation.[20]

The author—a theologian named G. R. Dunstan—argues that "mutual expectation is at the heart of professional ethics. . . . Society, and his professional colleagues, attach certain expectations to his role." Behavior is not determined by how the professional happens to feel at the moment, or spelled out in every detail by regulations. Conventions also impose limitations: "the first demand of community is limitation— an ethics which requires the limitation of self-interest where it conflicts with the interests of other persons or of the community itself." And, although it always sounds self-contradictory, the limitations must be self-imposed beyond the minimum standards established by law.

> A healthy community requires that the limitations essential to corporate life be, so far as possible, inward and voluntary; the product of conscience, conviction, inward persuasion, and belief, and not imposed from without.

Conventions embody expectations and impose limitations, but Dunstan argues that they result in liberation—"liberation for the individual and the conditions of freedom for the community."

> Where there is a convention of honesty and fair dealing, buyer and seller can negotiate together without crippling suspicion or fear. . . .
>
> As in personal behaviour, so also on the social level: it is worth reflecting how much more constricted social life would be—how much less free—were not so much of it governed by an extensive conventionalized morality.

The autonomy of the professional is based on the conventions that we can take for granted: Our expectations make possible the professional's latitude. The cost of not having those conventions accepted and understood are at the source of the explosion of medical malpractice insurance costs, to cite only the most familiar example. The loss of professional freedom of action is obvious: Never act boldly in a patient's behalf; don't run risks in a patient's behalf; keep your own interests in mind.

My conclusion from Dunstan's discussion of convention is that it squares with my experience in various areas of professional life: journalism, diplomacy, teaching and administration, and grantmaking. Convention is also consistent with the theory of virtue. A virtue is defined as "an ethically admirable disposition of character"; the word *disposition* is crucial. Under normal circumstances a person can be expected to behave in a certain way. If the way of acting happens to merit praise for its moral quality, it will be considered virtuous.

Other writers make the same point. John Dewey, for example, identified *persistence* as one of the aspects of virtue; more recently, James D. Wallace spoke of *conscientiousness.*[21] The point is fundamental: What counts is not the isolated act; what counts is reflective habit. Doing the right moral thing at the right time and in the right place requires reflection on each case, and when that reflection becomes a disposition, it is called a virtue.

Is "enlightened self-interest" a virtue?

Enlightened Self-Interest

The conventions of grantmaking are based on a rationale of enlightened self-interest. I quoted Frank Abrams earlier on "self-interest tempered with a broadening sense of social consciousness." I found that quotation in a book written in 1956 by Richard Eells of Columbia University: *Corporation Giving in a Free Society*. Eells lists seven principles of corporate philanthropy, and this is the first one:

> The corporate donor's motive should properly be one of enlightened self-interest that reflects the socially dimensioned purposes of the enterprise.[22]

Bearing in mind what was said earlier about conventions, enlightened self-interest as a principle will be spelled out in written statements that are widely shared by grantmakers. In the course of preparing this essay I came upon a "check sheet" for the corporate contributions committee of a large corporation (that has since been swallowed up by a larger corporation). The list is almost identical to another offered in the same book—*Corporation Giving*, by F. Emerson Andrews[23]—and I think we can take it as representative. Although it is 35 years old, I have seen many like it in recent years. The list is an effort to spell out the conventions that will guide the committee in making decisions about grants and their recipients.

1. Is the cause a worthy one?
2. Will the contribution benefit [the company] directly or indirectly?
3. Is the request likely to lead to other similar requests in the future? Is this objectionable?
4. Does the organization have widespread acceptance and support?
5. Is it efficiently and honestly managed?
6. Is the immediate need significant or does the organization have substantial reserve funds?
7. Does it aid all kinds of people, or is it restricted in its operations?

8. Is the request consistent with our place in the community?
9. Will there be a public relations reaction if we give or do not give?
10. Will the contribution advance the community and public relations of the company?
11. Are important customers, dealers, or other business contacts interested in the solicitation?
12. Are other organizations in the community similar to ours supporting the soliciting organization, and if so, in what amounts?

If grantmakers are to be ethically alert, what kinds of questions should be asked about that list of questions?

• Which of those questions might be thought to be self-interested (or *self-regarding*, as the philosophers say)? Which of them might be thought of as "enlightened"? Questions 2 and 8 through 11 are clearly focused on the company rather than the recipient.

• Questions 4 through 7 seek to determine whether the organization is worth investing in and whether the funds are really needed.

• Only the first question deals with the cause itself.

• Some grants are useful but not important, according to question 6. That suggests that a small grant to a large and successful capital campaign, for example, might be unimportant in that context but that the same amount of money given to a small and struggling organization could be important to its very survival. Grants that are token grants are not "bad" in some absolute sense, but they are often the result of laziness or timidity. They are examples of poor stewardship.

• Might the answer to question 1 ever be so compelling that the answers to questions 2–12 should be brushed aside? How might we go about weighting the 12 questions?

• Questions 4 and 5 are the source of the criticism of mainstream corporate philanthropy and the mainstream nonprofit organizations supported by business. Where do innovation or risk appear on the list? Should corporations limit their bets to favorites and sure things?

• Question 5, about "efficient and honest management," calls to mind the frequent efforts to put a ceiling on fundraising expenditures by nonprofits. Yet every effort to do so brings out the difference between the fundraising costs required of a new and unknown organization in a controversial field and the fundraising costs that claim a share of the resources of established organizations serving traditional causes.

The tendency of the fundraiser is to explain away the shortcomings; the tendency of the grantmaker is to make them more important than they are. When are we deceiving each other? When are we deceiving ourselves?

The term *enlightened self-interest* was not coined until the late 18th century. Until then the word *prudence* was popular, but since Aristotle, prudence has often been described as "wisdom" or practical reasoning. What is intended is the idea that morality requires action based on reflection, what Dewey described as "severe inquiry and serious consideration of alternative aims."[24] Prudence is self-regarding (egoistic); benevolence is other-regarding (altruistic).

After a long and difficult discussion of the inadequacies of thinking about corporate grantmaking in terms of virtues and vices, a seminar participant put these thoughts on paper in a letter to me:

> I do not believe that a paradigm based on traditional concepts of right and wrong is adequate—or useful—in dealing with current motivations and practices of corporate grantmaking. New language and a new model of ethical behavior must be crafted to deal with the changed dynamics in today's corporations.
>
> A revised paradigm should identify a new balance point between altruism and self-interest and define parameters for corporate giving that tap and blend the best of both motivations. Though difficult to craft, this approach would take advantage of the complexity inherent in corporate grantmaking today. In many ways, this model would be characterized by compromise.
>
> In summary, new motivations and practices are not in themselves amoral . . . or unethical. It is our challenge to

develop a code of ethics that works with today's realities, without losing the commitment of business to "do the right thing" in situations devoid of self-interest.

Combining the self-regarding with the other-regarding, as enlightened self-interest implies, is difficult. For one thing, the word *enlightened* tends to have an elastic quality. It is often a fudge word, useful to have on hand because it can be reshaped when circumstances call for it. It will mean one thing when the CEO is being addressed; another when speaking to a volunteer from an arts organization. The problem I have with the position just outlined is that the overall pattern of behavior today is indeed changing, and is changing strongly toward the self-interested side of the scale. The "new balance point" tips the scale away from other-regarding and toward self-regarding. The result is a diminished concern, even a disregard, for the purposes served by the philanthropic part of the corporate enterprise.

The author of that appeal for a new model of ethical behavior in grantmaking wants desperately to preserve the other-regarding aspect. What sort of "commitment" does one expect to find in the new environment to "do the 'right thing' in situations devoid of self-interest"?

A moral philosopher, observing and then reflecting on the argument, might argue that self-interest is deeply grounded in human nature, and that it is by definition the dominant characteristic of the marketplace. By inference, then, it is plausible to expect that the most powerful forces at work in a corporation will always be those of self-interest. Other forces and constraints will be necessary in order to restrain that self-interest and to keep it from destroying itself.

It is not intended to show disrespect in arguing that one need not be concerned about the corporate determination to pursue its self-interest. The problem has always been that of trying to broaden that self-interest, to lengthen the time horizon, to take into consideration those who fell outside the direct benefits of the self-interest. Frank Abrams's "broadening sense of social consciousness" and Richard Eells' "socially dimensioned purposes of the enterprise" are *other-*

regarding, even if the rationale for them is put in the form of long-term and indirect benefits to the self.

But the point is well-taken: Either we need new language and a new way of thinking about corporate morality and the ethics of corporate grantmaking, or we need to clean the barnacles of misuse from the traditional language and values. Or some of both.

The Road Less Traveled

The title of this section is drawn from the extraordinarily successful bestseller by psychiatrist M. Scott Peck (who borrowed it from Robert Frost).[25] Peck offers a simple and evidently persuasive guide to behavior. He begins with a warning that *life is difficult*. Because life is difficult, we need disciplines to cope with it. He names four: delaying of gratification, acceptance of responsibility, dedication to truth, and balancing.

That list fits well with enlightened self-interest by putting "delaying of gratification" first. *Delaying gratification* is the psychologist's equivalent of the philosopher's *prudence*. *Acceptance of responsibility* may also apply to enlightened self-interest—if the corporation's sphere of responsibility is broad enough to include some of those who won't share directly in the benefits. But we should ask: Responsible *for whom?* Responsible *at what time?* Responsible *by what standard?*

Dedication to truth is very tricky in this context, for several reasons. "Honesty is the best policy," is often claimed as business policy but we reserve judgment until we observe the practice. The language of advertising and public relations undermine not only honesty but meaning. In much of the self-reporting literature about corporate philanthropy that I have read—and in much that I have written myself—the goal is *persuasion* rather than *truth*. Persuasion is self-regarding; truth-telling is other-regarding. There are those who have argued fervently for full reporting of corporate grantmaking activity, and companies are sometimes praised for making public information that used to be considered private company business. But such material usually has very little effect on the grantmaking policies and practices of the corporations involved. Most corporations see their reports instead as another opportunity to present the corporation in a flattering light—whether deservedly so or not.

Peck's notion of *balancing* is most intriguing of all. He refers to it as "the discipline of disciplines." Consider the discipline of balancing in the context of the traditional concept of character.

Character

Virtue is both a unitary idea and an aggregative one. There is virtue and there are virtues. Classical philosophy identified four virtues as "cardinal"—that is, as summarizing all the other virtues. (The word cardinal, I'm told, comes from the Latin *cardo*, or hinge.) Prudence, temperance, courage, and justice. *Prudence* is the disposition to think about the consequences and other aspects of alternative courses of action. (Gary Hart was imprudent.) According to John Dewey, *temperance*—which became a term of amusement when swamped in the rhetoric of Prohibition—meant to the Greeks "a happy blending of the authority of reason with the force of appetite."[26] It meant *self*-discipline. *Courage* is often advanced as the highest of the virtues, because if one lacks courage he lacks the will to act virtuously. But courage is double-edged: courage can be employed as prudence can in a bad cause. (Some terrorists are courageous.) *Justice* is the only one of the four cardinal virtues that has real contemporary popularity, and it has particular importance for grantmaking. In our day, *justice* means *fairness*.

The Greek list did not include the virtue of benevolence, by the way. We owe the powerful idea of benevolence as charity to religion rather than to philosophy. It is to religion, in fact, that we owe the rash notion of "love for humanity," which is the way philanthropy is translated. Religion is the source of the moral obligation to share one's surplus with the poor.

To add the virtue of charity to corporate grantmaking is

awkward, at best. ("Corporate philanthropy is not almsgiving," Eells wrote.)[27] We find other ways to rationalize the charitable, usually calling upon prudence. For example, as people argued in 1935 and again in 1970: "If we don't help to alleviate conditions in this city we're going to have a riot on our hands." Or, to paraphrase Frank Abrams and others in 1952: "If we don't provide more financial support for the private colleges, they'll go under, and then government will fill the vacuum. Not only will our taxes go up, but freedom will be lost."

The purpose of this quick summary of the virtues is to bring out the point that some of the virtues are sometimes in conflict (or seem to be). Justice and benevolence are often at odds. We seem unable to resolve the conflicts by arranging them in a hierarchy and subordinating everything to a single virtue. (Try it.)

And so we balance them.

Those who balance the virtues well are said to be virtuous or people of good character. A person of good character is someone who persists in the disposition to do the morally right thing. Such a person knows when deception is appropriate and when it must be avoided, even at great cost. A person of good character will be someone who will weigh the alternatives prudently and have the courage to choose and then to act wisely with conviction tempered by justice.

A person of good character will not have to have a rule book or a set of instructions to tell him how to make the right decision. The person will know the conventions of his profession, and he will be reliable about meeting the expectations that people have of him.

The person of good character will be a person with a conscience, a lively sense of the right thing to do and an itch to do it.

The problems arise when the conscience of the individual comes into conflict with the conscience of the corporation. It is easy to write, as I just have, about "doing the right thing," but how is one to behave when the personal perception is different from the collective one?

Corporate Character and the Individual Grantmaker

The important question that I've been building up to, of course, is that the things that I've just said about the qualities of character as they are attributed to persons might also be usefully applied to corporations. Corporations also have character—revealed in what is popularly called "corporate culture" these days. Corporate culture can strengthen the personal integrity of employees or undermine it. Corporations can fail in truth-telling so often that they are unable to be truthful even to themselves. Corporations can be prudent to the point of being cowardly, just as individuals can. Failure can be punished in a corporation in such a way that prudence becomes timidity.

I have seen the average of behavior in business and other organizations deteriorate under stress, and I have seen the average rise as well. It is that average of behavior among those who set the tone of a corporation that I'm talking about when I try to apply the notion of character to the business corporation, to stretch some of the useful ideas of individual virtue and personal character to collective action.

In the course of our seminar, someone referred to the grantmaker as "the conscience of the corporation." That is an awkward role at best. It seems self-serving and self-flattering. It puts the grantmaker in the position of moral superiority, which is presumptuous. It also puts the grantmaking function at a higher moral level than the mainstream of the business—which is accurate, and hence awkward at times.

There is a practical aspect to the place of conscience in the grantmaking function. Grantmakers are in touch with the community in important ways, but with aspects of the community and in ways that are very different from others in the same corporation. There is a generally positive mutual relationship of grantmakers with nonprofits. An effective grantmaker will have an easy rapport with a wide range of people whom others in the corporation would never know or deal with in an official way. The interaction of the grantmaker with other grantmakers is also valuable. (This is especially true when corporate grantmakers are in touch with grantmakers in foundations. My impression—as one whose corporate foundation experience gave him informal membership in both groups—is that the mutual ignorance of corporate grantmakers and independent foundation grantmakers is appalling.)[28]

The point is that the process of grantmaking is the source of valuable information—of intelligence, in the military and diplomatic as well as the marketing sense. The information is about values and ideas, the undercurrents of community life.

Because the information that grantmakers absorb deals with values, grantmakers cannot be indifferent to the interpretation put on those values. There is a moral requirement to try to interpret values fairly and honestly. Pandering to management bias or prejudice by telling management only what it wants to hear about the changing environment is a bad habit—a vice.

The grantmaker is one among many who shape the moral dimension of a corporation's culture, but someone with a very distinctive contribution to make that no one else is likely to. The internal as well as the external image of the corporation is shaped, as is that of the individuals involved, by patterns of language and behavior over time, by the subjects that are discussed and the seriousness they are given. Perfunctory discussion about grantmaking will gloss over ethical distinctions. The gaps between statements of ethics policy and ethical practices will then, sooner or later, become evident. Failures in ethical practice on occasion will be weighed against a larger pattern.

The larger pattern includes the basic standards of doing the company's mainstream business. The congruence between claims of quality appropriate to price, the interpretation of contracts and less formal agreements, the treatment of employees all involve ethical considerations that are at least as important as the ethical claims of corporate philanthropy. The difference is that corporate philanthropy enlarges the responsibility to include in the discussion the interests of those who will not directly benefit from the company's success. It is their claims and needs and rights that must be considered.

Conclusion

The first point of this essay is that enlightened self-interest is the core value of corporate grantmaking and that enlightened self-interest is ethically problematic in practice. It is an unreliable guide.

The second point of the essay is that to behave ethically as a corporate grantmaker requires continuing reflection on the ethical dimension of the work. Although many of the conventions of grantmaking can be spelled out and serve as a guide to behavior, there is no simple set of rules to follow.

These points are supposed to merge in reflection on such questions as enlightened self-interest. Why bother? Can reflection on the ethical dimension act as a guide to behavior? A long popular and respected book on ethics cautions us not to expect too much:

". . . . Ethics cannot serve practice in more than an advisory capacity. It cannot decide the issue itself."[29] In order to make sound decisions we need information about the specific case, enough information to determine whether or which general rules apply. For example, we will want to anticipate the impact of our decision on others; for corporate grantmakers, "others" includes a great many people, not just the recipient. Ethical thinking forces a careful consideration of the consequences of a decision. That in itself is a major step forward. Thinking about the longer term and indirect consequences of an act, you will recall, is a characteristic of the "enlightened" aspect of enlightened self-interest. To speak seriously of being enlightened is to bring the ethical dimension to the surface. Talking about enlightened self-interest, then, can have a positive value by forcing a corporate grantmaker to weigh the consequences for others against the consequences for the corporation, and not limit the analysis to benefits to the corporation.

"To make the gray areas less gray," as a friend challenged me recently, is difficult, but that is what decision-making is all about. Making decisions ethically involves the process as well as the result. Almost every decision is made in the context of uncertainty about the facts and the consequences. There is a tendency to resolve the ambiguity by pretending that the matter is clearer than it is. We seek to be consistent by forcing cases into predetermined and comfortable categories; we find such comfort in certainty that we blind ourselves to the ambiguity that won't go away.

In my experience, the most common expression of that tendency is to hide behind guidelines, to make them so precise and inflexible that they make the decisions for us. Reflection is time-consuming; making judgments is risky; having opinions invites criticism. The comfort-seeking grantmaker avoids contact with grantseekers and lets rules make the decisions automatically. All grantmaking thereby becomes reduced to the mechanical processes of a matching gift program.

Grantmaking should be the result of grantmakers who are engaged with grantseekers in a common enterprise—with each participant candid about the legitimate claims of self-interest on both sides. Some grants will be mechanical and *pro forma*, of course; some will be made simply to maintain continuing activities. The professional requirement is imposed by the need also to take risks, to explore, to innovate. Technicians can process paper; professionals exercise judgment and make decisions.

How do we judge professional performance? The problem in grantmaking is that there is no clear market test. It is also true that we cannot usually isolate the decision so precisely that we can measure its impact. The evaluation of professional performance in grantmaking requires a balanced assessment of style and consequence over time.

The word *balanced* was used to remind the reader of the earlier reference to M. Scott Peck's four virtues: delaying of gratification, acceptance of responsibility, dedication to truth, and *balancing*.[30] A grantmaker might sometimes engage in egregiously[31] unethical conduct and deserve to be fired for a single action, just as a grantmaker might make a lucky decision and be able to make all the claimants at the door happy at the same time. The more common condition will be one of success mixed with and limited by some failure; some good things will not happen to good people; some grant money will appear to have disappeared into the sand. These philanthropic misfortunes will be offset by spontaneous and sincere expressions of appreciation, of recognition of the enlightened quality of the company's self-interest. Some troubling problems in the community will be alleviated. Some young people will have a better chance.

The grantmaker throughout will have dealt with people in certain ways, treated them with respect or disdain, courteously or indifferently. The grantmaker will have won a reputation, among those rejected as well as among recipients, among peers in other companies as well as within the company. The grantmaker will have stood firm on some issues and accommodated other priorities on other issues. The grantmaker will have recommended some risky or awkward grants because of the quality of the idea or the merit of the people. The grantmaker will have pressed for increases in program funds for what his evaluators conclude are substantive rather than empire-building reasons.

The grantmaker will be a person of good character. There is no universally *accepted* ethical system, even though there are ethical systems that lay claim to universal validity. To be a person of good character will be to present a very different portrait in one culture than in another. Most of us are thus required to make a choice about the ethical pattern of behavior we will follow. Most of us fabricate a working ethic out of our personal upbringing, experience, and interaction with others we respect and think to be of good character. Occasionally our ethical beliefs will reflect study of ethical philosophers.

That is not an easy context in which to find one's ethical bearings. Persons of good character are those whose movements are corrected by an internal gyroscope. Their guesses will almost always be close to the target ethically—even if sometimes deficient in other ways.

Balancing. No single virtue is enough, no single aspect of personality, no single skill. To be of good character is like being liberally educated. The insight is best expressed in what I have found to be the most useful line to reflect upon in all the organizational literature:

"This general executive process is not intellectual in its important aspect; it is aesthetic, and moral."[32] If that point of view pervades your grantmaking, you will be able to make your own map.

The most common professional complaint is that daily pressures deprive one of "time to think." In the context of this essay, that would be revised to complain of the lack of time to reflect on being ethical—on asking what is enlightened about enlightened self-interest. The only employer for whom I ever worked who made time available for the express purpose of discussing ethical matters was not a university or a government agency but a business corporation. The corporation required an annual discussion at the smallest unit level—about 20 people on the average—of the ethical policies of the company, of shared understanding of conflict of interest, of ethical problems raised by employees. These were not moral rearmament sessions, but as practical and down-to-earth as all the other business of the company.

Although those sessions and the distribution of the ethics policies of the company were about all that was done, *neither* were done as a matter of regular practice in universities nor in government. Government requires employees to read documents and to sign them, forever confident that such rituals influence behavior. The affectation of universities is the pretence that everyone is ethically sophisticated to start with—a striking example of self-deception. Some companies and agencies offer formal codes of ethics, but reading a code is like reading a regulation: unless the ideas and values are internalized, their written form is itself a form of deception.

I cannot accept the desperate view that ethical values and moral behavior are formed in early life and that all subsequent efforts at moral education are a waste of time and money. One of the reasons why ethical problems have become so much a matter of public concern is that we do so little to help people become more ethically sensitive and alert.

To explore ethical problems calls for some familiarity with

the working definitions of the principal approaches to ethical problems—of other people's approaches as well as our own.

There is a dangerous tendency to assume that one is ethical—that one understands the principles of ethics and behaves morally—and that other people understand them in the same way. We act as if there is a "common morality" that we can all readily fall back upon. There isn't.

There is more often ethical confusion than ethical consensus on issues. Any issue of a daily newspaper should make that clear. The common morality—unexamined—is as undependable as enlightened self-interest—unexamined.

Finally, the reason ethics is so important to grantmaking is that grantmaking itself is a normative, other-regarding, moral activity. Each grant is an assertion about the way the world *should* be. Anything so important is not likely to be simple or easy or even finished.

NOTES

I am grateful to the Council on Foundations for the opportunity to participate in the seminar on the ethics of corporate grantmaking. The group was interested, involved, candid, and concerned. It is reassuring to think of them as representative of the quality of the field (and so I will think of them that way). Judith Healey of the Minnesota Foundation was the key organizer. Judy and Alice Buhl of the Council were especially helpful in offering suggestions about this paper. Seminar participants Nicholas Goodban (Chicago Tribune Foundation); Peter Hutchinson (Dayton Hudson); Carol Reuter (Pillsbury), and James Shannon (General Mills) were altruistic—downright supererogatory—in gifts of time and comments.

1. Joseph W. Towle, editor, *Ethics and Standards in American Business*, Houghton Mifflin, 1964, pp. 20–29.

2. Richard Eells, *Corporation Giving in a Free Society*, Harper and Brothers, 1956, p. 1.

3. Paul Desruisseaux, "Harvard Will Seek $30-Million for Pro-

gram on Business Ethics," *The Chronicle of Higher Education*, April 8, 1987, pp. 27, 29.

4. Elizabeth M. Fowler, "Industry's New Focus on Ethics," *The New York Times*, August 11, 1987.

5. Based on an informal conversation with Irving Kristol.

6. Cf. Allan Bloom, *The Closing of the American Mind*, Simon and Schuster, 1987, pp. 141ff.

7. Bernard Mayo, *The Philosophy of Right and Wrong*, Routledge and Kegan Paul, 1986, pp. 8–9.

8. Adapted from the work of Mark Pastin, Arizona State University.

9. Ronald Milo, *Immorality*, Princeton University Press, 1984.

10. Sissela Bok, *Lying: Moral Choice in Public and Private Life*, Pantheon Books, 1978.

11. Cf. the essays by M. F. Burnyeat and David Wiggins in Amelie Oksenberg Rorty, *Essays on Aristotle's Ethics*, University of California Press, 1980.

12. Erik Erikson offers still another distinction in *Insight and Responsibility* (Norton, 1964) when he speaks of moral rules as based on "a fear of *threats* to be forestalled," and ethical rules to be based on "*ideals* to be striven for. . . ." (p. 222).

13. H. Ward Fowler, *Modern English Usage*, 2nd ed., edited by Sir Ernest Gowers, Oxford, 1965, pp. 170–171.

14. J. Barton Bowyer, *Cheating*, St. Martin's Press, 1982.

15. Ibid., p. 61.

16. For an insight into the differences between male and female attitudes to rules and their interpretation, see Carol Gilligan, *In a Different Voice*, Harvard University Press, 1982.

17. Eric Berne, *Games People Play*, Grove Press, 1964.

18. Bowyer (see note 14), p. 432.

19. Bernard Williams, *Ethics and the Limits of Philosophy*, Harvard University Press, 1985, p. 9.

20. G. R. Dunstan, *The Artifice of Ethics*, SCM Press, 1974, from Chapter 1, "Community and Convention," pp. 1–17.

21. John Dewey and James H. Tufts, *Ethics*, Henry Holt, 1909, p. 404. James D. Wallace, Virtues and Vices, Cornell University Press, 1978.

22. Eells (see note 2), p. 135.

23. F. Emerson Andrews, *Corporation Giving*, Russell Sage Foundation, 1952, pp. 340–341.

24. Dewey (see note 21), p. 418.

25. M. Scott Peck, *The Road Less Traveled*, Simon and Schuster, 1978, pp. 15, 18.

26. Dewey (see note 21), pp. 405–406.

27. Eells (see note 2), p. 136.

28. The Council on Foundations is to be complimented on its determined efforts in recent years to bridge the gap between the two subcultures.

29. A. C. Ewing, *Ethics*, Free Press, 1953, p. 17.

30. Peck (see note 25).

31. Maxwell Nurnberg, *I Always Look Up the Word "Egregious,"* Prentice-Hall, 1981.

32. Chester I. Barnard, *The Functions of the Executive*, Harvard University Press, 1938, p. 257.

The Role of Philanthropy in the Future of Higher Education

I know from personal experience that the tensions between "public" and "private" are serious, and at times flare up in controversy. Foundations (corporate and independent) have an undetermined role to play as mediators, agitators, advocates, reactors, and diplomats. I have left the perspective unaltered—at the time I presented the essay, I was president of Exxon Education Foundation. Including this essay here is in no way intended to reflect the present views of my former colleagues.

This essay was presented to a group of college and university presidents of the nation's most complex system of higher education as part of "Year 2000: A Colloquium on the Major Policy Directions for Higher Education in New York," sponsored by the Association of Colleges and Universities of the State of New York, Tarrytown House Executive Conference Center, Tarrytown, NY, September 15, 1986.

Donald Gaudion, then CEO of Sybron Corporation and chairman of the board of the University of Rochester, spoke to an informal meeting of this organization about a dozen years ago.

He said that he liked to affect an academic style when he met with his corporate board, and a corporate style when he met with academics. That way he managed to keep both groups uncomfortable, annoyed—and attentive.

Speaking to us in the early 1970s, Gaudion said that the major point he would make is that different times call for different styles of management. In a growth economy, managers have to be risk-takers, innovators, experimenters. In a "mature" economy, on the other hand, managers have to be able to concentrate on cost-cutting, efficiency, productivity.

We were then in a "mature" industry. Gaudion advised us that in his industry, under such circumstances, the emphasis was on "eliminating bleeder products."

Higher education has been a mature industry in New York for a very long time. Enrollment has been soft; the demographic trends have ranged from just bearable to downright disheartening. The great expectations of the 1960s were deflated within a decade.

It was at about that time that the Board of Regents created a commission on "the financially troubled institution" in higher education. We examined a great mass of material and concluded that many public and private colleges and universities could be said to be in trouble. And, although we informally referred to ourselves as "the euthanasia committee," we discovered that generalizations were very difficult to apply to specific institutions.

When I came to Exxon Education Foundation a decade ago, I gradually came to understand that foundation work is the application of practical wisdom, gleaned from long experience in testing theory against practice. I brought with me some convictions that were based largely on my experience in higher education in New York. Fortunately, being in higher education in New York means being in the midst of one of the richest and most diverse systems of higher education anywhere in the world.

One conviction that I brought with me to Exxon Education Foundation was that Donald Gaudion was right: *Different conditions require different kinds of presidential behavior.* In some periods we most need the vision and enthusiasm of leadership, while in others we need the tough-minded and tightly focused values of management. Few people are switch-hitters, able with equal dexterity to perform both as leaders and as managers interchangeably, as circumstances require. Most of us have personalities that limit our adaptability. We tend to overstate our ability to function well in situations we find unpleasant, dull, or beyond our competence—just as our critics tend to understate that ability.

One responsibility of foundations is that they must pass judgment on the characters and abilities of the people with whom they deal. That means passing judgment on whether the institution is well led and well managed.

A second conviction that I brought into foundation work from my experience in higher education in New York was that *individual institutions have a great deal to say about their own destinies.* Service on the "euthanasia committee" convinced me of that, and observing the extraordinary will to survive of a number of colleges facing disaster since then confirms that it is dangerous to go into mourning while the patient is still alive. Some colleges are willing to live in a permanent condition of struggle; in some depressed regions of the country, these institutions are a symbol of hope. Whatever the averages and trends may imply, individual institutions can often find a way to counter them.

David Riesman once advised me that a foundation involved with higher education should invest in individuals rather than in institutions. Because of the power of leadership, he said, some of the most interesting and promising new developments in higher education emerge in some of the most unlikely places. Individual presidents and deans are the most important people in the developmental life of a college or university; they know how to enlist and utilize the talent that is available.

I then learned that talented and interesting people often move from one place to another, and take their charisma with them. Leadership is not enough.

We have long operated on the conviction that we must

try to direct our funds toward good ideas in the hands of capable people supported by their central administration. I have had no reason to change that view—to believe that we can focus only on the idea, the person, or the institution and neglect the other variables.

Ten years ago it seemed evident that a common problem facing higher education was the disorder surrounding general education. That judgment seems in retrospect to have been well founded. Since then, almost 70% of all colleges and universities report that they have been engaged in reviewing and often reforming their programs of general education.

General education is a complex world of its own. To have an interest in it means more than encouraging debates of educational philosophy. Foundations may wish to encourage efforts to strengthen general education, but colleges—and especially universities—are ill-designed for that purpose. The goals of higher education are driven primarily by forces rooted in the disciplines and the professions, and to challenge that structure is often to invite frustration if not failure.

Foundations must choose specific aspects of general education, as the Sloan Foundation has done so well with its program on technology and as Exxon Education Foundation has attempted to do with its support of foreign language teaching and learning. Much as Sloan discovered with the rising interest in re-thinking the place of science and technology in general education, we found a decade ago there was promise of a national revival of interest in foreign language study after a dismal decade of abandonment and know-nothing rejection. The presidential task force known as the Perkins Commission seemed to signal a renewed interest and commitment.

(At the same time, people in foundations as well as people on campuses know all too well that the field of foreign language study is notoriously fragmented and fractious.)

In foreign language and in other fields, we also learned another very important lesson: that it was not sufficient to work with individual scholars and institutions. Because of the structure of the university and the conflict between specialized fields and general education, we have found that working closely with educational organizations and associations is increasingly necessary to pursue the objectives of our foundation.

In addition to general education, the methodology of teaching and learning, and the management of higher education, we have encouraged efforts to cut across the barriers that have balkanized the campus. Integrative studies, interdisciplinary and multidisciplinary studies, and international studies have all been prominent in our thinking.

It occurred to me that we might be most helpful to you in sketching out the strategies we follow as well as where we think our future emphasis will fall and the kinds of priorities that we think will emerge. How do we mesh our strategies with yours? How do we relate strategic planning in education to strategic planning in philanthropy?

Foundations and corporations such as those represented here today have achieved prominence for two reasons, it seems to me: They have philanthropic investment strategies; they set patterns that individual givers can follow. Because these foundations are staffed by professionals, so-called, they are able to develop strategies, to consider numerous alternative opportunities, and to monitor results.

The very word *strategy* implies a long-term perspective. Strategizing tends to diminish emotional influences. Individuals often respond to relief efforts intended to reduce suffering, but foundations and corporations do not. The Ethiopian famine is a good example, and the immediate response to the survivors of the volcanic eruption in Cameroon is another. Strategic philanthropy aims at understanding the underlying causes of those terrible problems in terms of the social and political as well as the natural forces at work.

Education is a long-term process, one that should require strategic thinking. Donald Gaudion, at the ACUSNY discussion I mentioned earlier, spoke of the "product cycle" in his industry (medical and dental equipment). The time from the first development of a product until a decision to drop it, he said, was a span of just three years. When he looked at the development of curricula and degree programs in a university, on the other hand, the time frame seemed vastly longer, and there seemed to be no point where a decision could be made to eliminate anything.

Educational philanthropy has three choices: It can focus on the immediate alleviation of problems resulting from falling enrollments and budget deficits; it can commit its resources to sustaining what is already functioning and functioning well, and make grants in support of base budgets and incremental improvements; or it can focus on root causes and seek to influence long-term change.

Most philanthropic foundations are engaged in all three kinds of activities, although the myth is that we are only engaged in the third—in ferreting out the sources of difficulty and developing innovative solutions to them.

To be involved in the long-term growth and development of education means trying to be aware of the larger environment. That environment presents three issues at the moment, which I will discuss as illustrations of a foundation strategy. One is immediate, a second is medium-term, and the third is long-term.

"Immediate" for me means the next five years. "Medium-term" I define as extending over the next decade or so. "Long-term" extends to say, 2015, when the graduates of the coming academic year will be about the average age of those present here.

The immediate issue is the impact of tax reform on philanthropic resources and giving patterns.

The medium-term question is about governance—about the evidence of what I will call for purposes of provocation "creeping capitalism" in public higher education, following a long period of what others once called "creeping socialism" in private higher education.

The third and long-term question is the changing character of American society, and what those changes mean for educators now as well as for your successors.

Tax Reform

Our foundation will not become involved in the first issue. As a company-sponsored foundation, we avoid involvement with specific tax policy issues.

The educational question involved that touches on your interests and ours is the question of public understanding of tax policy and philanthropy. My impression is that Congress was handicapped by its own ignorance in trying to weigh the effects of the proposed changes in tax policy on philanthropy. I hope that somewhere within the philanthropic community will be found the resources to support continuing historical as well as analytical research in this field.

Governance

The second issue, over the next decade or so, is the complex of issues so well illustrated in New York's "system" of higher education. I have always believed—perhaps in a partisan way—that New York greatly benefits from its diverse conglomeration of colleges and universities. My own advocacy was always intended to sustain the system rather than to yield to the temptation to argue for one sector's interests to the fundamental detriment of the other.

I borrow from John T. Flynn's attack on "creeping socialism" a generation ago to remind you that it was in the period beginning in the late 1960s that private higher education in New York sought and was given access to public revenues. These days, in this state and elsewhere, an as-yet unrecognized phenomenon that might be called "creeping capitalism" is under way in the public institutions.

The publicized aspect of this is the emergence of major capital campaigns among the great public research universities. (New York lags behind California, Minnesota, and others in this competition.) The unpublicized aspects include the appearance of aggressive and increasingly sophisticated fund-raising efforts among state colleges and community colleges.

We have increased the share of our grant funds that will be allocated to help institutions improve their fund raising. We hope to see an increased effectiveness among the small liberal arts colleges that are in greatest jeopardy. We also hope to see the public institutions begin to catch up with the private colleges and universities in their efforts to raise money from alumni and parents. We believe that trustees should play a more prominent role, and that there should be a wide-spread effort to improve the professional standing of development officers.

But it is very clear that we will have to see a more balanced appreciation of fund raising—both its great potential and its real limitations—among all of those directly involved with higher education.

A second aspect that has gone largely unnoticed is the philosophical change implicit in what has taken place: the change in management philosophy and governance of the state university system.

A generation ago, the private institutions were quite content with being private and the public with being public. Each saw its virtues as unambiguously offsetting its limitations; for the most part, neither talked much about its limitations. Public institutions today see the need for greater flexibility and diversity, flexibility almost by definition associated with private higher education. Private institutions, decreasingly able to sustain themselves by tuition income and philanthropy, discovered 20 years ago the need for a more secure financial base—a degree of security primarily associated with public higher education. The result is the model of tuition support and other base budget funding that New York provides through its enlightened legislation each year.

Students of such matters should be encouraged to follow these trends and to project alternative sets of consequences. It may be that foundations can be most helpful in a mediating and convening capacity, along with other interested but concerned bystanders. Our foundation's role thus far has been to encourage continuing dialogue and the development of reliable empirical information that policymakers may draw upon with confidence. We are unlikely to go beyond that.

The Changing Character of American Society

The third issue—the changing demographic profile of American society and education—is the one that most intrigues us at the moment, although being a long-term problem it is probably least urgent from your point of view. It also has two aspects, the first educational, the second more broadly cultural and social. It comes to our attention because we have a program in elementary and secondary education and because we have an interest in "social thought and discourse."

First, the educational aspect:

We are persuaded that the quality of higher education is eroding from below. The quality of learning varies dramatically among ethnic minorities, but especially among those groups in which the population is growing most rapidly.

Some of us believe that there is an opportunity over the next few years to address some of the most serious issues facing pre-college education. The short-term costs involved are such that questions of political will must be considered.

What is most important is that we know what we are talking about. Important information is now available about student performance and about what takes place in the school that policymakers have lacked in the past. We need to expand that information and then to interpret it with great care.

Similar work will then be necessary at the higher education level. My principal associate in these matters, Scott Miller, believes that we need a massive study of higher education analogous to John Goodlad's study of the elementary and secondary system: *A Place Called School*[1] should be followed by *A Place Called College*.

The second aspect of this issue is the rapidly changing ethnic profile of American society. There are profound changes in age groups, geographical changes related to long-term restructuring of the economy, the continuing impact of technology on birth rates. Beyond these are changes in the relative position and influence of ethnic groups, including the relative decline of the Anglo-European group that has dominated American life for more than two centuries.

These changes are reflected in empirical data that are becoming increasingly familiar to all of us. What is stickiest, however, is not the empirical but the normative. These changes will one day begin to add even greater complexity to the question, What *should* be taught? That question is even

more complicated than it was almost 60 years ago, when
Charles Beard and some others published a book entitled
Whither Mankind? Everett Dean Martin, who wrote the essay
on education, complained that "There are few places in
America where anything may be mentioned in the public
school that is not displeasing to Methodist preachers, the
Catholic Irish, leading politicians, grocers, or any organized
group."[2]

Martin was also distressed as most of us still are by the
polarization of cultural and vocational education: "The
practical problem of orientation [to work] cannot be divorced
from the end of the struggle for value."

The question of who will receive a liberal arts education
as well as advanced professional education becomes an important social issue. Will we be able to bring the young people
of greatest promise from minority groups into the mainstream of the society on something approximating equal
terms? Thus far we haven't done very well, in spite of our
good intentions.

The long-term question is what we should be teaching
teachers to teach children not yet born. What do we *now* believe it is most important to pass on to them? Skills and
methods, without content? Which content?

Were we to ascertain among ourselves that the most important obligation we have to future generations, whatever
their ethnic makeup, is to pass on a free, open, and democratic society, what would we teach? What are the values of
the rising non-Western ethnic groups? What are they most
likely to contribute to the mix of values?

Assuming that we can define ourselves, *What do we believe?*

Conclusion

These three issues—tax reform, governance, the changing
character of American society—are intended to show some
interrelationship. Each one requires more study, more information, more analysis. Each one involves issues of governance, of who will make which decisions about what is

taught and learned, and to whom. Each one raises long-term consequences, some of them touching on our most basic values.

The frustration of being a president is knowing that all those *other* people out there are worrying, talking, and arguing about *those* issues, while you're trapped at your desk or at a head table someplace, worrying about budgets, drug abuse, athletics, and labor contracts. Not only that, those other people don't even have to come to conclusions, to make decisions, and to suffer the consequences. *They* can worry about 2015 A.D. without any concern for 1988 or 1991, while your only concern with 2015 A.D. is written into a construction financing agreement.

Perhaps one thing *we* can do is worry about you, at least part of the time: what you think is most important, how you think you can be of greatest service, how some modest financial help can push things along.

NOTES

1. John Goodlad, *A Place Called School*, McGraw Hill, 1983.
2. Charles A. Beard, ed., *Whither Mankind: A Panorama of Modern Civilization*, Longmans, Green, 1928, p. 370.

Research on the Independent Sector: A Progress Report

Virginia A. Hodgkinson
Vice President, Research
Independent Sector

Dr. Virginia A. Hodgkinson, Vice President for Research of Independent Sector, has become the best known person in her field. Although it is under her direction and with her personal effort that Independent Sector publishes important reports on the condition of philanthropy, it is through Virginia's *Work in Progress* that she finds herself at the center of a rapidly expanding network of research. The following essay gives a clear indication of the encouraging array of scholarship and empirical work under way in this field.

The year 1987 marked the Independent Sector's fifth Spring Research Forum. The first forum "Since the Filer Commission" was held in the spring of 1983 to assess the condition of research since the Commission on Private Philanthropy and Public Needs had completed its work in 1975 and published its *Research Papers* in 1977. This forum also launched the research program of the Independent Sector (IS). The goal of this research program was and is to stimulate the development of an identifiable and growing research effort that produces the body of knowledge necessary to accurately define, describe, chart, and understand the sector and the ways it can be of greatest service to society.

The purpose of this progress report is to provide a broad review of research activity on philanthropy and the independent sector, the support for such research, and the achievement of progress toward the broad goals of the IS research program. It is not designed to provide a critique of the scholarly work completed or in progress, but rather to point out where significant scholarly activity is occurring, some commitment made by academic institutions or major research organizations to research and academic programs on nonprofit organizations and philanthropy, and to note where major gaps still exist. Because one of the major functions of the Independent Sector research program is to encourage and document ongoing research, this review is organized according to the plan approved by the IS Research Committee to accomplish that function. As such, this essay looks at the sector as a whole, and more particularly at the efficacy of the IS research program to achieve its goals to encourage, support, and document a growing research effort.

The IS Research Program is guided by a Research Committee under the chairmanship of Robert Payton, former President of the Exxon Education Foundation and, more recently, a Scholar in Residence at the University of Virginia. Under his leadership, this committee developed a series of strategies designed to stimulate research and to increase the support of research on this sector. These strategies include:

1. Establishing a research community through the annual research forums and publication of the *Working Papers*

from the forums and *Research-in-Progress* to document
work in progress

2. Stimulating the development of bibliographies and
   searches through former literature
3. Encouraging the development of the bookshelf on philanthropy, voluntary action, and nonprofit activity by
   encouraging and documenting the publication of works
   relating to this sector
4. Building the resource base on the independent sector
   in order to stimulate social science research
5. Identifying major research gaps, and encouraging research to fill those gaps
6. Encouraging the establishment of endowed chairs and
   academic centers to maintain intergenerational support for both teaching and research on the sector across
   the humanistic disciplines, the social sciences, and in
   professional schools of public administration, business
   management, and law
7. Increasing support for research and teaching on the
   independent sector

Establishing a Research Community

Because the Independent Sector represents over 600 national voluntary organizations, foundations, and corporate
responsibility programs, it essentially works through the
voluntary service and commitment of its members to achieve
its program goals. The research program not only needed to
seek the support of IS members, but also the interest of the
academic community at colleges and universities across the
United States and abroad.

An important element of developing a body of knowledge
in any area is to provide opportunities for scholars to meet
with persons of similar interests and to have a regular process
of publishing new research, usually through journals and
books. Such a situation is more difficult in an area where
most of the research is multidisciplinary in character, and
very few scholars are scattered across several disciplines,
each with its own scholarly professional association and

journals. In order to address a major gap in the ability of scholars to know and to communicate with each other, the annual research forums were established. Since 1984, these forums have been co-sponsored by the United Way Institute. These annual forums have been very well received by the scholarly community as well as the leaders from national voluntary organizations and donor organizations. They provide scholars with an opportunity to present their research and representatives of voluntary and donor organizations to learn about current research. Furthermore, they provide an opportunity for all three groups to discuss future research needs, to ask new questions, and to refine older questions.

Each year the quality of research, and the number and variety of new researchers in the field who are invited to present papers, have measurably improved. Since 1982, over 150 scholars have been invited to present papers at these Spring Research Forums, but where the early sessions primarily focused on the research that needed to be done, since 1985, a substantial part of the programs of these forums have been devoted to reporting findings from current research. The limited publication of *Working Papers* containing the papers for discussion at each of the forums have been purchased by researchers, libraries, and other voluntary and donor organizations for further use. Many of the papers included in the annual *Working Papers* are published later as articles in journals or as chapters in books.

Another strategy that is used to build a research community is the annual publication of *Research-in-Progress*. This volume includes an annual compilation of current research on philanthropy, voluntary action, and not-for-profit activity. Its purpose is to identify researchers and describe current research on issues of concern to the independent sector. Our goal in publishing this series is to provide an avenue for sharing information among researchers in the sector. These researchers may have common interests, but currently there are very few scholarly publications and little opportunity through professional associations to meet one another. *Research-in-Progress* covers research across a great range of disciplinary and interdisciplinary endeavor, from theoretical research on the role and functions of the nonprofit organizations to analyses of the motivations of giving, to special industry studies on particular subsectors of the independent sector, such as hospitals and schools. As such, it provides researchers, students, and practitioners with a convenient compendium of work underway, as well as recently published articles, papers, and books.

Since the first edition of *Research in Progress* was published in 1983, over 1,800 research projects have been summarized: 282 in the 1982–1983 edition, 403 in the 1983–1984 edition, 511 in the 1984–1985 edition, and 441 projects in the 1985–1986 edition. Although multi-year projects are relisted each year with a progress report, over 60% of the projects listed in each addition are new projects, for a total of about 1,100 new research projects over this period. As such, the volume stands as a record of research activity on the sector for any particular year.

Research-in-Progress has rapidly become a basic reference in the field for researchers, voluntary organizations, and donor organizations. Originally, donor organizations were concerned about funding duplicative research efforts. Researchers, on the other hand, had to start from scratch with each study because they had difficulty in knowing or in accessing research currently underway. This document has provided a handy starting point for researchers and practitioners alike. It has led to several collaborative efforts in research; and it has provided a reference point for determining the amount of or the lack of research on a topic in various areas.

Opportunities for more scholarly meetings also have increased. The Program on Non-Profit Organizations has offered weekly seminars on current issues that many researchers have attended. Other academic centers also are providing seminar series and planning conferences, such as the Institute for Nonprofit Management at the University of San Francisco and the Center for Philanthropy at the Graduate Center at the City University of New York. As these and other new centers develop their programs, they will provide more opportunities for scholars to meet together.

In 1985, the Association of Voluntary Action Scholars expanded its mission to include membership of scholars broadly interested in research in volunteering, citizen participation, philanthropy, and nonprofit organizations. This expanded mission will provide scholars in the field with access to a professional association that holds a yearly conference. This association also has expanded the purpose of its journal, edited by Jon Van Til of Rutgers University, to include scholarly papers on the wider topics of philanthropy and nonprofit organizations. The title of the journal has been changed to *Nonprofit and Voluntary Sector Quarterly* to reflect this wider interest and to provide researchers in the field with more opportunity to publish articles within their scholarly interest.

The Development of Bibliographies

One of the major obstacles to encouraging research on the independent sector is building a basic body of literature. The problems stem from the lack of key words to identify subjects dealing with philanthropy or nonprofit organizations in traditional bibliographical systems, such as the Library of Congress system or *Dissertation Abstracts*. To this end, finding the literature and identifying the key words under which such literature is classified across a variety of disciplines is an important activity in establishing the body of knowledge that already exists. Supporting and evaluating this literature in annotated bibliographies by topic and/or by particular discipline or area of study is another important activity, for research has shown that readily available bibliographies are valuable tools to stimulate research. Several bibliographies are in progress or have been published in the past five years.

Brian and Ann O'Connell produced an excellent bibliography as part of *America's Voluntary Spirit* (The Foundation Center, 1983). This bibliography lists publications on philanthropy, voluntary action, and nonprofit activity for the past 300 years.

Robert Bremner, author of *American Philanthropy* (1960)

and member of the IS Research Committee, updates annually a key word system for identifying work on the nonprofit sector from the Union Catalog of Manuscripts. Copies of his work are available through Independent Sector.

Steven Wheatley of the American Council of Learned Societies is updating a bibliography on the history of philanthropy. This bibliography was originally commissioned as part of the Princeton Conference on the History of Philanthropy held in 1956. Part of the 1986 Spring Research Forum was devoted to celebrating that conference and its impact on the history of philanthropy, and IS is partially supporting the completion of this bibliography.

The Program on Non-Profit Organizations (PONPO) at Yale University also has supported bibliographical research. As part of its *Working Papers* series, it has produced bibliographies of research on management of nonprofit organizations; a bibliography on motivations for giving, primarily in the area of psychological research; and a bibliography of current research on philanthropy and the nonprofit sector abroad. Independent Sector has agreed to update this international bibliography as part of its *Research-in-Progress* series.

More recently, the Association of American Colleges has been supported by the American Association of Fund-Raising Counsel Trust for Philanthropy and other foundations to prepare a bibliography on philanthropy particularly for use by faculty and students interested in teaching and studying philanthropy at the undergraduate level. *Philanthropy and Voluntarism: An Annotated Bibliography* was published in June 1987 by the Foundation Center.

There are two bibliographical projects in progress at Independent Sector. The first is an annotated bibliography on the motivations for giving and volunteering, which is multidisciplinary in nature. The first purpose of this bibliography is to evaluate whether there are some generalizations that can be made about motivations for giving and volunteering. The second purpose is to determine what gaps exist in our knowledge about motivations, what areas of research hold the greatest promise for filling in those gaps, and what the priority projects are that ought to be part of a research agenda on motivations. Independent Sector has taken responsibility for running and coordinating this particular project because of its enormous importance, generally in providing ways in which giving and volunteering can be measurably increased in America. Some of the generalizations that emerge from a review of this research on motivations can be further tested in a series of national studies on giving and volunteering that IS is sponsoring over the next five years.

The second bibliographical study concerns the study and relationships of religious institutions to philanthropy. In an effort to stimulate research on a variety of issues relating to religion and philanthropy, IS staff members are compiling an initial bibliography on this topic. Other scholars who are working on the development of research agendas in this area are David Watt at Temple University, Ann Fraker at Indiana University, Robert Wuthnow at the Woodrow Wilson School at Princeton University, and David Hutchinson at Harvard University. These collaborative efforts should result in a published bibliography and an agenda for research developed by scholars in the field to stimulate interest in such research.

Although the Yale Program, in its series of books ranging from the *Handbook on Nonprofit Organizations* to international studies, is making an enormous contribution to the field by paying attention to both bibliographies and scholarly evaluation of former and current research across a variety of topics and fields, several other bibliographical projects need to be encouraged. Through both PONPO's work and the work of new academic centers currently being started, such attention to bibliographies should provide scholars with reference points across a variety of topics relating to philanthropy, thus stimulating further inquiries more quickly. Until recently, scholars working on nonprofit sector research were forced to reinvent the wheel because bibliographical resources were not readily available. Furthermore, as such scholarship grows, researchers should be able to bring about improvement in the key words used in the major bibliographical search systems to allow scholars to access scholarly work on philanthropy and the nonprofit sector more easily.

The Foundation Center is currently conducting a feasibility study to determine whether there is enough need to design a bibliographical system on publications about the independent sector. Should this project prove viable, it may be possible to build a key word system building upon bibliographical work currently completed or in progress that would be enormously useful to both scholars and practitioners interested in this field.

Developing a Growing Bookshelf on Philanthropy, Voluntary Action, and Nonprofit Activity

Several years ago, John Gardner, who chaired the Organizing Committee of IS, mentioned that studies of government and business filled enormous space on the shelves of most libraries, but studies of the independent sector barely filled one shelf. It is not enough to stimulate an interest in research on the independent sector; one must also encourage the publication of that research into books which take on a life of their own. Brian O'Connell remarked that when he was building the bibliography for *The Board Member's Book*, very few of the good books were still in print, and that most of the information on boards in the independent sector were written in what librarians call "ephemeral" literature. One of the major goals of Independent Sector's Research Program is to document the development of a basic body of knowledge on this sector. There is no more permanent, nor durable, form than published books on library shelves for use by other scholars and new generations of students.

Therefore, it has been a major concern at IS not only to provide publications that synthesize knowledge already available in a more permanent form, but to stimulate and encourage other scholars and organizations to become more concerned not only with the publication of current research, but also with the reprinting of former classics that are out of print and not readily available. During the past five years, increasing attention has been paid to the publication of books by IS, Yale's PONPO, and the Foundation Center. And the publication of books by researchers is an indication of the growing interest in the field.

Both the writing and the publication of books is a lengthy and expensive process. This is particularly true if the books address issues encompassing the whole independent sector, and what this sector means and does. It is even more true in an area that has a long history, an enormous diversity of functions, but very little recent research. But good books on the sector cannot be written without good research. And good research, particularly in a neglected area of study, takes time. Several books are just being written as a result of research projects described in the 1982–1983 volume of *Research-in-Progress.* Of course, there have been numerous journal articles and several hundred working papers over this period. After nine years, seven edited volumes on various aspects of the nonprofit sector are just coming off the press as a result of the research supported by Yale's PONPO, although the work of individual scholars associated with the Yale Program has resulted in over 30 books published or under contract for publication. In 1997, as interest in research on this sector continues to grow, there ought to be several good books annually published addressing important issues that will improve our understanding of the role, functions, and contributions of the independent sector to American society and other cultures.

There also has been a concern with reprinting the classic literature of the sector that has been long out of print. The University of Chicago Press reprinted Robert Bremner's classic history *American Philanthropy* (1960) in 1985, and published a revised and updated edition in 1987. The purpose of Brian O'Connell's *American Voluntary Spirit* (1983) was to produce a collection of classic pieces written about philanthropy and voluntary action spanning 300 years. More recently, Richard Magat, President of the Hazen Foundation, agreed to become the new series editor for Transaction Books' series Society and Philanthropy. The purpose of this series is to reprint classics on philanthropy in the social sciences. The first book in the series, *Wealth and Culture* by Eduard C.

Lindeman (1935), was just published with a new introduction by Richard Magat. More projects to reprint such classics ought to be encouraged, because some of the most important research on the voluntary sector was published before 1940.

Building the Resource Base on the Independent Sector

A major stumbling block to stimulating social science research on the independent sector has been the lack of regular data collection on institutions, their programs, functions, and finances; on employment and occupations in these institutions; and on giving, volunteering, and the motivations for individuals who give and volunteer. As *The Nonprofit Handbook*, edited by Walter Powell of Yale University, clearly shows, many talented social scientists have developed definitions and theories about the role and functions of the sector, but there are few large-scale empirical studies to test these theories. In fact, an even more formidable stumbling block than lack of data is the lack of a common language with which to describe, chart, and understand this sector of American society. In order to address the enormity of these issues, several strategies were developed to provide social scientists with a better resource base and to provide them with access to statistical studies as they became available. Three major strategies were developed to address these issues: (1) the reviewing of what information was available and identifying major information gaps; (2) the development of the National Center for Charitable Statistics to improve the collection and reporting of data from federal, state, and private sources; and (3) the sponsoring or encouraging of surveys in areas where information was not collected. The decision of the Research Committee was that the development of basic resources needed more direct effort and a clear agenda.

A REVIEW OF CURRENT INFORMATION: SETTING THE AGENDA

Dimensions of the Independent Sector: A Statistical Profile is a biennial publication (first published by Independent

Sector in 1984) that synthesizes completed statistical research on the sector. It provides a framework to measure the
size, scope, and dimensions of this sector from various data
collections and national surveys. As such, it serves as a useful
reference book that summarizes what we know, as well as
outlining the gaps in our knowledge about the sector. This
publication in its current form became possible because of
baseline research on employment and earnings done by Gabriel Rudney and Murray Weitzman for PONPO at Yale University (1983). That research allowed for the development of
a framework for measuring the size of the nonprofit sector
as part of the American economy. Many of the information
gaps noted in the first edition of *Dimensions* are now being
addressed, including: (1) more information on giving and
volunteering by individuals; (2) a survey of religious institutions; (3) the creation of a national sample to chart the
finances of nonprofit institutions and foundations; (4) the development of a national classification system; and (5) a
change on the 1990 Census to allow people to report whether
they are employed at a nonprofit organization. The 1986 edition of *Dimensions* charted this current progress and reported
on the new studies that occurred between 1982 and 1985.

THE NATIONAL CENTER FOR CHARITABLE STATISTICS

The National Center for Charitable Statistics (NCCS),
started as a special program of the National Charities Information Bureau in 1980. It was incorporated in 1982 as a
501(c)(3) organization under the sponsorship of the Council
on Foundations, Independent Sector, the National Charities
Information Bureau, and the United Way of America. In 1983,
the management of NCCS was moved to Independent Sector
and in 1986, at the request of the NCCS Board and with the
approval of the IS Board, NCCS became a program of Independent Sector.

The NCCS program is a unique commitment to track the
scope of the charitable sector in the country through a continuing effort to improve and expand the reporting of statistics on charitable organizations by both federal and state

governments and to make these statistics publicly available. It also stimulates the collection of statistics on giving and volunteering through private research efforts. It serves as a national repository of those statistics. It provides access to these statistics through the sale of computer tapes, the provision of computer runs, and occasional publications.

The core activities of NCCS are: (1) improving the collection of statistics by the federal government on charitable organizations; (2) assisting and encouraging states to computerize the data on the 990 forms; (3) developing and implementing a national classification system on the nonprofit sector; (4) serving as a national repository, both historical and current, of statistics on computer tapes relating to charitable organizations; and (5) publishing periodic reports on statistics of the sector.

Improving the Reporting of Statistics by the Federal Government. In 1980, NCCS secured the agreement from the states and the federal government to use a single 990 form. Not only was this accomplishment important for charitable organizations to reduce the cost and effort of separate reports, but it gave us a base for a national database on the nonprofit sector. The NCCS now is working with states to agree on a single state supplementary form for the 990's.

In 1983, NCCS also commenced its work with both the U.S. Department of Treasury, the Internal Revenue Service, and the U.S. Bureau of the Census to improve its reporting on nonprofit organizations. NCCS also tried to convince IRS to code more than the name, address, and total revenues and assets on the 990 master file. While carrying out these activities, NCCS started to check more thoroughly about how accurately even those two numbers were coded on the master file. In 1985, NCCS noticed that the 1983–1984 IRS master file of 990 forms for 501(c)(3) and 501(c)(4) organizations had massive errors. We asked the IRS to investigate. The IRS appointed a task force from the Statistics of Income (SOI) Division to investigate the problems. The SOI team found that the data recorded on the 990 tapes had massive error problems due to the coding errors in the IRS regional centers. At the request of NCCS, the IRS agreed to develop a system to eliminate these coding errors which they estimate will take two to three years. In the meantime, at the request of NCCS, they have removed the master file tapes from public use. This is the *only universal* database on charitable organizations that file tax returns, but we are providing public support for this effort to assure more accurate reporting by the federal government in 1988 and beyond. The task to persuade them to increase the items it codes from those forms will still be with us, but we hope to generate more public support in the interim for these efforts.

During this period, the SOI Division launched a program to collect annual samples of private foundations and tax exempt organizations. The last time such a national sample was collected was in 1975, which directly resulted from the efforts of the Filer Commission. In the fall of 1985, SOI started the collection of these samples from the 1982–1983 year. For the first time, it looked like the charitable sector was to have a longitudinal database.

However, in the spring of 1985, the SOI received a 25% budget cut for Fiscal Year 1986. Because these samples were not mandated by federal legislation, future collections would be cut. Fritz Scheuren, Director of SOI, asked NCCS to go into partnership to save these samples. NCCS called a meeting of executives from government agencies, foundations, and corporations to discuss this issue. It meant raising $125,000 a year for two or possibly three years to provide the 25% cut needed to save these samples. By December 1985, NCCS raised $250,000 to save the samples for 1986 and 1987.

By going into a contractual relationship with the SOI, NCCS will be able to implement its national classification system on these samples. It has been able to save the only longitudinal database on financial statistics of foundations and charitable organizations because the Statistics of Income Division currently plans to conduct enlarged samples of all nonprofit organizations annually starting in 1989.

The Development of a National Classification System for the Nonprofit Sector. One of the stumbling blocks to stimulating social science research even if sufficient government information were available was the lack of a way to classify nonprofit, tax-exempt organizations by purpose. Nor was there a common language to accurately define and describe the voluntary sector in the United States.

In 1982, the National Center for Charitable Statistics realized that the development of such a system was a first priority in order to improve research and data collection on this sector. It appointed a National Classification Task Force chaired by Elizabeth Boris, vice president for research at the Council on Foundations, to design a plan to develop such a system for the nonprofit sector. After several meetings, the Task Force recommended that Russy D. Sumariwalla, Senior Fellow of the United Way Institute, direct the project. In 1987, after extensive pilot testing in several hundred national nonprofit organizations, the National Taxonomy of Exempt Entities was released.

Soon after its release, NCCS, in collaboration with the IRS, developed a plan for its implementation by 1990. NCCS will classify 900,000 nonprofit organizations on the IRS Master File of Exempt Entities, and the IRS will classify new organizations and revise its systems to accommodate the new system by 1990. When the classification system has been implemented, social scientists studying the nonprofit sector will begin to have the kinds of analytical tools that have been available to them for the stalemated study of business and government since the 1930s, when the Standard Industrial Code was created.

The States Computerization Project. NCCS launched its states computerization project in 1981 in an effort to record more data from the 990 forms. Bill Levis of the National Charities Information Bureau staffed this effort until 1985. Currently, Frank Swenson, former head of the Charities Registration Office in New Jersey, directs this effort. The states computerization included development of a software package for use by states, technical assistance to the states during the computerization, and, in some states, assistance with raising funds for hardware among local donor organizations.

By the end of 1986, five states were fully computerized: New York, California, Minnesota, New Jersey, and Connecticut. Partial computerization of the 990 forms have been completed in Nevada, Illinois, Indiana, Maryland, New Hampshire, and Connecticut. Partial or full computerization is in progress in Virginia, Massachusetts, and Pennsylvania. We are currently working with North Carolina, Texas, and Wisconsin to start state computerization efforts there.

NCCS is unique in its effort to serve as a national repository for statistics on the nonprofit sector. These statistics come from both public and private sources. NCCS collects both federal and states tapes on the 990 forms. It also encourages funders to donate the tapes of major private surveys to the Center. Currently, the tapes of the first SOI samples of private foundations and tax-exempt organizations are housed at NCCS. The Rockefeller Brothers Fund donated the tape from the Yankelovich, Skelly and White national survey of the Charitable Behavior of Americans to NCCS and the Americans Volunteer 1985 conducted by the Gallup Organization and commissioned by the IS research program will be available through NCCS. The Urban Institute will also donate the tapes of its survey from the Nonprofit Sector Project after the research has been completed and the findings disseminated.

Efforts are being made to get copies of major earlier studies to complete the library. The purpose of the repository is to provide a single tape library to house these studies. In the past, master 990 files were destroyed after a year and are no longer available to the public. Former research files from the Filer Commission still are in the hands of individual researchers and NCCS is trying to get copies of these older tapes.

Without such a repository to serve the sector, it is extremely difficult and costly for social scientists to consider conducting research on this sector. Therefore, as the years pass, NCCS will serve as a national computer library for the nonprofit sector.

To Provide Data Services to Organizations. One of NCCS's major functions in the years ahead will be to provide computer tabulations for a variety of purposes to organizations and researchers. Until this year, NCCS has been limited to providing mailing labels and occasional samples for researchers. However, once the classification system is in place, and with the new tapes from the SOI studies, and the giving and volunteering surveys, NCCS will have a rich repository of information for researchers.

To Publish Periodic Reports of Statistics on the Sector. In 1985, NCCS published *Non-Profit Service Organizations: 1982*, discussed earlier. In 1987, NCCS published a series of state directories on the finances of nonprofit organizations in New York, New Jersey, Minnesota, California, and Connecticut.

NCCS believes in the critical importance of the development of an information system for the whole nonprofit sector. Its striving to secure more and better information on the charitable represents a major endeavor to build a national repository to provide statistics on the sector. If all the 990 forms in the states with reporting requirements and the federal government are computerized using the NCCS classification system, the sector and the public in general will finally have a common language with which to define, chart, describe, and understand this neglected sector of American society. These data can be used for social science research, reports on financial trends of various organizations, public information, public policy research, and the development of financial indicators for use by managers of nonprofit organizations. The NCCS Program Plan constitutes a major effort toward meeting those information needs and filling the statistical void on charitable organizations.

STIMULATING THE COLLECTION OF DATA NOT OTHERWISE COLLECTED

Another strategy to improve the resource base on the independent sector is to sponsor, support, or encourage the collection of data that are not collected by the government. This includes both studies sponsored by Independent Sector, and providing encouragement and support to a variety of organizations to engage in the regular collection of information on various aspects of the nonprofit sector. Independent Sector is sponsoring regular national surveys on giving and volunteering, a national survey on the activities and finances of religious institutions, and is assisting and encouraging cities and states to conduct local and regional surveys of giving and volunteering behavior. Independent Sector also has supported and encouraged the continuing research on tax policy and its impact on giving by Lawrence Lindsey of the National Bureau of Economic Research and Charles Clotfelter of Duke University.

Another ongoing study that is improving our understanding of the diversity and complexity of this sector and building the resource base for other scholars is the Nonprofit Sector Project at The Urban Institute. The Nonprofit Sector Project, directed by Lester Salamon, is the only major national research project on nonprofit human services organizations (at 16 sites around the country) that has been conducted. As a result of this research, new definitions of the sector (particularly in social services) are emerging, information on scope and activities of nonprofit organizations and their sources of support are becoming available, and a profile of the complex interrelationships or partnerships that nonprofit sectors engage in with both the public and private sectors is being revealed. This project is the only study that charts changes in programs, financing, employment, and volunteer service in this sector. As such, it has provided new information that will be useful in improving the collection of data on nonprofit organizations at the federal level, on charting new trends in programs, and in determining the vitality of nonprofit organizations over time. In the future, information from these surveys should provide social scientists with an enormously valuable set of empirical data for testing various concepts developed to explain the role and functions of this sector in the economy and in the political structures of the society.

Other regional studies are also providing insights into the structure, impact, and functions of philanthropic institutions and nonprofit organizations in relation to communities. Of particular note is the continuing work of Julian Wolpert (Woodrow Wilson School, Princeton University); Thomas A. Reiner (University of Pennsylvania); and Joseph Galaskiewicz

(University of Minnesota). These studies provide a more in-depth analysis of the impact of philanthropy on particular communities. There is a need for more sociological studies of communities and regions, particularly cross-sectional studies that examine the interrelationships of government, business, and the nonprofit sector.

Two other major studies will provide valuable information about foundations and the philanthropic behavior of the wealthy. A study co-sponsored by the Council on Foundations and the Program on Non-Profit Organizations at Yale University examines the formation of foundations during this century. Part of this massive study involved a survey of wealthy individuals, accountants, and legal advisors to the wealthy, and an analysis of recent bequests to determine the philanthropic behavior of the wealthy and their attitudes and perceptions about starting their own foundations. *America's Wealthy and the Future of Foundations*, edited by Teresa J. Odendahl (The Foundation Center, 1987) provides detailed analyses of these studies.

Another study conducted by Paul Schervish at Boston College also involved a national survey of wealthy individuals to probe how they use their wealth and what their motivations are to engage in philanthropic activities. These two studies, along with the Yankelovich, Skelly and White survey on charitable behavior of Americans (1984) commissioned by the Rockefeller Brothers Fund and the Gallup survey of Americans Volunteer (1985) commissioned by Independent Sector, provide baseline information to encourage researchers to look seriously at issues of the values, attitudes, and motivations of Americans in their giving and volunteering behavior, and as such provide a rich resource base to stimulate further research.

Corporate giving grew faster than other types of giving during the 1970s, and by the 1980s, annual corporate giving equaled foundation giving. Other than an annual survey of corporate giving *(Annual Survey of Corporate Contributions)* conducted by the Conference Board and The Council for Aid to Education, which focuses on the top 1,000 corporations, good information on the universe of U.S. corporations and their giving was not available until Hayden Smith analyzed corporate giving using special runs from the IRS corporate tax files. *A Profile of Corporate Contributions* (1982) gave detailed figures on corporate giving for 1977. An update covering corporate giving in 1983 is forthcoming.

Corporations give more than cash and equipment. They help nonprofit organizations in many ways ranging from providing loaned executives to encouraging their employees to volunteer in their communities. However, little is known about the scope of these activities. To address the issue of non-cash corporate giving, Alex Plinio, president of the Prudential Foundation and a member of the IS Research Committee, interviewed corporations over a period of years, and wrote, with Joanne Scanlan, *Resource Raising: The Role of Non-Cash Assistance in Corporate Philanthropy*, in which he catalogued such corporate activity and estimated its values.

The last study of the scope and extent of employee volunteering in corporations was *Volunteers in the Workplace* (1979), the first comprehensive study of the nature and scope of the efforts of corporations and organized labor to involve workers as volunteers in their communities. The study, conducted by Volunteer, the National Organization that provides technical assistance and information services to the volunteer community, was urged to repeat this historic study on a regular basis. In 1986, it published an update, including a new national survey of volunteers from the workplace, in *A New Competitive Edge: Volunteers From the Workplace*. All of these studies are starting to provide a more complete picture of corporate participation and giving in the community.

The United Way of America also is conducting and producing research on the social service agencies in America that receive little attention in government information collections. Over the past five years, the United Way Research Division has developed a sophisticated community information gathering and sharing network that is useful to assess community needs.

The purpose of supporting the development of data collection on this sector is to produce more resources for social science research, for public policy deliberations, and for the dissemination of information to the public. Because data collection systems need careful thought, more investment, and demand long-term investment, there is a need for organizations (such as The Foundation Center, the National Center for Charitable Statistics, and the National Bureau of Economic Research) and research institutions (such as The Urban Institute and The Brookings Institution) to devote substantial efforts and time in the planning, examination, coordination, and review of a system of information regularly collected that will provide a meaningful and accurate description of this sector and its relationship to the American society and economy.

Identifying Major Research Gaps

As many researchers who have started to investigate various aspects of this sector know, finding gaps in our knowledge is easy. What is more challenging is to design a series of questions that will start to fill the voids. And, even more challenging is that the attempt to answer one question suggests a thousand more. The Program on Non-Profit Organizations at Yale University started with the challenges ten years ago. *The Nonprofit Sector: A Research Handbook* (1987), edited by Walter Powell, provides cogent analyses of what researchers primarily working in the Yale program learned over the past decade, as well as the enormous gaps in knowledge that remain. This research handbook provides a road map for future exploration in many of the social sciences.

The IS Research Committee tried not only to focus on research gaps, but to develop a series of strategies to encourage research in major areas where there seemed to be little interest in scholarly investigations. As described earlier, the long-term collection of data and information was one major area. In 1983, other than research in economics, and the law relating to nonprofits, scholars reported at the first Research Forum that there was very little sustained research activity in history, philosophy, psychology, anthropology, the humanities, or religious studies. One could not find a course on philanthropy, or even a part of a course on philanthropy, in the catalogs of major institutions of higher education. Furthermore, along with the neglect in the teaching of philanthropy, educational institutions were no longer emphasizing voluntary service as part of an education for responsible citizenship. Members of the Research Committee developed several strategies to encourage research in a variety of areas.

One of the major weaknesses in our knowledge about this sector was a lack of histories. *American Philanthropy*, by Robert Bremner, (University of Chicago Press, 1960) still was the only general history available. Peter Dobkin Hall at Yale University published *The Origins of American Culture* (New York University Press, 1982); Kathleen McCarthy published *Noblesse Oblige* (University of Chicago Press, 1982); Stanley Katz and Barry Karl have been working on a history of foundations and their impact on American public policy in the 20th century. Merle Curti's book *Philanthropy in the Shaping of American Higher Education* on higher education and philanthropy abroad, published over two decades ago (Rutgers University Press, 1965), had not been updated. No one had written a history about American religious institutions and their contribution to the development of the nonprofit sector. Although McCarthy's *Noblesse Oblige* did address American public values and attitudes toward philanthropy, primarily in Chicago through the beginning of the 20th century, not much attention generally had been paid to the impact of religious values on American philanthropy. Yet most of the sector's organizations could trace their origins to religious institutions. Although Hall published a history on the relationship of the creation of nonprofit organizations to American culture up to 1900, more attention needs to be paid to the role of voluntary associations in modern American culture and to its impact on the values, attitudes, and beliefs of Americans. Without such studies as a foundation for understanding the role and evolution of this sector, both in the United States and abroad, scholars labor without a cultural memory.

To address some of these major gaps, Robert Payton, Chairperson of the Research Committee, spent two years lecturing to faculties at colleges and universities about the need to address these issues. He also wrote *Major Challenges to Philanthropy* (Independent Sector, 1984), which has become a classic discussion paper to encourage the study of the philanthropic tradition. He also encouraged, inspired, cajoled, and sought support for conferences on the history of philanthropy at Columbia University and a conference for social philosophers to examine these issues. The papers from the conference convened in New York by the Social Philosophy Policy Center of Bowling Green State University were published in the May 1987 issue of *Social Philosophy and Policy*, and also will be published as a separate volume (Transaction Books, 1988).

Since 1983, working through the Research Committee members, particularly Stanley Katz, President of the American Council of Learned Societies and Robert Bremner, Professor Emeritus of History at The Ohio State University, a research forum was held focusing on the theme of history of philanthropy (1985) and a Center for the Study of Philanthropy was established at the Graduate Center of the City University of New York (1986). With Kathleen McCarthy as the Center's first director, the history of philanthropy will receive some attention. And, Peter Dobkin Hall still remains at the Program on Non-Profit Organizations at Yale University, where he is preparing two new histories for publication, one on corporate philanthropy and one on nonprofit institutions.

Through the work of Robert Lynn, senior vice president for religion of the Lilly Endowment and a member of the IS Research Committee, a new program has been established at Independent Sector and at the Lilly Endowment to stimulate the study of religion and philanthropy. This project includes sponsoring a national survey on the activities and finances of religious institutions; preparing a bibliography on religion and philanthropy; and supporting religious scholars at Harvard, Princeton, Temple University, and the School of American Culture Studies at Indiana University to develop research agendas in this area. Through these and other activities, the Research Committee is actively working to stimulate more scholarly interest in this area.

After learning that several studies showed declines in altruism and voluntary service among college students, Howard R. Swearer of Brown University convened a coalition of college presidents to found "Campus Compact: The Project for Public and Community Service" in 1986. The purpose of Campus Compact is to reemphasize the value of public service as part of undergraduate education. Campus Compact, staffed by Frank Newmann, President of the Education Commission of the States, has over 100 participating colleges and universities as members. Each of the participating members: (1) agrees to a campus self-study program of public service activities available to students and (2) commits their college or university to increasing students' public service opportunities both for credit and as part of campus activities. This college compact has been enormously influential in just a short time to increase volunteering among college students.

In 1986, the Association of American Colleges, supported by the American Association of Fund-Raising Counsel Trust, an IS member organization, instituted an award program for faculty who were willing to design courses on philanthropy. The awards were open to all disciplines in the arts and sciences. Both the faculty members and the institution had to make a three-year commitment to teach the course. Nine winners were selected in the first round, and new awards will be made for two more years.

Some attention has been paid by political scientists to the role and functions of the nonprofit sector in American life. Lester Salamon has started to examine political theory in relation to his research on the nonprofit sector project, and Jennifer Wolch of the University of Southern California is conducting research on the distribution of resources to the nonprofit sector in the context of political decision-making. James Douglas' *Why Charity?* (Sage Publications, 1983) provided insightful analysis of the political rationale for the nonprofit sector that resulted from initial research done at Yale University. But the larger questions about the structure of the American public and the role of voluntary organizations in conducting public business need far more attention.

David Mathews, President of the Kettering Foundation and a member of the IS Research Committee, has sponsored research on the meaning of *public* in America, on citizen participation and problem solving, and on the political functions of the nonprofit sector. The Kettering Foundation has been doing and supporting research in this area, but much more needs to be done. Another study by Robert N. Bellah *Habits of the Heart* (University of California Press, 1985) has been extremely influential in demonstrating the movement of Americans toward individualism and away from public commitments. Helmut Anheier (Rutgers University) and Brian Smith (Massachusetts Institute of Technology) are conducting research on the role and functions of voluntarism and nonprofit activity in other political systems. But much more remains to be done to trace the comparative role and functions of voluntary organizations and voluntary service in various political systems.

For several years, the IS Research Committee studied various models of knowledge development and dissemination, and finally selected the method the Hastings Center had used with great success for several years. (Willard Gaylin of the Hastings Center was a member of the IS Research Committee.) The Hastings Center had pulled together the best materials dealing with medical topics and ethics that could be used in a variety of courses within several disciplines. They then developed a short unit outline for each particular topic or issue, and included this in a packet along with copies of pertinent articles and a short bibliography of readily accessible materials. These packets then were made available to faculty and students (for a small fee) for inclusion in appropriate courses. Once a field was sufficiently developed—and books and texts were readily available—the packets were discontinued.

It is our intent to develop several packets over the next four years on a variety of issues and areas, such as education and philanthropy, religion and philanthropy, philosophical thought on charity, philanthropy and altruism, and so on. These packets will be developed by a variety of guest editors, drawn from various academic centers addressing the study of philanthropy and voluntarism, and a few will be done directly at the Independent Sector.

Through this effort, we hope to stimulate further research, increase the teaching of philanthropy in a variety of disciplines, and produce an increased demand for more information so that in the years ahead more books and courses will result, eventually broadening the knowledge bases in these areas of inquiry.

In trying to address major research gaps, the IS Research Committee has actively participated in encouraging scholarly attention to a variety of issues. From the very beginning, however, it was clear that attention without funding support would not result in much serious work. Therefore, both directly and indirectly, stimulation of research has also meant seeking support for such work.

Establishing Academic Centers

When the Independent Sector research program was established, the only academic program focusing on the study of nonprofit organizations was the Program on Nonprofit Organizations (PONPO) at Yale University. It was established in 1977 under the leadership of John Simon to generate an interest in independent sector research, of which, as Simon stated, our knowledge was like "the dark side of the moon." In the ten years since its establishment, PONPO has attracted over 200 scholars and graduate students to study the role, character, functions, and impact of the voluntary or nonprofit sector both in the United States and abroad. These studies have led to nearly 120 working papers, several books, and a series of volumes emanating directly from the Yale program covering several areas including economics, arts and culture, private education, research, and international comparison, among others. The Yale program was and is enormously important as an academic institution encouraging the development of theory and knowledge about this sector. As such, PONPO has made an enormous contribution to the development and stimulation of research on the independent sector over the last decade.

The IS Research Committee, on which John Simon serves, has had from its first meeting a continuing interest in supporting research on the independent sector at colleges and universities in order to establish a tradition of teaching about this sector. Support of research leads to teaching, to new doctoral students, and to further research, thus fostering the inter-generational chain of knowledge. Therefore, in addition to supporting research, the Committee realized that more opportunities were needed for researchers to fill academic positions, receive tenure, and establish the importance of this sector as worthy of intellectual attention at academic institutions.

Two major strategies were developed to increase interest in the study of the independent sector at academic institutions: (1) encouraging the establishment of endowed chairs to secure long-term faculty positions; and (2) establishing academic centers for the study of philanthropy. Most of the following academic centers and endowed chairs with a commitment to research that have been established over the past five years have IS support. In many cases, the involvement of IS through its Research Committee and the Effective Sector Leadership and Management Committee has been active in the launching of these centers.

- The Center for Nonprofit Management at Case Western Reserve University with an endowed chair
- An endowed chair for the study of "public" at the Hubert Humphrey Institute of Public Affairs, University of Minnesota
- A Center for Philanthropy and Voluntarism with an endowed chair at Duke University
- The Center for the Study of Philanthropy at the Graduate Center of the City University of New York
- The Institute for Community Leadership and Nonprofit Management at Virginia Technical Institute and State University
- Program on Nonprofit Management at the State University of New York–Stony Brook
- Center for Public Service–Tufts University

- The doctoral program in Nonprofit Management at the Graduate School of Public Affairs at the University of Colorado
- Institute for Nonprofit Management at the University of San Francisco
- The Institute for Public Policy and Administration, Union for Experimenting Colleges and Universities
- A master's degree with emphasis on the nonprofit sector in the Graduate Public Policy Program at Georgetown University
- The Center on Philanthropy at Indiana University
- The Center for Special Studies at Rhodes College with an endowed chair

Centers are in the planning stages at Boston College, the University of Missouri, and the University of Rochester.

Three established centers will add an emphasis on the study of philanthropy and nonprofit institutions through their newly appointed directors. Robert Payton is pursuing his studies of philanthropy at the University of Virginia; Lester Salamon has become director of the Institute for Policy Studies at Johns Hopkins University; and Carroll Estes, a member of the IS Research Committee, has added a research emphasis on nonprofit organizations serving the aging at the Institute on Health and Aging at the University of California–San Francisco.

The IS Research Committee held a meeting for directors of current and emerging centers in May 1987 to provide a meeting ground for center directors to share their research interests, work on research agendas, and discuss problems about curricula and courses about philanthropy. Although an enormous amount of progress has been made in the past five years, most of these centers are just starting, do not have many staff openings, and may not survive without adequate funding.

Of more than 200 scholars who were in the first edition of *Research-in-Progress* (1983), 173 scholars are still conducting research on the nonprofit sector. Very few faculty hold positions within their disciplines for their specialization on nonprofit institutions. Most faculty, even our most distinguished researchers, maintain their academic reputations because of their research in other areas of inquiry. In order to sustain the progress being made, far more effort and attention has to be given to the continuing support of researchers, academic centers, and the establishment of endowed chairs. These efforts will allow talented faculty to give more sustained attention to research pertaining to the nonprofit sector and philanthropy. Therefore, this part of the IS Research Committee's effort is of central importance in building long-term commitments and support.

Increasing Funding Support for Research

Another major objective of the IS Research Program is to stimulate the funding for research on the independent sector. Several strategies have been devised by the IS Research Committee, both formal and informal, to achieve this objective.

First of all, leaders from donor organizations and corporations are members of the IS Research Committee and provide guidance and leadership to assist this strategy. Of members of the Research Committee, Robert Payton while at the Exxon Education Foundation, Robert Lynn of the Lilly Endowment, Fred Billups of The Pew Charitable Trusts, and Alex Plinio of the Prudential Foundation have moved to encourage their own foundations to provide more support to the study of philanthropy and education, philanthropy and religion, and the building of statistical studies on philanthropy. Each year, some members are rotated off the Committee and new members are added. In this way, new persons from the donor community become acquainted with the general need for research on the nonprofit sector. So the first strategy has involved education and encouragement to donors to provide some funds within their organization's specific mission for the study of this sector.

Foundations and corporations that have entered the field of funding for research and the development of statistical resources on the nonprofit sector over the past decade are:

Aetna Life and Casualty
   Company
Aid Association for Lutherans
American Association of Fund-
   Raising Counsel Trust
Atlantic Richfield Foundation
Bankers Trust of New York
The Bush Foundation
Carnegie Manhattan Bank,
   N.A.
Chevron U.S.A., Inc.
Commonwealth Fund
Conoco, Inc.
Dayton-Hudson Foundation
Equitable Life Assurance
   Society of the United States
Exxon Corporation
Exxon Education Foundation
The Ford Foundation
General Electric Foundation
General Mills Foundation
Gulf & Western Foundation
George Gund Foundation
Evelyn and Walter Haas Jr.
   Fund
Marian and Peter Haas Fund
IBM Corporation

Robert Wood Johnson
   Foundation
W. K. Kellogg
Lever Brothers
Lilly Endowment, Inc.
The Mandel Foundation
Merck Company Foundation
Metropolitan Life Foundation
Mobil Oil Corporation
Stewart Mott Foundation
Northwest Area Foundation
NYNEX
The Pew Charitable Trusts
Prudential Foundation
The Piton Foundation
Rockefeller Brothers Fund
The Rockefeller Foundation
Shell Companies Foundation
Alfred P. Sloan Foundation
Spencer Foundation
Sun Company, Inc.
Texaco, Inc.
Time, Inc.
Whirlpool Corporation
Robert W. Woodruff
   Foundation

The second strategy has been to actively encourage some researchers to pursue their research interests. Independent Sector staff help to identify funders for these researchers, and in many cases, write letters of support to donors on their behalf.

The third strategy is to provide meeting ground opportunities for leaders of donor organizations to meet with researchers—the annual spring research forums. This strategy has produced more interest on the part of the donors to fund various research projects of these researchers. In fact, because there is always good attendance from donor organizations at the research forums, we believe our investment in these conferences has been well worth it. Each year, I hear from several researchers that they had been more successful in getting project funding as a result of donors taking an interest in their work after attending the forum.

A fourth strategy is to respond to donor queries on proposals submitted to them. So many foundations and corporations do not have staff that are well acquainted with research on the independent sector. We publish *Research-in-Progress* to help them as well as researchers review research that is currently going on in a particular area. We do not make statements about research priorities, except in those areas where IS is directly encouraging research on a public issue or on statistical collections. However, our assistance through *Research-in-Progress* has led to funding support in some areas, where a staff person may have not pursued reviewing a proposal for lack of information.

A fifth strategy is to hold an invitational meeting for donors at each IS Annual Meeting and Assembly. At these meetings, we review the need for research and have proposed strategies for research funding. These donors' meetings have been very useful to us and to the Research Committee in considering new ways to interest donor organizations to support research on this sector.

A sixth strategy is to encourage the establishment of endowed chairs and centers for the study of philanthropy at academic institutions to support further research on this sector. Independent Sector originally proposed that Case Western Reserve set up a multidisciplinary program on management of nonprofit organizations. Brian O'Connell and Sandra Gray worked for two years with Case Western Reserve on their Center for Non-Profit Management, including providing consulting assistance and providing assistance with donors who might fund the program. Brian O'Connell also has worked with Harlan Cleveland at the Hubert Humphrey Institute of Public Affairs to establish an endowed chair there. In fact, Kenneth Dayton provided the first challenge grant for the establishment of the chair.

After donors' meeting at the IS Meeting in 1984, John Day,

executive director of the Duke Endowment, wondered how the Endowment could contribute to the support of research on this sector out of its mission. The result was a plan to establish a Center for the Study of Philanthropy at Duke University which would include an endowed chair. The current program plan includes research on the nonprofit sector, conferences and retreat sessions for leaders in the sector, and a commitment to continue its research on tax policy and charitable giving under the leadership of Professor Charles Clotfelter. The Duke Endowment provided a challenge grant to start the funding, and our most recent report is that Duke University is one third of the way toward their funding goal for the Center. These efforts also have led to donations by individuals.

Another result of the annual meetings was that Russell Mawby, president the Kellogg Foundation, invited Brian O'Connell, Sandra Gray, and Virginia Hodgkinson to meet with grantmakers in Michigan to discuss how the study of philanthropy and nonprofit organizations could be encouraged at the local and state levels. We were recently informed by the Kellogg Foundation that they have held several meetings with donor organizations in Michigan to explore how they can encourage academic institutions and faculty at those institutions to give increased attention to research and teaching on the independent sector.

By increasing funding for research, new and talented researchers can be attracted to this sector. They, in turn, will attract students, and an inter-generational knowledge chain will be started. That is why endowed chairs are important. That is why interest on the part of major foundations is important to provide leadership in this neglected area of study, for gaps in research on this sector range across a host of disciplines from philosophy to the impact of philanthropy on science, to public policy, and to economics.

Although increased funding support for research has occurred, it falls far below the actual need to stimulate significant activity at colleges and universities. A recent letter from one of the researchers working on historical studies of the sector eloquently stated the difficulty facing talented and committed researchers in this field:

Moving towards a more durable research product may require that funders seriously rethink their goals. What, for example, is meant by "a basic body of literature?" Is it a series of isolated research initiatives undertaken for proximate purposes? Or, is it an ongoing and self-renewing enquiry which continually addressed both the applied and basic research issues affecting a field of activity or a set of institutions? If it is the latter, what kinds of funding strategies are likely to produce it?

Sustained enquiry requires sustained support—not merely support research, but underwriting the institutional infrastructure of conferences, journals, research programs, and teaching positions which attract the best scholars into a field and maintain communication between them. INDEPENDENT SECTOR's annual *Research-in-Progress* and Research Forum's *Working Papers* and Yale's *Working Papers* and books represent important steps in the right direction, the kind of sustained funding that would attract and hold the interest of teachers, researchers, and graduate students has not yet materialized.

. . . Institutions have been happy to accept the "soft" funding dispensed for research in the area. But none have been willing to make enduring commitments to nonprofit research. Without enduring commitments, particularly teaching positions, younger scholars will be unwilling to blight their careers by working in a field that offers them no prospects of employment or advancement.

These comments warn us that in spite of the progress made in the last five years, there is still an enormous challenge ahead to persuade institutions of higher education about the importance of permanent commitments to research and teaching about philanthropy. Certainly, we have started to establish a base for future progress, but during the next five years we will need an enlarged effort to institutionalize the gains we have made. This effort must include a substantial increase in philanthropy literature, increased dissemination of research findings, recognition on the part of government to improve its collection and reporting of data on nonprofit institutions and the people they serve in order to provide the basic resources for social science research, in-

creased support for academic centers, and faculty special-
izing in research in this area.

The first decade of the Program on Non-Profit Organization at Yale University and the first five years of the Independent Sector Research Program have stimulated an interest in and increasing support for research on the sectors.
During the next decade, we should assure the establishment
of long-term attention and institutional commitments in order to sustain support for research and teaching about this
sector.

Afterword

Philanthropics

This book is about a domain of knowledge. My proposal is that we call it "philanthropics," a coined word intended to be parallel and analogous to *politics* and *economics*. Philanthropics would be the domain of inquiry concerned with the organization, methods, and principles of voluntary action for public purposes.

William Drennan has written an unpublished book entitled *Neonyms*, a book about words that he has coined to address aspects of modern life. Although he gleefully mixes Greek roots with Latin prefixes and suffixes and vice versa, some of his coinages are promising, for example, *anaclysm*, to identify "a momentous, constructive upheaval, especially in politics"; while some are less so, for example, *chronoflake*, as the category of "someone who keeps offbeat hours."[1] John Money, according to an advertisement of Prometheus Books, writes about *sexosophy*. Scholars have given us *victimology* recently, and *narratology* as "the theory of narrative." Professor DeVito's textbook *Communicology* (Harper & Row, 1982) is now in a second edition. Mortimer Adler coined *propaedia* and *micropaedia* to embrace his new design of the *Encyclopaedia Britannica*.

Some important new domains have failed to arrive at consensus about a label for their field: *Women's studies* and

These notes are adapted from a paper prepared for a conference at the Duke University Center for the Study of Philanthropy and Voluntarism, November 1986.

feminist studies may ultimately become *gender studies,* forever offending those who would limit gender to grammar.

Rhetoric seems unkillable, perhaps because its rivals are words like *communicology.* "I believe it was the Edinburgh logician Sir William Hamilton who said that a good new term is like a fortress to dominate country won from the forces of darkness; but those forces never sleep and will strive by their Philosophical Arm to recover lost territory."[2] William H. Riker has defined "heresthetics" "to refer to a political strategy. Its root is a Greek word for choosing and electing. . . . And this is what heresthetics is about: structuring the world so you can win."[3]

The *Oxford English Dictionary* includes *philanthrope* for philanthropist (as in *Too Late the Philanthrope*), and *philanthropism* was once proposed to identify "the profession or practice of philanthropy; a philanthropic theory or system."

I came to the notion of *philanthropics* first while reading a book on *dogmatics,* and was encouraged when later coming upon this passage in the introduction to Friedrich Schiller's *On the Aesthetic Education of Man:*

> The systematic study of art, of its nature, effects, and its function as a distinctive value in human life, was not yet fifty years old. It had been started by A. G. Baumgarten when he founded what he called a new "science" and christened it *Aesthetica* (1750). From the very beginning the name gave rise to misconceptions.[4]

Misunderstandings have occurred even before the coinage of the word *philanthropics.* First, insistence that the philanthropic tradition constitutes a domain of knowledge has prompted immediate suspicions that I am proposing to create an academic department. The place of the study of philanthropy in the university is a subject worthy of a separate essay, but I am most fearful personally that philanthropy might drift into academic isolation much as international studies and Afro-American studies have. I like the analogy to aesthetics because aesthetics fits comfortably within art history and philosophy as well as fine arts; *philanthropics* has even more opportunities.

The word *philanthropy* as presently used qualifies as what W. B. Gallie once called in a well-known essay an "essentially contested concept."[5] The book entitled *Philanthropics* (to which I will turn after this book is completed) will include an essay on the competing conceptual claims that are obscured behind the word *philanthropy* (and charity, too, of course—but the claims differ in some important respects). I once discovered that in the *Encyclopedia of the Social Sciences*, published in 1936, the index, under the entry *philanthropy*, says "see *charity*." In the *International Encyclopedia of the Social Sciences*, published in 1967, the entry *charity* in the index advises the reader to "see *philanthropy*."

Teaching About Philanthropy

It is also presumptuous for me to discuss the teaching of philanthropy because as I write this I have not yet done it. That is, I have not yet taught a course on philanthropy open to undergraduates, an ambition I hope to realize in the near future. Should that happen, I will join a growing number of college and university faculty members who are confronting philanthropy as a classroom challenge for the first time.

An insight into the likely character of teaching undergraduates about philanthropy may be gleaned from the winning entries in the competition sponsored by the Association of American Colleges. Fifty-one entries were received in the first round, and nine grants were awarded. The courses will be offered for the first time in the 1987–1988 academic year, and all that is available at this point are the proposals themselves. The winning entries received grants to sustain the courses over a three-year period of development, and funds could be used for purposes collateral to the courses themselves, as well as for released time. I have reviewed the 9 winning entries (as well as the other 42), asking myself a set of who–what–when–how–where and even why questions.

The winners come from an array of institutions: Regis College, Chapman College, Baruch College of City University of New York, Harvard University, Georgetown University, Northwestern University, Seton Hall University, Babson

College, and Illinois State University. Fields of study range across American studies, economics, government, philosophy, and several interdisciplinary combinations.

Mary Oates at Regis College wants to offer the course "to deepen student understanding of the character, historical evolution and significance of philanthropy in American life." Chapman College, in the words of its president, G. T. Smith, considers "a life of service to others" as one of the six "central commitments" of its program.

Richard Freeman of Harvard will treat philanthropic behavior as "an important component of American capitalism." Freeman adds that

> If the course is successful, it will place the issue of philanthropic and volunteer behavior, and the humanistic and moral underpinning of such behavior, into economics, currently one of the university's largest majors, and will alter the perspective of students toward the role of non-profit–seeking behavior in a free enterprise economy.

William Brandon and Kenneth Fox of Seton Hall University, both political scientists, want their students to analyze the "social and political consequences" of the origins of philanthropy. They also say they want to "prepare our students to play a role in current policy debates about the appropriate roles for government and the private sector." Albert Anderson and Fritz Fleischmann at Babson College, along with some others, see in the study of philanthropy an opportunity to bring out the tension between individual success and individual responsibility in American culture.

Some of the courses, then, are intended to influence student behavior later in life as well as to expose them to the tradition. Chapman College believes that there is "self-fulfillment through service." Baruch College's course will try to inform students about the interaction among individuals, corporations, and public agencies. Margaret Wyszomirski and Leslie Lenkowsky of Georgetown offer their course in the context of a public policy program.

Even so, none of the winning entries includes an explicit intention to make use of the campus's own nonprofit sector, nor does there appear to be a special effort to engage in the courses themselves the faculty members and administrators who help to guide the campus nonprofits. The interaction of the campus and the classroom, even in the weak academic tradition of "co-curricular" studies, is not apparent in these proposals. Although some of the courses will draw on outside resources, most of them will not make important use of practitioners other than as occasional lecturers.

Most of the courses will be lecture courses, alas, with some extra effort given to discussion sections. Some will be offered in seminar format. Guest lecturers will be common. Babson and Illinois State will seek to involve the broader campus community, by offering some of the lectures as public lectures or, in Illinois State's case, conducting a campus-wide workshop.

All of the courses were designed for upper division undergraduates (with Georgetown allowing for the possibility of some master's students). Courses designed for first- and second-year students—similar to Gettysburg's freshman colloquy on social justice and individual responsibility—did not appear. The profile of institutions would suggest a male and female population aged 20 through 22. Regis's course has a particular interest in the role of women and others "outside the mainstream" in philanthropy; Illinois State has express concern about the international influence of philanthropy; and several institutions will try to relate the course to foundations and nonprofit organizations. Most of the courses will be team-taught, and in some cases the teams will include lectures by outsiders.

The question of the organizational locus of philanthropy in the curriculum is obviously not one to be argued in such a competition. The academic culture devotes its primary political energies to quarrels over turf and territory. Only a handful of institutions—none of them among the entrants in the first AAC competition—have established academic centers for the study of philanthropy. Those that have carefully respect prior academic claims by insisting on joint appointments between philanthropy and established disciplines. The various interdepartmental and interdisciplinary forms of centers, institutes, and committees hold part of the future in their hands, assuming they achieve an adequate financial base and adequate enrollments.

The more interesting question is that quoted earlier from the Harvard proposal of Richard Freeman. There is an important intellectual issue in the establishment of the place of philanthropic behavior in economics. As Freeman's proposal makes clear, his course will confront students with difficult issues for philanthropy, such as those relating to free-rider problems, public goods, and notions of the evolution of cooperation based on analysis of the prisoner's dilemma. Philosophy and religious studies have yet to establish such a beachhead. Political science accounts for philanthropic organizations under its rubric of interest groups, but there has been little exchange of ideas between the two fields.

The tentative conclusions to which I have come are these:

• The study and teaching of philanthropy can be used to illuminate other fields, just as these other fields can illuminate our understanding of philanthropy.

• Both specialized and interdisciplinary approaches are important.

• I see little evidence that the value of active learning as a pedagogical approach to the study of philanthropy has been recognized. The effort to use the study of philanthropy as a way to instill values or to make implicit values explicit—to surface the deep-seated dialectical tensions of philanthropy—will fail unless there is a better fusion of theory and practice.

• There are abundant opportunities for field work and for the involvement of practitioners. Students should be able to observe firsthand what it means to be a philanthropic "professional."

Educating Ourselves

The field of philanthropy is filled with organizations, some of which are directly concerned with the welfare of the field itself. Independent Sector, the Foundation Center, the Council on Foundations, and United Way of America are among the best known. There is also a myriad of other professional or-

ganizations that seek to enhance the professional development of their members: the Council for Advancement and
Support of Education (CASE), for example, is well-known in
higher education for the enormous array of courses and
workshops it offers its members.

The nature of the meetings of professional organizations,
of course, is such that emphasis is on the technology of the
profession rather than on its philosophical basis, historical
development, or ethical practices. Independent Sector commissioned *Major Challenges to Philanthropy* to contend with
that problem. CASE has developed a code of ethics, as have
other organizations that think of their members as full-
fledged professionals.

The question of what professionals in philanthropy should
know about *philanthropics*—about *the organization, methods,
and principles of voluntary action for public purposes,* in case
you've forgotten—needs wider consideration and discussion.

The educational model I propose would be close to the
professional's home base. It would bring together professionals from the nonprofit world, from all sides of the desk—
grantmakers, fund raisers, managers, trustees—and scholars
from diverse disciplines. It would require of them a limited
commitment of time: perhaps three or four hours at a session,
eight or nine times a year. The commitment would also be
a commitment of long duration: at least several years. Participation in such a group would call for an occasional personal contribution: a paper, a lecture, or a presentation of
some sort that might be defended against collegial critique
and examination. On occasion, these materials might be
published, and often made available for teaching.

The characteristics I have just outlined are roughly those
that have emerged and survived over the four decades that
the University Seminars at Columbia have played such an
important role in the intellectual life of New York as well as
of the University itself. These are among the issues that we
struggled with as we attempted to create the Columbia University Seminar on Philanthropy.

Not everyone would want to join such a group, nor would

everyone be able to make an appropriate contribution. Judgment has to be exercised on the sticky question of membership. Some people would have much to take away from their participation, but little to leave behind. Some are not in sufficient control of their lives and schedules to meet the requirements of regular attendance. Some people are not good at discourse that is more rigorous than that of a lively cocktail party. Others are not interested in any subject with enough intellectual intensity or focus to sustain their interest over time.

The questions of membership should thus also address (1) intellectual background; (2) facility in group discourse; and (3) breadth of interest in the subject.

The seminar that brings practitioners and scholars together on a continuing basis is a model that can be replicated in every community in America that houses an accessible college or university. At this point in time, there are no more than a handful of true experts in philanthropy in the entire country—even academics of narrow intellectual orientation with little hands-on experience, and practitioners with a wealth of experience and little grasp of the principles that guide their work.

What we have instead is a large and unevenly educated population concerned with philanthropy or interested in it with little or no opportunity to discuss it seriously. After four years' experience with the Columbia Seminar on Philanthropy, I am convinced that it is the best model to meet the needs of the field of philanthropy as a whole. I am also convinced of its usefulness in coming to grips with some of the underlying and intractable issues that confront us.

The most serious challenge to such a study is the problem of the agenda. What will claim first priority? What is "the subject" as far as the particular group is concerned? Part of the answer depends on what people have done to provide themselves with a base of experience or knowledge or both. Those details will vary widely from one group to the next.

This is as it should be in the American philanthropic tradition.

Prospective

After a philanthropy seminar (of fund-raising professionals) not long ago, someone asked me what one should read
to pursue an interest in the subject. I was stumped. What
one reads next depends on what one has already read. And
we have all read many things about philanthropy, albeit
without realizing we were doing so. (Dickens's *A Christmas
Carol* comes first to mind.)

Even so, I've fretted over the question ever since. The obvious things are there, at least for me: Robert Bremner's
American Philanthropy (University of Chicago Press, 1960; a
new edition is in preparation); James Douglas's *Why Charity?*
(Sage Publications, 1984); the several works of Merle Curti
and his colleagues (including Curti's essay in *The Dictionary
of the History of Ideas*).

But the movement of ideas means that topics and themes
of little interest to one generation may become compellingly
important to another. Philanthropy has emerged from a place
of relative obscurity to one of increasing respectability as
well as current interest. The next decade will see a substantial
increase in philanthropy research: in its most obvious manifestations of voluntary giving and voluntary service, but also
in deeper study of the role of voluntary association in shaping
the national agenda.

The research needs are at least as great conceptually as
they are empirically. Analysis of the ideas and methods of
philanthropy lags well behind empirical research at this
stage. Even while the millions of participants in philanthropic practice do their work through hundreds of thousands
of organizations, others are just beginning to examine the
assumptions on which the system rests.

We are beginning to see increasing interest in comparative
studies as well. The European traditions from which we borrowed our own practice are in the process of being redis-
covered at home. The Japanese have recently become more
interested in their own philanthropic practices and traditions, and in this area, as in most others, will quickly become
important actors. Philanthropic funds from the Middle East

have brought political controversy with them; recent controversies over politically oriented centers at Stanford and Georgetown indicate how complicated it is to shelter diverse philanthropic agenda on a campus.

Comparative studies prompt us to look at the diverse religious origins of charity and philanthropy, and to ask about the place of these activities in the ideologies of secular states. I have been cautioned recently for making too much of the American tradition of philanthropy and not giving significant recognition to philanthropic traditions in other societies. To consider philanthropy a virtue (as I do) is assumed to imply criticism of those who don't practice it as we do. Defensiveness about other peoples' philanthropy is usually voiced in behalf of Third World nations and cultures. More careful ethnic studies would reveal patterns of philanthropic behavior in these cultures that would cause us to be more modest in our claims. I have observed the extraordinary hospitality of Africans toward strangers, for example, and the one-way transfers that take place among extended families and tribes, and there is obviously something at work in those societies akin to what we call philanthropy.

Having said that, and attended carefully to the criticism, it is time we put some substance into the argument. I don't think much is known about philanthropy on a comparative or cross-cultural basis, and we should begin to pull together what we do know and start filling in the gaps in our knowledge.

One place to begin—I keep telling my friends at NYU, City University, and Columbia—is in the New York Metropolitan Area. There is as much ethnic diversity within 25 miles of Midtown Manhattan as one could find in any thousand-mile radius elsewhere, yet so far as I know there are no doctoral students out there conducting surveys and interviews and gathering material.

People can't teach without materials, and scholars are producing those materials in increasing volume. Even so, the central text in one of the notorious controversies in American philanthropy—the John D. Rockefeller gift that prompted the famous "tainted money" article by Washington Gladden[6]—

isn't conveniently available and hasn't been widely discussed among those of us most closely involved in analogous problems. Parallel to Brian O'Connell's celebratory anthology (*America's Voluntary Spirit*, The Foundation Center) should be a collection of essays that reveal the deep-seated controversies of our field: *Tainted money* is one; *factionalism* is another; *desert*, a third.

Philanthropy is an amorphous subject (or group of subjects). The University Seminar on Philanthropy at Columbia has been able to pursue its work for four years without agreeing upon a satisfactory definition of terms. There is also no agreed-upon taxonomy, no body of theory to be tested.

Yet because philanthropy exists—there really *is* something out there—one can only conclude that the next few years will be years of improved understanding.

I find that I can best think about the future of research in philanthropy by thinking about ideas discovered beyond the imprecise realm of the subject as it is usually identified. I am greatly impressed by the diversity of work that is germane to the study of philanthropy that has been written with other purposes in mind. Occasionally someone writes a book that reaches a wide audience: Waldemar Nielsen's best seller *The Golden Donors* (Dutton, 1985), Robert Bellah and associates' *Habits of the Heart* (University of California Press, 1985). Other things come along that seem to catch the interest of a scattered collection of us. As a lifelong believer in the idea of general education, I think it is useful that we be alert to insights that appear in other fields so that we might begin to build a shared body of literature.

Some of the things I have read recently or have scanned and plan to read more carefully in the immediate future (*pace* Professor Bosanquet) indicate—to me, at least—the wonderful range of possibilities:

• Robert H. Walker's *Reform in America* (University Press of Kentucky, 1984) prompts me to look much more carefully at the interaction of philanthropy and reform in American life. Walker traces the idea of reform across areas as diverse as banking and finance, abolition and civil rights, and utopian communities. He proposes a taxonomy of reform that may be helpful in constructing a taxonomy of philanthropy.

• Franklin I. Gamwell's *Beyond Preference* (University of Chicago Press, 1984) is a bold effort to find a secure base for voluntary association. Gamwell examines the work of economist Milton Friedman and philosophers Alan Gewirth, John Dewey, Alfred North Whitehead, and Charles Hartshorne in the course of offering his own conceptual framework. Gamwell wants to base his own theory on a defensible metaphysics.

• Robert E. Goodin's *Protecting the Vulnerable* (University of Chicago Press, 1985) examines our moral duties and the mechanisms we develop to meet them.

• Lawrence C. Becker's *Reciprocity* (Routledge and Kegan Paul, 1986) offers a study of reciprocity as a fundamental moral virtue.

• Amartya Sen's *Poverty and Famines: An Essay on Entitlement and Deprivation* (Oxford University Press, 1981) includes a chapter on "the Ethiopian famine"—the famine of 1972–74, however, not the famine of 1984–85. (The Columbia Seminar has devoted a year and a half to consideration of the response to the recent famine as an informal case study of philanthropy in action.)

• A Polish scholar at the University of Warsaw, Stanislaw Ehrich, has written *Pluralism On and Off Course* (Pergamon Press, 1982), a rare opportunity (for me) to look at an eastern European perspective.

• The sociologist Donald N. Levine of the University of Chicago, an authority on Georg Simmel, has written *The Flight From Ambiguity: Essays in Social and Cultural Theory* (University of Chicago Press, 1985). I found it helpful in many ways; thinking about "strangerhood," for example.

• Michael Ignatieff, in *The Needs of Strangers* (Viking, 1985), writes with occasional elegance and sharp insight about the thorny idea of *desert* and the "complex human emotion" of pity, "mingling compassion and contempt," and draws from King Lear, Augustine, Pascal, and Adam Smith, among others.

• Dante Germino's *Political Philosophy and the Open Society* (Louisiana State University Press, 1982) builds on the work of Eric Voegelin. Germino's discussion of the idea of *metaxy* ("the between" the human and divine) offers a tantalizing insight into the realm of the philanthropic.

I find that I need to go back to some other things. I want to read much more deeply in and about Aristotle, the Stoics, Thomas Aquinas, Jeremy Bentham, and Henry Sidgwick. I continue to remain hopeful that someone will compile an anthology or guide to philanthropy in literature. Beyond Norris Pope Jr.'s *Dickens and Charity* (Columbia University Press, 1978), I know of no guides to the work of authors who have shaped public attitudes toward charity and philanthropy. Is there a comparable study of Balzac, for example? Of Jane Austen? Of Kurt Vonnegut and other contemporary writers?

Professor James Childress, a colleague at the University of Virginia, and I will co-chair a project funded by the Lilly Endowment on the place of philanthropy in world religions. We hope that it will help all of us find our way in traditions unfamiliar to us. I have yet to find a collection of essays that would introduce me to the basic writings or other manifestations of the values on which non-Western religions and cultures have developed their philanthropic practices. That should be a piece of cake for anthropologists and other students of comparative religion (my perennial nominee is Clifford Geertz, whose field experience ranges across Islam from Indonesia to Morocco).

I am also hopeful of finding (for example, in the recent writings of Jon Elster for Cambridge University Press) an insight into what Marxists think about philanthropy (if they were ever to take it seriously and not simply repeat clichés).

Finally—although that is merely a phrase indicating that I am about to end this piece, not that I'm going to shorten my reading list—I would like to understand the link between philanthropy and personality. Could one find common personality traits among people engaged in philanthropic work? How would the personality traits differ between those, say, who work as grantmakers in foundations and those who work abroad in relief agencies? Do the volunteers brought together by the independent sector share characteristics of behavior as well as values? How does personality affect career patterns? Relationships among professionals and volunteers? And so on.

For the new inquirer into philanthropy, then, I would draw from the following insight into academic learning: In *Human Beings,* the British psychologist Liam Hudson told of discovering that successful students in the humanities varied quite widely in their IQ scores. They also differed in their work habits and in the range of their reading.

> The inter-correlations between these three variables were, effectively, nil. I noticed, though, that among the most successful each student was *either* high in I.Q., *or* very widely read, *or* exceptionally hard-working. . . . Only if he lacked all three of these qualities was a student in academic difficulties.[7]

Most of us have at least one of these academic virtues going for us. We think we know where we want to go. All we need now is a map.

NOTES

1. Don Oldenburg, "Not Ready for Prime-Time Dictionary," *Washington Post,* August 7, 1987.

2. P. T. Geach, *The Virtues,* Cambridge University Press, 1979, pp. 75–76.

3. William H. Riker, *The Art of Political Manipulation,* Yale University Press, 1986, p. ix.

4. Friedrich Schiller, *On the Aesthetic Education of Man,* Elizabeth M. Wilkinson and L. A. Willoughby, eds., Oxford University Press, 1982, p. xx.

5. W. B. Gallie, "Essentially Contested Concepts," *Proceedings of the Aristotelian Society,* (NS) vol. 41, 1956, pp. 167–198.

6. Washington Gladden, *The New Idolatry,* McClure Phillips, 1905.

7. Liam Hudson, *Human Beings,* Jonathan Cape, 1975, p. 39.

Index

277

42932